"In my lifetime, the world has changed significantly, but leaders have not. The norms of leadership remain individualism, self-interest, and unbridled ambition. Take note—the next generation is not going to follow that approach anywhere. The time for change is now. Let this book show you the path forward so you might better steward the people and the organizations entrusted to your care."

—**Cheryl Bachelder, former CEO, Popeyes Louisiana Kitchen, Inc., and author of** *Dare to Serve: How to Drive Superior Results by Serving Others*

"In this book, Stephen M. R. Covey takes us to the next level of leadership—how to trust and inspire. Having known Stephen since 1993, I can safely say that what he writes about in this book comes from personal experience in having paid the price for living, or violating, some of the principles that he so eloquently advocates. As he so correctly says, the single biggest barrier to becoming a Trust & Inspire leader is that we think we already are one. He surmises correctly that if any change happens, it is at best from an authoritarian style of leadership to a kinder and gentler, enlightened style of leadership. The underlying paradigm of Command & Control remains! The single most important lesson that this book teaches me is how to 'show' to be a Trust & Inspire leader than to 'tell' how to be one. That requires humility and a willingness to fail and be vulnerable. Such a trait in a leader inspires the people to take the leap from success to significance."

—**V. S. Pandian, Chairman, Leadership Resources (Malaysia)**

"Stephen M. R. Covey has brilliantly zeroed in on the heart of today's leadership challenge . . . migrating from a Command & Control model of leadership to more of a Trust & Inspire model mindfully designed to unleash the greatness of every individual and every team in your organization. An absolute leadership masterpiece."

—**Douglas R. Conant, former President & CEO, Campbell Soup Company; founder of ConantLeadership; and bestselling author of** *The Blueprint*

Business Authorities

"A beautifully written page-turner, full of engaging stories. *Trust & Inspire* integrates the author's personal experiences with research-backed insights to show how to lead in a world that has never been more in need of leadership. Quoting Eleanor Roosevelt, Covey reminds us that 'A good leader inspires people to have confidence in the leader; a great leader inspires people to have confidence in themselves.' Powerful words. Better still, he offers a playbook for how to make it happen."

—**Amy C. Edmondson, Harvard Business School professor, and Thinkers50 #1 Thinker in the World**

"*Trust & Inspire* is a paradigm-shifting book that will change work and lives. Stephen M. R. Covey compels us to move from a Command & Control to a Trust & Inspire leadership style. By respecting people, and unleashing them, he shows how you'll inspire people to become their best selves, enabling people to bring their full potential to work and relationships. A fantastic follow up to *The Speed of Trust*, this book will benefit any leader and transform any team or organization."

—**Christine Porath, Georgetown University professor, and author of** *Mastering Community* **and** *Mastering Civility*

"Purpose-driven work is fast becoming a prerequisite to meaningful innovation and sustainable business performance. You can't micromanage people to purpose-driven work, you really can't even motivate them to it—they've got to be inspired. *Trust & Inspire* offers a hands-on approach to connecting with people and connecting to purpose."

—**Rosabeth Moss Kanter, Harvard Business School professor, Thinkers50 Lifetime Achievement Award, and author of** *Think Outside the Building*

"To trust is to believe in the core capacity of people. Not just some people, and not because of specific credentials. Simply by standing in that spot in the world only one stands, each of us has value to add. Trust that."

—**Nilofer Merchant, Thinkers50, former tech executive of Apple, et al, and author of** *The Power of Onlyness*

"If you're a business leader, this book should be a fixed staple on your virtual bookshelf. Stephen M. R. Covey's *Trust & Inspire* holds a beautiful treasure chest of visionary, thought-provoking insights, ideas, and powerful tools helping leaders adapt to a fast-changing hybrid future."

—**Martin Lindstrom, Thinkers50, and** *New York Times* **bestselling author of** *Buyology* **and** *The Ministry of Common Sense*

"Not only do we need to disrupt ourselves, we need to disrupt the way we lead. *Trust & Inspire* is the ultimate disruption of traditional Command & Control leadership—and it's desperately needed today. As we lead in this new way, we'll succeed in growing our companies by first growing our people."

—**Whitney Johnson, Thinkers50, LinkedIn Top Voice 2020, and bestselling author of** *Disrupt Yourself*

Healthcare, Government & NGO Authorities

"The best leaders recognize a responsibility to become sponsors for those they lead and serve. There's nothing quite so empowering and inspiring as really having someone believe in you and then giving you the opportunity to succeed. *Trust & Inspire* powerfully captures the essence of this kind of leadership—and the collaboration and innovation it leads to. But more importantly, it frames and gives a roadmap for how you get there."

—**Jill DeSimone, President, U.S. Oncology, Merck**

"I pursued a career in healthcare to serve and care for people. From my early career as a critical-care nurse to my current role as a president and CEO, I have learned that caring for individuals as whole persons is the key to healing, building genuine relationships, and creating meaningful impact. *Trust & Inspire* is a must for any leader who wants to be inspired and to know the framework to care and motivate their team members not only as employees but as whole persons. Genuinely caring for others as unique individuals and as whole persons will not sacrifice performance in the organization but will inspire and ignite individual and organizational performance to the highest level. I highly recommend this magnificent book for anyone who wants to build real trust and inspire others to excel both personally and professionally."

—**Candice Saunders, President and CEO, Wellstar Health System**

"A move from Command & Control to Trust & Inspire is exactly the kind of shift that is needed in leadership today. Stephen M. R. Covey powerfully articulates this new way to lead with a transformative approach that is highly relevant for our new world. *Trust & Inspire* not only brings new insight to empathy, empowerment, and trust, but also frames inspiration as an accessible, learnable skill—for anyone. In our new world of work today, no leader can afford not to have this book."

—**Bill George, former Chairman & CEO, Medtronic; Senior Fellow, Harvard Business School; and author of *True North***

"Since I first read *The Speed of Trust*, I have been a huge fan of Stephen M. R. Covey. Now, with *Trust & Inspire* he is outlining a transformative approach to great leadership. Every leader, every manager, every person interested in how best to connect with others, should read this book! It will be the defining book for leadership in the twenty-first century."

—**William H. McRaven, 4-Star Admiral & Commander of United States Special Operations (Retired); former Chancellor, University of Texas system; and #1 *New York Times* bestselling author of *Make Your Bed***

"I have really enjoyed reading *Trust & Inspire*—it is a captivating, compelling work from the lucidly erudite pen of Stephen M. R. Covey in which he lays out, from rigorous research and vivid examples, what instinctively we all know delivers for us with those we most like to be with. Trust is that mysteriously elusive but hungrily pursued 'rock-solid fact' of our interactions when you know you can see it, and yet it can be the vacuous and painful absentee from fractious experience. To inspire is to light a fire in our souls that moves us beyond strategy and even reason into actions of impact. This immense work is a framework for confident relationships in every place, and its easy-to-read manner will grip executives and decision makers with the keys to innovation and the grit of purpose that everyone in business or public life now seeks with urgency."

—**Lord Dr. Michael Hastings, CBE (member of UK House of Lords); Professor of Leadership, Huntsman Business School, Utah State University; Chairman, University of London School of Oriental and African Studies; and former Global Head of Citizenship, KPMG International**

"Having worked in public service for nearly thirty years, including in all three branches of the federal government, I can state unequivocally that the very best public service leaders are themselves governed by a sense of their stewardship of the public trust and a commitment to the public good. *Trust & Inspire* is exactly the kind of leadership required in government today. In this book, you'll find practical tools for tapping into the deep sense of purpose and contribution that drives meaningful impact and strengthens others to do the same. This book is needed—and profound."

—**Max Stier, President and CEO, Partnership for Public Service**

"We succeeded at Grameen Bank because contrary to traditional banking, we were not interested in the past of our borrowers, we were committed to building a new future with them. I believe all human beings are packed with unlimited creativity. It is for precisely this belief that we have succeeded in our work. Like seeds, people come with all the potential needed to accomplish extraordinary things. Like the gardener described in this book, the job of leaders is to create an environment where the seeds of greatness within people are able to flourish. *Trust & Inspire* powerfully demonstrates how to cultivate this kind of growth in any setting."

—**Muhammad Yunus, 2006 Nobel Peace Prize winner, and founder of Grameen Bank**

Education & Family Authorities

"I never get tired of truth. As a college quarterback, I learned firsthand how to lead through Command & Control. Now as the president of a university, I am daily tempted by the false comfort of shortcutting messy and complicated relationships by convincing people I am right and railroading my ideas through in the name of 'collaboration.' But truth helps me resist. I knew instinctively the truth that trust is the key to effective leadership, but I *internalized* it when we brought Stephen M. R. Covey to Pepperdine to lead our first leadership retreat under my tenure several years ago. His *Speed of Trust* principles for building trust transformed the foundation of our leadership team. That is not hyperbole—it is the truth. It is timely for us now to expand on this trust work by modeling those principles and inspiring our management teams to greatness—to turn outward and create a Trust & Inspire culture. Once again, Stephen M. R. Covey provides the truth and path to get there in this high-impact toolkit for truth-seeking organizations."

—**Jim Gash, President & CEO, Pepperdine University**

"*Trust & Inspire* is the future of education. Both the challenges we face and the ones coming that we haven't even thought of yet require a new level of collaboration, innovation, and partnering with teachers, staff, students, families, and communities that the traditional education system simply isn't designed for. What this exciting book makes clear is that the capacity to solve these challenges already lies within those we lead, serve, and teach. They are ready for our trust and ready to be inspired. This book will help you do both."

—**Cathy Quiroz Moore, Superintendent of Schools, Wake County Public School System**

"*Trust & Inspire* is a must-read for every educator! Stephen M. R. Covey encourages us to rethink how we lead for the changing world in which we live while inspiring us to reconsider the skillsets and school culture needed for this generation of students. He gives us tools and strategies to unleash our own greatness while inspiring the greatness in others."

—**Muriel Summers, former Principal, AB Combs Leadership Magnet Elementary School (only two-time winner of the #1 Magnet School in America)**

"As a leader in public education, I continuously strive to ensure our school system is improving in many ways, including academic achievement, financial stability, capital improvements, and student safety. While these areas of focus are all critical for success, perhaps the most important is establishing and improving culture and climate. In his book *Trust & Inspire*, Stephen M. R. Covey does an excellent job conveying this same belief and emphasizes the importance of relationship building, servant leadership, and empowering others. *Trust & Inspire* is a must-read for superintendents, principals, and other district/school stakeholders who want to purposefully focus on developing their own leadership style and those within their organization."

—**Dr. Andrew Houlihan, Superintendent of Schools, Union County Public Schools**

"*Trust & Inspire* should be the new handbook for every person with the desire to lead others more effectively. In his compelling book, Covey has given us a thoughtful, practical, and inspiring guidepost for leading teams, families, schools, and organizations. As a leader in public education for over twenty-five years and a teacher of leadership, I am often asked, 'What is the one book you would recommend on effective leadership?' *Trust & Inspire* is now that one book. It invites us to see the potential for greatness in others and then provides the roadmap for creating trust and inspiration for those we are privileged to lead."

—**Dr. Candace Singh, Superintendent of Schools, Fallbrook Union Elementary School District**

"We often forget how important we are in the lives of those we raise, teach, and serve. We have the ability to help them see their potential and become greater and more capable than either they, or we, could imagine. Most people want to lead and empower in this way, but simply don't know how. *Trust & Inspire* lays it all out. Every parent, every teacher, every leader needs this book."

—**Esther Wojcicki, educator, journalist, parenting expert, and bestselling author of *How to Raise Successful People***

Personal & Professional Development Authorities

"Many leaders are looking for a style that's more uplifting and empowering than Command & Control, but few are clear on where to start. This book is brimming with ideas on how to bring out the best in people."

—**Adam Grant, #1 *New York Times* bestselling author of *Think Again*, and host of the TED podcast *WorkLife***

"Covey addresses a welcome change in workplace culture and leadership from carrot-and-stick motivation to trust and inspiration. While recent, this shift reflects the timeless and true human need to do things because we want to, and because we think we can, and because we understand their greater purpose."

—Angela Duckworth, founder and CEO, Character Lab,
and *New York Times* bestselling author of *Grit*

"For fifty years we have heard that we need to move away from Command & Control leadership. But nobody has named what we should do instead! That's what Stephen M. R. Covey boldly and brilliantly does in the words, and the book, *Trust & Inspire*. Isn't that what we want? Fifty years from now nobody will speak of Command & Control without saying 'Trust & Inspire.' It's going to become a part of our language, a part of what management itself means. As a great leader himself, Stephen will, through this book, unleash the greatness within you."

—Greg McKeown, author of the *New York Times* bestseller *Effortless*,
and host of the podcast *What's Essential*

"Stephen M. R. Covey has done it again! *Trust & Inspire* is the practical guide to how anyone can lead in our ever-changing workplace. In a refreshing shift from the Command & Control structure, Covey provides the insights to empower us all to lead anytime, anywhere."

—Erica Dhawan, author of *Digital Body Language*

"I love *Trust & Inspire*! It is the future of leadership. Master what Stephen teaches, and you will transform your power to choose your destiny—both personally and professionally. It is the secret to unleashing potential—yours and others'. His best work yet."

—Tony Robbins, #1 *New York Times* bestselling author

"Thoughtful, immensely practical, and timely. A vital read as we face the new realities of work. Energy and joy—these two dimensions change everything when it comes to human performance and, in turn, our personal, business, and educational outcomes. While we can all find some degree of each of these things on our own, really big potential is only unleashed when we build meaningful connections with our ecosystem, enhancing others and empowering greater resilience. *Trust & Inspire* helps us tap into those renewable sources of both energy and joy to create positive change in our world."

—Shawn Achor, *New York Times* bestselling author of *Big Potential*
and *The Happiness Advantage*

Leadership, Learning & HR Authorities

"I am convinced *Trust & Inspire* is the message leaders need to hear—now more than ever!"

—Kathleen Hogan, Chief People Officer and EVP, Human Resources, Microsoft

"For leaders to survive the new world, they must be ready to lead in a style that empowers, develops, and encourages their team. *Trust & Inspire* brings real examples and powerful principles to how leaders can take practical steps to becoming better mentors and more effective managers for their teams and organizations. A must-read!"

—Marshall Goldsmith, Thinkers 50 #1 Executive Coach, and only two-time #1 Leadership Thinker in the world

"In today's economy companies innovate or die, and employees no longer have to pay the 'a-hole tax.' Leaders must dispense with creativity-killing, soul-crushing Command & Control tactics and learn how to Trust & Inspire their teams to do the best work of their lives—and enjoy working together. Covey shows you how."

—Kim Scott, *New York Times* bestselling author of *Radical Candor* and *Just Work*

"People desperately want to find leaders who instill trust and inspire them to be their best without placing harsh controls on them. Stephen's newest book teaches a brilliant framework for unleashing the greatness in others through a simple yet powerful approach to leadership that will leave people feeling cared for and ready to get to work. An engaging and enlightening read!"

—Heather R. Younger, bestselling author of *The Art of Caring Leadership*

"More and more, the men and women in our workplaces are looking to do work that matters—to know that their daily contributions are making the world (and themselves) better. Covey's new book, *Trust & Inspire*, lays out a compelling argument for one of leadership's greatest truths: leaders should invest in and develop the potential of those they lead. Because when leaders develop other leaders, influence—and success—multiplies."

—John C. Maxwell, bestselling leadership author, speaker, and coach

"*Trust & Inspire* is important. It's the compelling answer to the traditional Command & Control and carrot-and-stick approaches to leading people. No one wants to get caught up in these industrial age management techniques, yet still today, almost everyone does. *Trust & Inspire* provides a practical framework and process for bringing out the best in ourselves—and the best in others."

—Frances Frei, Harvard Business School professor, and coauthor of *Unleashed*

Also by Stephen M. R. Covey

The Speed of Trust

Smart Trust

TRUST

&

INSPIRE

HOW TRULY GREAT LEADERS
UNLEASH GREATNESS IN OTHERS

STEPHEN M. R. COVEY

with David Kasperson, McKinlee Covey, and Gary T. Judd

Simon & Schuster Paperbacks

NEW YORK   LONDON   TORONTO

SYDNEY   NEW DELHI

Simon & Schuster Paperbacks
An Imprint of Simon & Schuster, Inc.
1230 Avenue of the Americas
New York, NY 10020

First Simon & Schuster trade paperback edition April 2023

SIMON & SCHUSTER PAPERBACKS and colophon are registered trademarks
of Simon & Schuster, Inc.

For information about special discounts for bulk purchases,
please contact Simon & Schuster Special Sales at 1-866-506-1949
or business@simonandschuster.com.

The Simon & Schuster Speakers Bureau can bring authors to your
live event. For more information or to book an event, contact
the Simon & Schuster Speakers Bureau at 1-866-248-3049
or visit our website at www.simonspeakers.com.

Manufactured in the United States of America

5   7   9   10   8   6

Library of Congress Cataloging-in-Publication Data has been applied for.

ISBN 978-1-9821-4372-5
ISBN 978-1-9821-4375-6 (pbk)
ISBN 978-1-9821-4376-3 (ebook)

To my mother and father,
Sandra and Stephen R. Covey,
who modeled to me what it means
to be Trust & Inspire parents and leaders

Contents

CONTENTS

Part Three: Overcoming The 5 Common Barriers to Becoming a Trust & Inspire Leader

Part Four: The New Way to Lead in a New World

TRUST

&

INSPIRE

Introduction

The highest temperature ever recorded on the face of the earth is a sizzling 134 degrees Fahrenheit. This record was set on July 10, 1913, in California's Death Valley.

Nothing grows in Death Valley because it's so hot and dry. Average rainfall is one to two inches a year. Not too long ago, a total of only half an inch of rain fell in *forty months*. No wonder it looks like such a barren wasteland.

Amazingly, all that changed in the spring of 2005. For no apparent reason, six inches of rain fell over a brief period in the winter of 2004. When spring arrived, observers were stunned to see a rich carpet of wildflowers completely covering the floor of Death Valley.

Maybe the place isn't dead after all. Maybe it's just dormant, waiting for the right conditions. In fact, the late Sir Kenneth Robinson, British author and international adviser on education, argued in a stirring TED Talk that it would be better called "Dormant Valley"—not as catchy, maybe, but a lot more accurate.

People are a lot like that. We have greatness inside each of us, though sometimes it is just as dormant as the wildflowers in Death Valley. The seed is always there—it just needs the right conditions to flourish.

Like those six inches of rain, truly great leaders can create the right conditions to awaken the potential within a person. Approaching leadership like a gardener, these leaders recognize that the power is in the seed. They curate conditions in which a person can flourish—not unlike the soil, water, air, and sunlight that enable a seed to flourish. As a result, they see that person rise beyond every imaginable expectation.

Some of us have been fortunate enough to be led by someone who has done for us what the rain did for the wildflowers in Death Valley. For the rest of us, however, we've lived a much different reality.

When it comes to the way we lead—in the workplace, in the classroom, at home—we've been repeating the same style of leadership for a long time. Many leaders still view their role as much more like a machinist than a gardener. They approach it first with the priority that there is a job to be done, and their role is to leverage the resources and people at their disposal to accomplish the task at hand.

Let's call this style of leadership "Command & Control."

Has this approach worked? When you think about it, does it work for you? Let me ask a more pertinent question—does this leadership approach work *on* you?

Probably not.

In fact, most of us have wanted a different way to lead and be led. But so far we've only been able to improve incrementally. We've known what we want to *move from*—Command & Control—but we're less clear on what we want to *move to*.

This book provides the answer.

In the vein of Socrates, who said, "The beginning of wisdom is the definition of terms," I suggest a simple term for the change we need:

Trust & Inspire.

Trust & Inspire is the new way to lead. Its goal is to unleash people's talent and potential—to truly empower and inspire them—rather than try to contain and control them. It's about trusting people to do the right thing and inspiring them to make meaningful contributions.

It's about connecting with people, through caring and belonging, so that we—and they—can successfully respond to our disruptive world. It's about then connecting people to purpose so they feel inspired not only by an organization's leaders, but also by a sense of purpose, meaning, and contribution in their work.

At its core, a Trust & Inspire paradigm flows from a fundamental belief in the potential and greatness inside people. Even—and especially—when it's unseen.

Command & Control is about getting things done, but it misses the potential power of the people who get those things done. Command & Control is about being efficient with people, trying to motivate them instead of inspiring them. It's about self-interest and competing rather than serving and caring. And if all else fails, it's about barking out the orders so everyone does exactly what they're supposed to do—not because they *want* to, but because they *have* to.

In short, it's about controlling people instead of unleashing their potential.

The game has radically changed, so why are so many of us still clinging to the old style of leadership? Operating from a Command & Control paradigm today is like trying to play tennis with a golf club. The tool is completely ill-suited to the reality, to the game being played.

I'd like to invite you to do a simple exercise: think of someone you know who might fit the description of a Command & Control kind of leader—a boss, manager, administrator, coworker, teacher, friend, coach, parent, or neighbor.

Now ask yourself, what is it like to work with this person?

I frequently do this exercise with an audience, and people are often surprised at the visceral reactions they have. You might be having that same kind of experience right now. Remembering someone who stifled you with rules and restrictions can fill you with frustration and exhaustion, sometimes even anger and pain.

Now think of someone you know who might be described as a Trust & Inspire leader, someone who believed in you and gave you opportunities and chances.

Ask yourself the same question. What is it like to work with this person? Remembering this kind of leader can fill you with gratitude, excitement, and a sense of confidence and fulfillment, even years later.

Command & Control in Action

Many years ago, I went on a sales call to a small, family-owned manufacturing company where I met with most of the company's executive team. As we sat down, they began to explain the positives and negatives that existed in their company culture.

After several minutes of back-and-forth between these executives, one man interrupted loudly, the exasperation clear in his voice, "Can we just get real here? Our biggest problem is that we're managed by a control freak!" The founder and current CEO—a guy everyone referred to as "Senior"—wasn't in the room, but his presence certainly was. Others in the room began to hesitantly chime in, agreeing.

"It's true, he can't let go of anything."

"He's constantly looking over our shoulder."

"He can't pass anything on. And it's time for him to pass it *all* on. Junior is ready."

After a bit of probing, I learned that "Junior" was the founder's son and heir apparent to the company. Junior had been working with the company since graduating college. He was well respected, and everyone felt it was time for him to take over. They all believed that his leadership would make the company more relevant and successful. Junior himself believed it, too—he'd told his father multiple times, "I'm ready, Dad. I can do it."

But despite Junior's confidence and the team's urging, Senior refused to let go.

"It's so frustrating not to be trusted; I can't imagine how Junior feels," one member of the team lamented.

"Well, it doesn't really matter how Junior feels if Senior doesn't feel Junior is ready," another said.

"But Junior feels ready?" I asked. "And you all feel he's ready, too?"

"Absolutely!" came the consensus. "We all believe in him, and we know he'd do a great job."

Suddenly the man who had originally broached the subject of their controlling boss smacked his hands down on the table in frustration and exclaimed, "For crying out loud, Junior is sixty-seven years old!"

I tried my best not to look as shocked as I felt.

I had imagined Senior to be in his fifties or sixties and Junior in his thirties or forties, sympathizing with how it might be hard for Senior to move on. Now it was downright comical to consider that Senior—who was most likely in his late eighties or nineties—still could not bring himself to cede control to his qualified and competent son, who had been working in the company for many decades!

From the dejected feeling in the room, it was also clear that Senior's need for control impacted not just Junior, but every aspect of the company. And it impacted results—the company wasn't thriving as Senior's leadership style was holding everything back. It was holding back his company's growth and progress. His employees. Even his own son.

Like Senior, most Command & Control people aren't bad people. Most are decent people with fine character and good intent. But far too often their style gets in the way of their intent.

Even when a leader is working toward a positive, beneficial outcome, a Command & Control approach leads to coercion, compliance, containment, and ultimately to stagnation. A Trust & Inspire leader, on the other hand, works toward that same beneficial outcome but does it through commitment, creativity, and the unleashing of talent and potential.

Here's the revealing thing: most of us are probably a lot more like Senior than we'd like to think. In fact, perhaps the single biggest barrier to becoming a Trust & Inspire leader is that we think we already are one!

Trust & Inspire in Action

I learned about Trust & Inspire as a child with my father, who was trying to teach me how to take care of our family's large yard. Some of you may be familiar with this story, from *The 7 Habits of Highly Effective People*, which my father had dubbed "green and clean."

My parents used to hold weekly family meetings. My siblings and I would gather—often grudgingly once we became teenagers—to hear about our parents' plans for the week or for new family activities or household chores. During one such family meeting the year I turned seven, Dad had asked us kids who would be willing to take care of the yard. I eagerly responded that I would. Not because I cared what the lawn looked like but just because I would've done anything for my dad.

After the meeting, Dad took me outside to survey the yard so I'd learn what the job required. It was at the beginning of the summer and our lawn was starting to yellow. "Son, your job is *green and clean*," he began. "Let me show you what *green* looks like—let's go over to our neighbor's house." We walked over and admired the cool, green blades on our neighbor's lawn. "That's the color we're after, son."

As we walked back to our yard, he said, "Now let me show you what *clean* means—let's clean up half of our yard." Together we picked up trash and debris on half of our lawn. As we paused, he pointed to the half we hadn't cleaned and said, "Notice how that looks compared to the area we just cleaned." Even for a seven-year-old, the difference was obvious. "What we just did is *green and clean*. Son, your job is *green and clean*. It's up to you how you want to do it. But I'll tell you how I'd do it if you want."

I realized I hadn't thought of the logistics of all this. "How'd you do it, Dad?" I asked.

"I'd turn on the sprinklers! But you may want to use buckets or a hose or spit all day long. It's up to you. All we care about is what, son?"

"Green and clean!" I exclaimed.

"What's green look like?" Dad asked. I pointed with enthusiasm to our neighbor's lawn. "Good. What's clean?" I pointed proudly to the area we had just cleaned up.

"Good. It's your job, son. Guess who your boss is?"

"Who?" I asked, my brow furrowing with confusion.

"You are!" Dad told me, and I smiled with satisfaction at that answer.

"Guess who your helper is?" he asked.

"Who?"

"I am! You boss me!"

"I do?" I asked eagerly, a smile sneaking across my face at the thought of being in charge.

"If you ever need help and I have time, you just tell me what to do, and I'll do it!" He smiled. "And guess who judges you, son?"

This time I nodded knowingly and pointed to myself.

"Right, you judge yourself. How do you think you judge yourself, son?"

"Green and clean!" I proclaimed proudly.

"Good! Why don't you think about it for a day or two and let me know if you want to do it."

When Saturday rolled around, Dad asked how I felt about the proposed deal. "I'll do it!"

He took my hand and shook it firmly. "Deal!"

But I did nothing, for days on end. It wasn't my plan to do nothing. Honestly, I think I just forgot. Or there was something more fun and exciting happening over at the neighbors' so I did that instead.

When Tuesday morning rolled around, my father was hit by the heat of the summer day as he walked out the front door to head to work. He looked at the neighbor's yard—green and clean, freshly manicured. He looked at our yard—yellow and burning up, garbage on the side lawn, three feet from his car.

He was willing to cut me a little slack. Not working on Saturday or Sunday made sense. But Monday? He told me later how he was ready to yell, "You get out there! Get over here and fix this!"

He knew that the moment he did that, he'd likely kill my initiative. He knew I'd clean up the yard if he came down on me hard, but what would happen the next day when he wasn't there? Instead he bit his tongue and decided to see what the yard looked like when he got home from work.

Later, when he drove home, our yard came into view as he rounded the corner. It was more cluttered and yellow than ever, and I was across the street playing ball.

"Hey, son! How's it going?"

I waved at him and replied, "Just fine, Dad!" And I was just fine—I was playing ball! I definitely wasn't thinking about the yard.

We had agreed that we'd walk around the yard twice a week so I could show Dad how it was going. He decided to make good on that deal. "How's it going in the *yard*, son?" he called out.

In that moment, I stopped being fine. I hesitated, eyes darting away as I held the football in my hands. "Uh . . . just fine?" I squeaked out.

Dad bit his tongue and went in the house. He dug deep, reminding himself why he was doing this: *Reaffirm my purpose: raise kids, not grass*, he thought to himself.

After dinner, he put his hand on my shoulder and asked, "Why don't we walk around the yard as we agreed, and you can show me how it's going?"

My lip started trembling. By the time we got out to the front yard, I was openly bawling. "It's so hard!" I moaned, even though I hadn't done a single thing.

Dad spoke softly: "Anything I can do to help, son?"

"Would ya?" I tentatively asked.

"What was our agreement?"

"That you'd help me if you had time," I said cautiously.

"I've got time!"

"You do? Okay—I'll be right back!" I ran into the house and came out with two garbage bags. I handed one to Dad, and we cleaned up the yard together.

I asked for help only a few more times that summer. It was my job. I gained ownership and a sense of pride in holding myself accountable. As for Dad, he took the time to set up the agreement and reaffirm it. He didn't backslide on it when he saw mistakes. He kept believing in me and holding me accountable in the way agreed.

And me? *I felt trusted.* I felt trusted by someone important to me—

my dad. Because I felt trusted, I did not want to let my dad down. I was too young to care about money or status or appearance. But I did care about my dad, so being trusted by him was very inspiring to me. I responded to his trust in me, and I took care of the yard. It was green, and it was clean.

While the yard looked great, more importantly I felt great. I gained confidence in my ability to keep the yard green and clean and I was eager to continue to do so. I experienced firsthand the power of being trusted, and this simple interaction at age seven became a defining moment for my understanding of leadership.

A good leader inspires people to have confidence in the leader; a great leader inspires people to have confidence in themselves.

—ELEANOR ROOSEVELT

The truth is, we all want to be trusted. To be trusted is the most inspiring form of human motivation. People who trust those they lead bring out the very best in them—and in all of us.

Trusting others is among the most important of our life's works.

Similarly, people yearn to be inspired. It can feel as vital to our existence as air is to our lungs. In fact, the word *inspire* comes from the Latin root *inspirare*, which means "to breathe into." Put another way, *inspire* means to bring life into something that is lifeless. So, to inspire someone is to breathe life into them.

Yet most people today are dangerously low on inspiration. In those precious moments when it touches us—like watching a child take a first step or runners cross the finish line at a marathon—it feels like a breath of fresh air.

To inspire is to take an experience and imbue it with purpose, to take a job and make it meaningful. It is to encourage a worker to become a creator, an employee to become a colleague, a vendor to become a partner, a group to become a team. As leaders, our job is to inspire the people around us—they want it. We all do. I'm reminded of this beautiful statement by the humanitarian and philosopher Dr. Albert

Schweitzer: "In everyone's life, at some time, our inner fire goes out. It is then burst into flame by an encounter with another human being. We should all be thankful for those people who rekindle the inner spirit."

When we inspire other people, we rekindle the inner spirit, both theirs and ours.

When we inspire other people, we breathe new life, purpose, and passion into them and us. We offer a new perspective, not only of their work and world but also of them as humans. Because we genuinely see greatness within them, they begin to see possibilities for themselves they hadn't previously considered—or even seen. They look beyond artificial limitations.

Inspiring others is among the most important of our life's works.

Being a Trust & Inspire leader provides a lens for seeing and living life—a way of being—not merely a tool that you use when convenient. Both you and the people you lead feel that they can and should be both trusted and inspired. Both of you believe they can create meaningful contributions and find a sense of purpose. Both of you believe that together, you all can produce something far greater than anyone could on your own.

Face it: has Command & Control *ever* truly worked for people? Has it ever been effective in a family setting? Did teachers hitting students with rulers for misbehavior ever truly encourage or inspire students to want to learn? Were employees ever inspired to work harder when their company implemented the time clock or installed employee "surveillance software"? Command & Control might have gotten compliance from kids, students, and employees in the past, but it certainly did not spark creativity, excitement, inspiration, or commitment. And it most certainly won't do any of those things today.

Intellectually, we understand this. And yet in spite of all our progress, the reality is stark: most leaders today are *still* operating with the old style of Command & Control. We've just become far better at it, much more advanced and sophisticated in its manifestation—implementing a style we might call "Enlightened Command & Control." But our fundamental beliefs of how we see people and leadership haven't changed much. Far too many of us are still falling back on an outdated, Industrial Age approach to address today's challenges.

What about you?

If you're still trying to win by containing people instead of unleashing their potential, by motivating others instead of inspiring them, by focusing on competing and self-interest above caring and service—you're playing tennis with a golf club.

The game has changed.

Pick up a racquet. I'll show you how.

PART ONE

The Future of Leadership: From Command & Control to Trust & Inspire

It's time for a new way to lead.

For decades, we've been getting away with a tired, out-of-date leadership style that we've patched and propped up to try to make work for our changing world. But incremental improvements within a flawed paradigm will no longer work. While our world has changed, our way of leading has not. It's time for a new style of leadership—one that is relevant for our times.

Not only has the world changed, so has the nature of work itself, along with the work*place* and the work*force*. *Inclusion*, *collaboration*, and *innovation* are no longer simply buzzwords but are the price of entry to being successful in our current as well as every future reality. Our constantly disruptive environment continues to create infinite choice and possibilities for a rapidly evolving, dispersed, and diverse workforce.

This workforce demands a new kind of leader—a leader who can see, develop, and unleash the greatness in every person. A leader who can model authentic behavior with humility and courage. A leader who can inspire others to willingly give their hearts and minds because they want to contribute meaningfully to something that matters.

Anyone can be this kind of leader. Everyone needs this kind of leader. Every child, every home, every classroom. Every colleague, team, organization, industry, and country.

This new way to lead works in any era, in any context and circumstance, in any industry and role. It works with any job to be done, amid change—anytime, anywhere, in any relationship.

A leadership style for the ages, a leadership style that is timeless.

Indeed, a new way to lead: *Trust & Inspire*.

CHAPTER 1

The World Has Changed, Our Style of Leadership Has Not

In a few hundred years, when the history of our time is written from a long-term perspective, it is likely that the most important event these historians will see is not technology, not internet, not e-commerce. It is an unprecedented change in the human condition. For the first time—literally—substantial and rapidly growing numbers of people have choices. For the first time, they will have to manage themselves. And society is totally unprepared for it.

—PETER DRUCKER

I was fortunate to share the stage at public seminars with my late father, where he began almost every session by posing two simple but provocative questions to the audiences:

"By a raise of hands, how many of you believe that the vast majority of the workforce in your organization possess far more talent, creativity, ingenuity, intelligence, and ability than their present jobs require or even allow them to contribute?"

Invariably, almost every hand in the room went up.

Then he asked, "And how many of you believe that the vast majority of the workforce in your organization are under immense and growing pressure to produce substantially more for less?"

Again, almost every hand in the room went up.

Just think about it: in city after city throughout the world, there was nearly universal agreement that the vast majority of the people in most organizations face enormous and growing expectations to produce substantially more for less in an increasingly complex world. Yet they are simply not able, or even allowed, to use a significant portion of their talents and abilities to do so.

Let that settle in for a moment.

The difference between what we are doing and what we're capable of doing would solve most of the world's problems.

—MAHATMA GANDHI

In order to bridge this gap, we can't continue to "manage" people in the same way we have in the past. It's time to change, for leadership to catch up with how we've changed. In a world characterized by profound disruption, we can't continue to rely on a management style that has become dated and ineffective. Both the type of work being done (service and knowledge work in a collaborative, team-based way) and where it's done (whether on-site, hybrid, or virtual, working from home or anywhere), we need a new way of leading. Where the workforce is more diverse than ever before, and multiple generations have radically different expectations, we need a new way of leading. Where choices and options have grown exponentially into near-infinite choice, we need a new way of leading relevant for our times.

With unprecedented choices and constant change, people are unlikely to be moved by, or ultimately even tolerate, leadership that doesn't match today's world. And yet the vast majority continue to lead, to parent, to teach, to coach with the same Command & Control style that brought us through the industrial age.

The world has changed. Our style of leadership has not.

As I work with people and leaders from around the world, I often hear expressions of frustration and concern related to the need to adapt:

My boss is constantly looking over my shoulder and second-guessing my decisions. Our company talks a lot about building a positive team culture—but I don't see it. Why did they hire me if they don't trust me?

I'm a manager at a company where I know several of my direct reports are also freelancing on the side. They say they like the autonomy and extra income of the gig economy but need the security of a salaried job. I feel like I'm not getting their best effort. How do I win their hearts and minds when I can't pay them any more than I already am?

Working from home has been great in a lot of ways, but it also makes me feel less connected to my colleagues. I don't feel like I reach the same level of creativity when I'm working alone—and it's not nearly as energizing. How do I bridge the gap?

My company talks a lot about the importance of diversity and inclusion, but beyond talking points, I'm wondering if they mean what they say? And how to be involved in these types of changes I'd like to see?

How can I be an effective boss and keep my people? It seems like these new generations don't mind leaving a company at the drop of a hat.

I like my job, but honestly, I don't feel like my work matters. It's hard to find meaning when the work you do doesn't feel significant. And if it doesn't feel important to me as a manager, how much less important must it feel to my employees?

Working from home has been nice for my team, but it has also made accountability a lot more difficult. How do I balance holding others accountable without looking like I don't trust them or that I'm just micromanaging them from a distance?

I lead a global team and struggle with cultural differences. The truth is, I have never left my own country. How can I lead and inspire people from different cultures when I lack experience?

I'm so frustrated by the state of politics and lack of civility in my country, and I'm convinced it's seeping into our work culture as well. How can I bring about change or make a difference when I don't know who or what to trust?

I'm worried about raising my kids in this modern age. It feels like they grow up so much faster now than when I was a kid. How can I teach them to navigate our new world today when I don't have all of the answers myself?

These statements reflect real concerns people have about the challenges we face today, that we'll attempt to answer and help navigate in the book. What would you add to the list?

The question is not whether we are able to change but whether we are changing fast enough.

—ANGELA MERKEL

These mega changes we are experiencing are a result of what I call the "Five Emerging Forces." These forces of change are sweeping through our world and impacting our work and our lives in unprecedented ways. We might try to avoid or ignore them, but they will not ignore us.

The Five Emerging Forces

1. The Nature of the *World* Has Changed

Technological innovations are bringing about extraordinary changes; not only is the *amount* of change unprecedented, but so is the pace or *rate* of it. In addition, the *type* of change—characterized by disruptive technologies—is impacting every society, industry, organization, and person. These technological innovations are happening in all areas, including the biosciences, artificial intelligence, machine learning, robotics, automation, virtual and augmented reality, digitization, nanotechnology, the internet of things, 3-D printing—the list goes on and on. These changes are converging and blending in what is being called "the Fourth Industrial Revolution."

On top of this rapid technological disruption, never before in history has so much knowledge and information been available. Scott Sorokin in *CIO* magazine notes that up until 1900, experts estimated that human knowledge doubled with every century. In 1982, it was estimated that knowledge doubled every thirteen months. Now, forty years later, experts suggest that human knowledge doubles every twelve hours. This explosion of knowledge has changed the way we view the past and made us think differently about the future. It has made it impossible to be what Dr. Carol Dweck of Stanford calls a "know-it-all," as there is simply too much knowledge and technology to be ingested. Instead, a premium is being placed on becoming a "learn-it-all"—being able to learn, and even relearn, faster than ever before.

This overflow of knowledge combined with significant disruption—whether through technology or through a global pandemic—has led to major societal changes and brought some industries and companies to their knees. Technological innovation has created new business models and even entire new industries, and opened the doors for nearly limitless possibilities. The accessibility of smartphones alone has significantly changed the way we not only do business but how we live our everyday lives. We do not live in a stagnant world; rather, it is erupting with risks and opportunities to which we must constantly adapt—as human beings, as businesses, as families, and as communities.

2. The Nature of *Work* Has Changed

The *what* of work today has become increasingly knowledge- and service-based, with access to instant and simultaneous information. It is far more collaborative, innovative, and creative than ever before. Traditional manual or industrial-age work, while still important, represents less and less of the work being done as we've definitively shifted into a new era.

Increasingly, people are being asked to focus on work that requires more of their minds and less of their hands, while those who work with their hands are being asked to augment their work with their minds. As the nature of the world continues to change through technological innovations, this reality will only become more and more relevant.

Most significantly, the way the work is being done is increasingly collaborative, requiring people to work in flexible, interdependent teams—to create and innovate together.

3. The Nature of the *Workplace* Has Changed

In addition to changes in *what* kind of work we do, there are also major shifts happening related to *where* we work. Working from home or working from anywhere had been growing, even before the disruption of the global COVID-19 pandemic, which tremendously accelerated this trend. Today, it's fast becoming the norm, particularly in some form of blended or hybrid combination with on-site work—a truly dispersed workplace.

While working in flexible, interconnected teams, most have some element of operating virtually; in fact, many are entirely virtual. Team members, whether globally dispersed or working in proximity, may work on the same project and never meet physically face-to-face. The idea of a shared physical workplace is nonexistent for some organizations and becoming less relevant for others. The traditional hierarchal organizational structure is becoming flatter in order to push decision making down and increase speed and flexibility.

The net effect is that people are taking their work around the globe, free of the constraints of a conventional office. These new ways and places of working have led to, and will continue to lead to, changes in organizational structures and systems and will have a significant impact on workplace culture.

4. The Nature of the *Workforce* Has Changed

Our workforce is far more diverse than it has ever been before, filled with people from different generations, genders, races, ethnicities, sexual orientations, religions, cultures, backgrounds, experiences, and perspectives. The goal is to create an inclusive culture for all that enables us to maximize our diversity—our differences—as our greatest strength. The greater the contrast in our differences, the greater the potential for creativity and innovation.

One example of the changing workforce is the multiple generations working alongside each other, as many as five different ones. As younger generations, such as Millennials and Gen Z, populate a larger percentage of the workforce, they bring with them different experiences, perspectives, and ideas. They have different expectations of their work and of their bosses than the older generations. The social contract has changed. What people want has changed. A paycheck is not enough. It matters to people how they are led, and they want to know that their contribution really matters. This inherently changes the way not only that the workforce operates, but also the way our societies and families operate.

5. The Nature of *Choice* Has Changed

The advances in technology have taken us from multiple choice to infinite choice, as consumers and as team members and leaders. For consumers, there are literally thousands of options available at the click of a button when it comes to TV shows, movies, games, clothing, tools, food, and everything else. Access to literally anything from anywhere in the world has never been greater.

But perhaps the most impactful choices and options have exploded in job and working opportunities. Because of the rise of virtual work, people have far greater options to work with a company in a location other than where they live. The remarkable growth of freelancing and the gig economy has given people more flexibility and options. Based on growth trends, some experts predict that there will be more freelancers than traditional jobholders by 2023.

With this flexibility and increased choice, it's important for leaders and organizations to create the kind of culture that attracts, retains, and inspires people. Never have people had anything close to the same ability to choose what their life will be than they do now.

To illustrate, I recently spoke with a sales professional who said that during the pandemic, she decided that from now on she was going to live where she wanted to live. She also decided that she simply wasn't going to take a job that required her to travel frequently. As a consistently high-performing sales producer, she realized she no longer had to. She saw in this new way of working that she had an unprecedented number of choices and options to do whatever she wanted, with whomever she wanted, wherever she wanted. She could choose to work with an increasing number of companies that valued her. Going forward, she said, she'd choose the firm where she felt most believed in, trusted, inspired, and valued.

———

These Five Emerging Forces are at work in our world regardless of whether we see them or are even aware of them. These forces of change are swirling around our jobs, our schools, our families, and our communities. In order to thrive, let alone survive, in this whirlwind of change, we organizationally and as leaders need to adapt as fast as things are changing around us. If we fail to adapt, we will likely not be able to deliver on the two epic imperatives of our time—

the most essential and critical needs of every organization in this new environment.

The Epic Imperatives of Our Time

All organizations today have two epic imperatives to achieve. First is the ability to create a high-trust culture that can attract, retain, engage, and inspire the best people—and thus win the ongoing war for talent. In other words, *win in the workplace*. Second is the ability to collaborate and innovate successfully enough to stay highly relevant in a changing, disruptive world. In other words, *win in the marketplace*. As Microsoft CEO Satya Nadella succinctly put it, "Our industry respects innovation, not tradition."

The bottom line is that if we cannot deliver on these two epic imperatives, we won't be able to sustain success in our new world.

Today we have cell phones in our hands that are more powerful than the original computers that helped astronauts get to the moon. How ironic, then, that in practical application, we still manage and motivate people by applying the same "carrot-and-stick" tactics and techniques that were cutting edge before computers of any kind even existed!

Management thinker Gary Hamel pointed out that most of the essential tools and techniques of modern management were invented by people born in the nineteenth century, not long after the end of the American Civil War. If you put a 1960s-era CEO in a time machine and transported them to today, Hamel said, that CEO "would find a great many of today's management rituals little changed from those that governed corporate life a generation or two ago."

The world has changed—but our style of leadership has not.

The Five Emerging Forces show that we need to change the way we lead if we hope to stay relevant. Marc Benioff, founder of Salesforce, described the future as "a work anywhere, live anywhere environment," remarking how "we're in the future" already. This is true for those working within organizations, but also freelance or on their own. People can work remotely and live nomadically. This new way of working and living requires a new way of leading. To succeed in the war for talent, we must stay current, remain relevant, and become intentionally flexible—not just with technology, but especially with the shifting needs and expectations of our people.

The need to adopt a new way of leading has never been more important or relevant than today if we want to be effective bosses, good parents, and productive citizens. What has worked in the past simply won't work anymore. In order to influence those around us, we need to better understand the changing world in which we operate. We can successfully lead in today's world only if we reject the Command & Control style of yesterday's leadership and instead adopt a new style that's far more relevant and suited for our times—Trust & Inspire.

Trust & Inspire is about seeing, communicating, developing, and unleashing the potential for greatness within people—tapping into what's inside. It's intrinsic; it's already there. Our job is to bring it out, to ignite the fire within, and to create an environment where that's possible and welcome.

People want this kind of leadership, and they want it now. A recent Young Presidents Organization (YPO) Global Pulse study concluded that "forward-thinking business leaders are moving away from traditional, Command & Control style of leadership toward a new, people-centered approach." That people-centered approach is Trust & Inspire. It's what is needed to lead today. It's what is needed to advance organizations and society as a whole. It's what enables us to build teams, collaborate, and innovate. And it's what attracts and engages today's top talent.

The Impact of a Trust & Inspire Leader

Not that long ago, the tech giant Microsoft wasn't as imposing as it once was. In fact, it was beginning to fade. Innovation had all but ceased. Its culture was on the rocks. It was losing relevance in the marketplace as well as in the workplace.

In *Vanity Fair*, reporter and author Bethany McLean summed up Microsoft's situation at the time: "There's a sense in the world outside Redmond, Washington, that Microsoft's best days are behind it, that the sprawling colossus, which employs more than 100,000 people, doesn't know what it is, or even what it wants to be."

Ouch.

Then along came India-born Satya Nadella, who succeeded Steve Ballmer to become Microsoft's CEO in 2014. No one envied what Nadella faced. In fact, in a *Fast Company* article, Harry McCracken put it bluntly: "The Microsoft that Nadella inherited was regarded by both Wall Street and Silicon Valley as fading toward irrelevance"—which the market bore out, too. In 2014, Apple and Google were both flourishing to record valuations while Microsoft's stock price had plummeted, then languished to a standstill. The entire industry had moved from Microsoft's forte of desktop computers to smartphones, quickly leaving Microsoft behind as the market share of Windows on smartphones fell to less than 4 percent. Moreover, top talent was leaving. It was no longer perceived as a cool place to work. Any way you looked at it, the situation was bleak.

A foundational problem was Microsoft's culture. A cartoonist at the time depicted the company's organizational chart as a pyramid-shaped hierarchy; a hand stuck out of each spot on the pyramid, pointing a gun directly at one of the others. The implication was clear: this was war. Word throughout the industry maintained that the only way to "win" at Microsoft at the time was to take out those ahead of you.

Nadella immediately assessed what was going on and how it was affecting Microsoft's sustainability. In his memoir, *Hit Refresh*, Nadella described the era of warring gangs by saying, "Innovation was being replaced by bureaucracy. Teamwork was being replaced by internal politics. We were falling behind."

Changing Microsoft's culture was Nadella's number one goal as CEO. Why? Because as a Trust & Inspire leader, he understood the first epic imperative of our time: to succeed, you must win in the workplace by attracting, retaining, engaging, and inspiring the best people.

Nadella came in quietly and thoughtfully, with little to no swagger or hubris, and right away modeled a Trust & Inspire leadership style that ultimately transformed the company culture. He began by modeling the behavior he was seeking—humility, empathy, authenticity, personal growth, creativity, collaboration. His leadership paradigm was one of trusting and inspiring others—manifest by adopting a "growth mindset," not only for himself but also for others, unleashing them to become the driving force of Microsoft's success. He successfully revitalized the company's cutthroat culture, completely changing the trajectory of Microsoft.

The result? Nadella has inspired the care and admiration of the people he serves. An employee survey showed a 92 percent CEO approval. For a company of more than a hundred thousand employees, that's remarkable.

Above all, Microsoft again became perceived as a relevant and exciting place to work.

It didn't stop there. Nadella squarely took on the second epic imperative of our time, the need to collaborate and innovate in order to win in the marketplace. He reviewed Microsoft's mission and strategy and revamped them to enable greater teaming and collaboration and to enrich the organization. He inspired people to aim for more and trusted them to do what it took to achieve that goal. They began to collaborate internally, and they began to innovate again in new technologies and new markets.

The results speak for themselves: when Nadella became CEO, Microsoft's market value was around $300 billion. It now exceeds $2 trillion, the second company in history to pull off that high a valuation. It was a turnaround few would have believed possible.

Considered a has-been story just a few years ago, Microsoft became the world's cloud powerhouse. It was nothing short of a grand reinvention. And at its roots that was fundamentally due to the inspiring leadership style of their new leader—a style that unleashed people's potential and that enabled everything else.

Being a leader is a privilege you have. Your job is about being able to help people realize their best potential. That's what, in fact, is expected of you.

—SATYA NADELLA, CEO OF MICROSOFT

A teacher recently told me the contrasting experience of two principals she had worked for in back-to-back years. The first principal operated with a style we might call "benevolent" Command & Control. He was competent, nice, and respectful—but he didn't trust his teachers. He often threw them under the bus when it came to situations with parents. He told them one thing to their face and then did the opposite once they were gone.

Needless to say, the culture among the teachers and staff was draining and joyless, and the turnover rate at the school soared. Many teachers even left during the middle of the school year despite not having a new job to go to.

The next year the school got a new principal. She was a Trust & Inspire leader, believing in and trusting teachers from day one and recognizing the hard work they did. She connected with teachers, staff, and students and cared about the work and them. She was open and transparent, and connected them all to the larger purpose of the power of education.

Even though nothing else in the school changed—the copier still broke almost every day and the budget was tighter than ever—the change in the experience among the teachers, staff, and even students and parents was enormous. People felt energized and excited. They started to collaborate and innovate, and they came up with terrific programs for the school to implement. The turnover rate dropped dramatically. People wanted to stay because they felt trusted by the leader, and how she modeled building relationships of trust began to ripple through the school.

This leader rekindled the fire that inspired teachers to teach in the first place. And the students learned more and better than before as evidenced by their engagement in class and historic highs in their testing results.

Command & Control versus Trust & Inspire

Perhaps the best way to understand why and how Trust & Inspire leadership is more relevant and apt for our day is to see how it contrasts to the style of Command & Control, even its more sophisticated version of Enlightened Command & Control.

Command & Control leaders operate under a paradigm of position and power. Trust & Inspire leaders operate under a paradigm of people and potential. It might be easier to see in parenting, where Command & Control parents are the ultimate micromanagers—afraid to let go and give up control, always looking over their child's shoulder. Trust & Inspire parents are the ultimate leaders—trusting and supporting their children as those children take chances. The same goes for organizations. For many Command & Control leaders, the biggest challenge is simply being able to let go.

Command & Control leaders may get compliance, but typically not much more. While compliance is necessary, it's woefully insufficient.

Trust & Inspire, on the other hand, is about garnering heartfelt commitment that's freely and enthusiastically given. Commitment is worlds apart from compliance, and it leads to a much higher level of engagement, innovation, and inspiration while creating far greater outcomes.

Command & Control is transactional—get the deal, finish the job, stop an undesirable behavior, and do it fast. That's the notion of efficiency shining through. Trust & Inspire is transformational—it focuses on building relationships; on developing capabilities; on enabling, empowering, and growing people. And the irony is that not only is this the far more enduring approach, it's actually the more efficient way to get things done as well. Remember this: *with people, fast is slow and slow is fast*.

Over the years, I have been compiling a growing list of contrasts between these two overarching leadership styles. I'd like to highlight here a few of the comparisons that I believe will make the contrast clearer, and I'll provide a summary list of new contrasts at the end of each chapter as we learn more about a Trust & Inspire approach. You can find a comprehensive list in the Appendix and an ever-growing list online where you can add your own insights.

As you consider these contrasts, think about your own life. When have you experienced the concepts associated with Command & Control? And when have you experienced those on the side of Trust & Inspire? Perhaps more importantly, which side of the experience do you create for those you serve? For your coworkers? Your customers? Your students? Your kids?

COMMAND & CONTROL	TRUST & INSPIRE
Compliance	Commitment
Transactional	Transformational
Efficiency	Effectiveness
Status Quo and Incrementalism	Change and Innovation
Fixed Mindset	Growth Mindset
Coordination among Functional Silos	Collaboration among Flexible, Interconnected Teams
Control, Contain	Release, Unleash
Motivation	Inspiration
Manage People and Things	Manage Things, Lead People

Manage Things, Lead People

Before moving on, let's dig a little deeper into that last contrast: When you think of a *manager*, what is the first thing that pops into your head?

Now, what pops into your head when I ask you to think of a *leader*? Is there a difference in the things or people that come to mind? Perhaps that difference becomes all the more clear when you contrast what it feels like to be "managed" versus what it feels like to be "led."

The distinctions between management and leadership began to be delineated decades ago starting with Harvard Business School professor Abraham Zaleznik, who posed the question "Managers and Leaders: Are They Different?" The delineations have continued through Peter Drucker, John Kotter, Warren Bennis, Herminia Ibarra, and many more of today's influential thinkers. Yet, despite all our progress in overlapping and distinguishing between the two, the reality is that in today's society, the terms are still typically used interchangeably.

I'm a huge believer in great management. I also believe we need equally great leadership. While both management and leadership are vitally needed, we live in a world that is overmanaged and underled. In fact, most teams, families, and organizations today are overmanaged and underled. Why? There is a disproportionately vital dimension in the contrast between the two, both in definition and in practical application. And that dimension lies in the contrast between people and things.

People in positions of leadership are frequently referred to as *managers*. While many people are comfortable saying something like "Susan is my manager," it would feel very different to say, "Susan is the person in charge of managing me." No one would go into a job interview and say, "My name is Aaron, and I'll do a decent job, but I really need to be managed."

The definition of *manage* is "to handle with a degree of skill." Its etymology comes from the Latin *manus*, which means "hand," and from the Italian *maneggiare*, which means "to handle horses or handle tools." Nobody wants to be handled, much less admit to the idea that they really need to be handled by someone with a degree of skill—it's dehumanizing and feels outright controlling. It perceives and treats an employee as an object or thing instead of as a whole person with a body, heart, mind, and spirit.

Many things need to be managed, even handled with skill. One example is technology, to be used effectively to help us solve problems and improve efficiencies. Schedules need to be managed to be coordinated and aligned to help things get done. Finances need to be managed so revenue, taxes, expenses, payroll, and investments are tracked and in line. Inventories, processes, systems, structures, supply chains all need to be managed. Those are all resources, tools, objects—*things*. Things serve a purpose and are generally some form of tool for accomplishing a task. But because things have no autonomy or choice, they need to be managed well in order to be effective or valuable.

We need leaders who are great at managing *things*.

Here's the problem: those with a Command & Control mindset typically manage *people* the same way they manage *things*. The constant focus on efficiency often leads to managers treating people the same way they would treat a machine.

But when you try to manage people like you manage things, you deny the very qualities people possess that bring real, unique value and enable them to solve problems and make decisions in creative, productive ways outside of how you might. In contrast to things, people can be inspired and show empathy. People have autonomy and choice. In fact, people's greatest value comes when that autonomy is willingly and passionately given, engaged, and unleashed.

The same management thinking around control and containment that works so efficiently with things simply does not work effectively when applied to people. People don't want to be managed or handled. This approach no longer works in our world today (if it ever did). People won't stay at a job where they're being controlled or treated like a replaceable tool or component, as if they were exchangeable or replaceable. You can manage resources. You can manage systems. You can manage processes and procedures. But you cannot effectively manage people.

Managing people doesn't always go poorly, but it rarely goes well. People might perform well enough to get by, but how big is the gap between performance and potential? Few things demotivate or demoralize people more than being controlled and constantly being told what to do. Not only is that disempowering, it can also kill initiative.

Consider the parable of the flea. When fleas are initially placed in a jar, they jump right out of it. But if a lid is put on the jar, the fleas hit the lid when they try to jump out of the jar. Over time, the fleas will jump only high enough to avoid hitting the lid. When the lid is then taken off, the fleas are fully capable of jumping right out of the jar— but their previous conditioning stops them from doing so.

In many ways, Command & Control is the human equivalent of this type of conditioning. The limiting of potential is perhaps an unintended consequence of being managed like a thing.

Comparatively, the flexibility, trust, and autonomy inherent in the Trust & Inspire approach encourages and inspires people. It conditions them to see and develop their capabilities and potential. They feel invested, they feel energized, they take initiative—and while they don't want to be managed, they absolutely want to be led.

Operating with a Trust & Inspire mindset means you manage things and you lead people. You're efficient with things, systems, and processes (a great manager), but you're also effective with people (a great leader). This distinction is key to narrowing the gap between potential and performance. And it's also key to tapping into purpose and meaning. As my late colleague Blaine Lee always used to remind me, "Meaning is not in things; meaning is in people."

Motivation versus Inspiration

The other contrast I want to highlight between Command & Control and Trust & Inspire is the critical distinction between motivation and inspiration.

Despite all the advances we've made in how we view and treat people, we rarely focus on inspiring them. We'd like to, but it's not always easy to know how to really connect with someone or how to tap into something that lights a person up. We might also think that only charismatic people can inspire others.

So instead, we've made a science of *motivating* people. How do we motivate our teams to hit their sales numbers? How do we motivate a child to do better in school? How do we motivate ourselves to lose weight or finish a project? The prevailing operating premise behind motivation is that we need to be "moved" to do something.

Interestingly, nearly all efforts to motivate people can be summed up in two very basic approaches: *the carrot* or *the stick*. The carrot offers rewards; the stick threatens negative consequences. Gain or pain. To be clear, carrot-and-stick motivation generally falls under a Command & Control style. The approach is intended to manipulate a person's normal disposition in order to get what we want.

In reality, motivation isn't bad. In fact, it can be good. We all like to be motivated, but motivation has its limits. The best of what we need from ourselves and from others is only accessible far beyond the confines of where motivation alone can take us.

A carrot-and-stick approach worked reasonably well during the industrial age. People were predominantly focused on survival and stability, fulfilling the lower levels on Maslow's hierarchy of needs. It was also well suited to the type of work that needed to be done.

Building on the work of Douglas McGregor, William Ouchi, and others, author Daniel Pink, in his significant book *Drive*, explained that all forms of carrot-and-stick motivation are *extrinsic* motivators—things outside of us that get us to do something. He makes the compelling case that to solve the problems we face today, we have to move from extrinsic motivation to intrinsic motivation, focusing on the upper echelons of Maslow's hierarchy of needs: belonging, esteem, and self-actualization—and Maslow's later addition, *self-transcendence*. The idea is to unleash the inherent "drive" that is inside people instead of trying to drive people ourselves. As Pink put it, "Human beings have an innate inner drive to be autonomous, self-determined, and connected to one another. And when that drive is liberated, people achieve more and live richer lives."

Inspiration is all about helping people find their inner drive—their inner spark—and ignite it into a blaze of genuine excitement and passion. To inspire rather than require. To breathe life into rather than to suffocate or extinguish.

When you are inspired by some great purpose, some extraordinary project, all your thoughts break their bounds. Your mind transcends limitations, your consciousness expands in every direction, and you find yourself in a new, great and wonderful world.

—THE YOGA SUTRAS OF PATANJALI

While the Five Emerging Forces show how work, the workplace, and the workforce have significantly changed in our new digital age, the reality is that not a lot has changed in regard to motivation. Many, if not most, organizations still rely primarily on carrot-and-stick reward systems. Most schools do as well. And probably nobody does carrot-and-stick better than parents.

At the most basic level, carrot-and-stick is transactional: If you do X, then you'll get Y. If you behave well, you'll get a reward. If you behave poorly, you'll get punished. If you turn in your assignments, you'll get a good grade. If you don't meet your quota, you'll get let go. If you clean your room, you'll get your allowance. Take away the reward or the punishment—the external motivating factors—and more often than not, people stop the desired behavior.

Talk about the ultimate manifestation of Command & Control! We command an action, then we control the consequence. This requires little thought, little consideration, and little development of the person. And if we're not there, the person either doesn't know what to do or doesn't care. No real changes have taken place.

Command & Control leaders love carrot-and-stick, both because they know it well and because it works. At least, it *seems* to work for what they want. Carrot-and-stick can be used almost ad nauseam to get someone to complete a task or achieve a certain number. It can be productive. It can even be impressive. But it's not much different from teaching a rat to find its way through a maze or a dog to sit. Here's the catch, as Pink noted: "Do rewards motivate? Absolutely, they motivate people to get more rewards."

Extrinsic motivation offers short-term success, but it has proven to be deficient, or even detrimental, in the long run. Why? It can create crippling dependencies. It's conditioning, not developing. Behaviorism, not autonomy. That's why carrot-and-stick is often referred to as "the great jackass theory of motivation."

Why do you think cheating in high school and college is on the rise? The emphasis on grades and getting into a good college motivates students (and sometimes even parents) to cheat—on assignments, essays, and standardized tests. Even on admissions applications. A recent study showed that 86 percent of students surveyed admitted to some kind of cheating in school, and 54 percent of them said they thought cheating was okay. Some even thought it was necessary to succeed.

Talk about motivation backfiring! Many students are motivated to get a degree; some are inspired to get an education. There's a world of difference between the two, both in the chosen path and especially in the outcome. We need more than just graduates who have degrees of knowledge and achievement. We need educated people who have wisdom and passion and who want to make meaningful contributions.

When we inspire others, they might feel a sense of purpose and excitement. They feel that their work matters; more importantly, they feel that *they* matter. They don't want to fail because they are invested in and care about the project, not because they're scared of being punished. When they deliver results, they feel a sense of accomplishment that is more meaningful and fulfilling than receiving an extrinsic reward alone. The ownership and pride they feel leads to creativity and the desire to innovate—to achieve even better results.

This leads to long-term success and happier people whose holistic needs are being met.

When things are going wrong, the common refrain from managers is, "Why aren't my people motivated?" The managers blame employees, while starting to devise ways to motivate people. A humorous example of this comes from the TV sitcom *The Office*, when the manager, Andy Bernard—needing to meet a quarterly sales quota—tries to motivate his staff by coming up with some lofty reward. He somehow decides to offer to let them choose what tattoo to put on his behind if they hit quota. This is clearly a short-term solution, and even he recognizes there's only so many places he can get a tattoo.

Instead of asking "Why aren't my people motivated?" a far better question to ask yourself is "How can I better inspire those I lead?"

Too often we focus simply on cosmetic changes—a new system of rewards, like offering bonuses, or a new system of punishment, like putting a child in "time-out." Neither is necessarily bad, but neither changes inner motivation and drive. Neither makes others want to be better. Neither of them inspires. And in a new world filled with upcoming generations who care more about passion than they do about possessions, we would do well to abandon surface-level changes and lip service—and to focus instead on authentic inspiration, on breathing life into relationships, teams, and organizations.

> *There are only two ways to influence human behavior. You can manipulate it, or you can inspire it.*
>
> —SIMON SINEK, AUTHOR OF *START WITH WHY*

We can intentionally inspire others when we connect with people and connect to purpose. I'll never forget an impactful conversation I had with Indra Nooyi when she was serving as chair and CEO of PepsiCo. Through an all-encompassing leadership approach she called "Performance with Purpose," she had already inspired her people by connecting them to purpose, meaning, and contribution in their work. But what really struck me was how she also inspired others by personally connecting with them by genuinely caring about them.

She shared with me that during a visit to her family in India, she noticed the pride her mother felt when others praised her for raising Indra to be such a successful leader. She particularly noticed how others' praise was not to Indra for being a CEO but rather for her mother (and late father) who had raised her. "They told my mom, 'You did such a good job with your daughter. Compliments to you. She's CEO.' No one said a word to me."

Indra realized that the leaders of her own company had parents who deserved to hear the same thing about their children. The experience with her mother inspired Indra to write as many as four hundred personal letters annually to the parents of her senior executives. In the letters, she thanked the parents for their magnificent work in raising such good and capable sons and daughters.

Both the parents and the senior executives were sincerely touched by Indra's heartfelt letters. They were also *inspired*. People felt valued and seen as whole people, not just people who were compartmentalized for their work. One of her executives exclaimed, "My God, this is the best thing that's happened to my parents. And it's the best thing that's happened to me."

How would you feel if your boss sent a similar letter to your parents or spouse? Or even your children? Knowing that someone cares about us and recognizes the work we do is crucial to a fulfilled life, because it honors the whole person. Not only that, it inspires us.

Self-Reflection

Nothing creates dependency faster than Command & Control, while nothing drives or lights the fire within like Trust & Inspire. We can sway people to action, or we can inspire them to greater performance. Ask yourself:

- As a leader, do I motivate my team to compliance, coordination, and incremental improvement? Or do I inspire them to commitment, collaboration, and creative innovation?

- As a parent, do I talk at and micromanage my children? Or do I communicate with them, guide them, and trust them to make smart decisions?

- As a teacher, do I motivate my students to get the assignments turned in? Or do I inspire them to learn and to get an education?

Regardless of your situation, you can extend trust and you can inspire. As you come to see leadership as a stewardship and people as whole people, you can become the kind of leader that will succeed best in today's world.

If you're still trying to win by motivating people rather than inspiring them, you're playing tennis with a golf club. Remember that the game has changed.

You Can Choose to Be a Leader

Some of you might be reading this book and thinking, *Well, interesting start, but I'm not in a leadership role or position, so I guess this isn't for me*. I'm happy to say you are wrong, my friend! This book is for you because you *are* a leader. Leadership is a choice, not a position. Quite often, the most influential leaders are the ones without a formal title or position.

Consider Mohandas Gandhi. He never held a formal government or leadership position, but today he is commonly considered the father of modern India because of the influence of his leadership—all without a title.

A Pakistani schoolgirl named Malala Yousafzai stood up for women's rights against the Taliban and galvanized global support for the cause of girls' and women's education. Her work garnered her the Nobel Peace Prize at the age of fourteen, the youngest recipient ever—all without a title.

I have a friend named Pedro Medina, a businessperson in the Republic of Colombia. In 1999, Colombia was considered one of the most dangerous places on earth, plagued by kidnappings, terrorist acts, drug cartels, and social instability. While teaching at a local university, Medina asked his students how many of them were planning to stay in Colombia after graduation. Only a few hands went up.

That response pained him. He asked those who didn't raise their hands, "Why do you want to leave?" They responded, "We have lost hope. Can you tell us why we should stay?"

That question haunted him. He ultimately came up with very compelling reasons, and soon thereafter he founded an organization called *Yo Creo en Colombia*—"I Believe in Colombia."

The organization was a grassroots initiative whose primary purpose was and continues to be to increase trust and confidence in Colombia, first at home and then abroad. It reaches out to Colombians to advocate for the achievements, potential, and resources of the country and to leverage those "in order to build a fair, competitive, and inclusive nation." Since its inception, the foundation has touched hundreds of thousands of Colombians in 157 cities and 26 countries.

Medina created a powerful social movement—all without a title. He held no position that required him to create the organization. But his efforts not only took off at the grassroots level, they spawned significant structural and institutional changes at all levels, including the national level. Three years after Medina began his initiative, Alvaro Uribe, inspired by the impact of *Yo Creo en Colombia* and the numerous like-minded initiatives it inspired, was elected president of the country on the very platform Medina had articulated, *"restaurando la confianza"* (restoring trust). Uribe was also the first Colombian to be reelected president in more than a century.

Today there is still great work to do, but Colombia has made massive strides in restoring trust in security, investment, and social cohesion—the very things Medina set out to impact, all without a title or a formal position.

It doesn't matter if you're a full-time parent, an experienced administrator, a brand-new intern, a community organizer, or a CFO. You do not have to "supervise people" or be in a certain role or situation to be a leader. Author Keith Ferrazzi writes about "leading without authority," a situation in which team members "co-elevate" themselves and others to share in the leadership role of the team, even when they're not the formal team leader. You can be a leader to anyone and everyone around you. You can exercise your circle of influence to be a Trust & Inspire leader—even if it's only for yourself and is manifest only in how you lead your life.

As we move into the Trust & Inspire solution, keep in mind that this *is* for you, regardless of your role. You'll find examples from business, education, health care, government, military, nonprofits, sports, communities, and families. Even if the specifics of a particular example don't directly relate to you, the overarching principles always do. And by applying principles, you will be able to become a more relevant leader in today's world—even a Trust & Inspire leader. And when people are trusted and inspired, they rise to the occasion, develop capabilities, and reciprocate. They reach their potential and they find their voice, and help others then in turn do the same.

THE WORLD HAS CHANGED

Being trusted and inspired brings out the very best—the greatness—in all of us.

COMMAND & CONTROL	TRUST & INSPIRE
Extrinsic	Intrinsic
Require	Inspire
Suffocate	"Breathe Life Into"
Conditioning	Developing
Behaviorism	Autonomy
Leadership Is a Position	Leadership Is a Choice

CHAPTER 2

The Increasing Irrelevance of Command & Control

In these troubled times, we don't need more command and control; we need better means to engage everyone's intelligence in solving challenges and crises as they arise.

—MARGARET WHEATLEY, AUTHOR OF *LEADERSHIP AND THE NEW SCIENCE*

"Nothing fails like success."

I have long loved this phrase, but if it doesn't make sense, let me explain. That thought is often attributed to historian Arnold Toynbee, who chronicled the rise and fall of civilizations. He posited that when societies face challenges, they respond with creativity and innovation in finding successful solutions to those challenges. But over time, the nature of the challenge inevitably changes, yet societies too often respond to the new challenge with their old approach. Their once-successful response simply doesn't work in addressing the new challenge—hence the expression "Nothing fails like success."

It's natural to use a response that worked well in the past to solve new problems, especially if that response worked well multiple times. But with the changing nature of work, as the Five Emerging Forces reveal, we need a fresh response to new challenges.

Warren Buffett succinctly captured the choice we face: "Should you find yourself in a chronically leaking boat, energy devoted to changing vessels is likely to be more productive than energy devoted to patching leaks."

We are far past the point where we can continue to patch the leaky vessel. We need a new boat. We need a new way of leading.

Put another way, it's a new world of unprecedented change, and the boat that worked yesterday will sink today. The need to move to a new style of leadership—relevant for our times—has never been more important than now. We cannot afford to approach today's challenges with yesterday's solutions, only to find out again and again that "nothing fails like success."

A Case Study in "Nothing Fails Like Success"

Blockbuster Video is a simple illustration of "nothing fails like success." At its peak in 2000, Blockbuster was extremely successful; 84,000 employees worked in 9,000 stores, producing nearly $6 billion in revenue while serving 65 million customers all over the world.

At the time, almost everyone who watched movies at home rented them from stores. Then the technology started to shift. Instead of having to go to a store to rent a movie, customers could get DVDs in the mail through a new entrepreneurial company called Netflix. Blockbuster was slow to the game, having previously turned down the chance to buy Netflix, and then again to partner with them.

Next came streaming movies over the internet. The new business model Netflix utilized was a subscription service, first by mail and then streaming. No late fees were charged. Again, Blockbuster was slow to respond to the new challenge. They were afraid of cannibalizing themselves: they wanted to protect their previously successful business model of video rentals through their nine thousand stores, and they wanted to continue to collect late fees when people didn't return their videos on time.

By the time Blockbuster finally responded to the changing way of doing things, it was way too late.

Today, Blockbuster has only one store, in Bend, Oregon, and it is, quite literally, a relic of the past. Netflix led the digital streaming revolution and continues to be a dominant player. Even though they've been challenged by technology changes and new competitors, to date they've chosen to disrupt themselves before someone else did—and have since done so again and again. Put another way, when the challenge changed, Netflix's response changed with it.

We need to do the same with the way we lead people. Command & Control doesn't work anymore, it's a relic of the past. We need a new way to lead, relevant for our times.

As I mentioned earlier, the outgrowth of the Five Emerging Forces in our lives and world today brings with it two primary imperatives: *win in the workplace* and *win in the marketplace*.

Let's consider both of these imperatives and addressing them with a Command & Control style versus one of Trust & Inspire.

1. Win in the Workplace by Creating a High-Trust Culture That Inspires

The most impactful way to attract, retain, engage, and inspire the best people is through *culture*. This has always been true, but it's even more so in a world of infinite choice where people can live and work anywhere.

I'll never forget the experience a couple of years ago when I was working with the dean of an up-and-coming business school at a university on the East Coast. He told me how their university's Command & Control culture ended up damaging their ability to attract talent in a major way.

They were trying to recruit a superstar professor. They had a lot going in their favor to lure this professor to their school. The professor was very interested in living in the area, and the business school went all out to try to convince him that their school was a great fit. They rolled out the red carpet for him on his visit, involving meeting with key members of the school faculty and leadership in order to give him a vision of what was possible. He was impressed by the visit and indicated to the dean that he was strongly considering joining the school.

But when it came time for the professor to be reimbursed for his expenses from his visit, the dean ran into a snag. The professor had turned in his expense report with receipts but hadn't included a physical-paper airline ticket. School policy dictated that the physical-paper ticket needed to be turned in for it to be reimbursed. Sheepishly, the dean called the professor and told him that they couldn't reimburse him unless he had the receipt and the physical-paper airline ticket. The professor explained that he had used his phone electronically to board the plane and had never even gotten a printed physical ticket. Embarrassed, the dean told him that because of the school's travel policy they couldn't reimburse the trip without the physical-paper ticket. The professor was stunned and ended up not taking the job.

The school sent mixed messages—their behavior on the visit said enthusiastically that *we want and need you, and this is a good place for you*, but their inability to be flexible on the ticket reimbursement shouted *we don't trust you (nor do we trust any of our own people either)*.

Perhaps someone had abused the expense reimbursement system before, causing the school to create this travel policy in the first place. But like most Command & Control policies, it penalized the many because of the few. Worse, even the dean wasn't empowered to use good judgment to override the policy. This institutionalized lack of trust caused them not only to lose a great prospective professor, but also damaged their reputation among their current faculty as tales of this sorry story spread.

By contrast, a Trust & Inspire culture is the ultimate magnet for attracting top talent, because people are drawn to environments and cultures where they're trusted and free. Where they are inspired by a sense of purpose, meaning, and contribution. Anyone can offer decent pay, benefits, and other standard perks. But high performers want to be where they'll be trusted and are empowered. They've got plenty of options, but they are intensely attracted to organizations where their potential is seen, communicated, developed, and unleashed—and where they can be trusted and inspired to make a difference.

As I work with leaders everywhere, I consistently get asked, "How do we retain our Millennials?" The simple answer is to trust them. Borrowing the expression I've already given, I like to put it this way: Millennials don't want to be managed, they want to be led. They want to be inspired. They want to be trusted.

And guess what? It's not just Millennials. Every generation wants the same thing! While the data from the Great Place to Work Institute show that Millennials are twenty-two times more likely to stay in a company with a high-trust culture, the data also show that it's sixteen times higher with Gen X and thirteen times higher with Baby Boomers. The reality is this: people of all generations respond to being trusted—it's simply a better way to lead.

When people are trusted and inspired, they'll tend to stay; when they're not trusted and inspired, they'll tend to move on and seek out a place where they are.

I like the following expression: engaged employees plan to stay for what they can *give*; disengaged employees plan to stay for what they can *get*.

If we want to move the needle on engagement, trust is the number one factor that drives it—by far! A recent study from ADP Research Institute showed that people are fourteen times more likely to be fully engaged when they can trust their immediate leader. The next highest driver was being a member of a team, at a distant 2.6 times.

Too often, the underlying paradigm for many leaders who are struggling to increase engagement is still rooted in Command & Control. It's a style that's efficient with people, but it doesn't engage them. And what's the point of attracting and retaining people if we're not engaging them?

Nothing engages people like being trusted. Use yourself as Exhibit A. When you're trusted, what does that do to your engagement? What about when you're not trusted?

Is there a level beyond being fully engaged? Yes—it's being inspired. In fact, I believe that *inspiration is the new engagement*. A recent study from the consulting firm Bain & Company showed that inspired employees are the most productive employees by far—a remarkable 56 percent more productive than engaged employees, and a whopping 125 percent more productive than satisfied employees!

So not only will inspiration dramatically increase performance, but employee well-being will also be significantly greater. Inspiration feeds the whole person, not just the part of the person who works at the office. When people are inspired, they're happier and they produce more. Employee net promoter scores (eNPS) also increase as the employee experience is vastly improved.

The same thing happens in families. Contentment increases when family members are inspired in ways relevant to their life circumstances.

2. Win in the Marketplace through Collaboration and Innovation

As a result of the Five Emerging Forces and the ongoing need for relevancy, organizations are focused on the need for collaboration and innovation. We need breakthroughs and creativity in order to continue to compete, create value, and stay relevant in a changing marketplace.

Unfortunately, a style of Command & Control creates fear, and fear stifles all of these things as people hold back. Taking a risk makes people vulnerable—what if they fail or make a mistake? That's a scary thought in a Command & Control environment. So is the thought of collaboration. What if the people a person collaborates with can't be trusted?

People under Command & Control don't really collaborate, because collaboration requires risk, trust, and transparency. Instead, they coordinate; at best, they might be able to cooperate. In contrast, Trust & Inspire fosters conditions that allow people to move to a much higher level of true, creative collaboration where they voluntarily give and share.

Bottom line, you can't Command & Control your way to collaboration! I've seen leaders try to do so, but if people don't trust each other or the leadership or don't feel trusted themselves, they simply won't collaborate. They'll hold back, giving only what is necessary.

People often use the word *collaboration* when what they really mean is *consensus*. People begin to catch on, and meetings where people are supposed to "collaborate" are seen for what they really are—nothing more than low-trust coordination. It's exhausting, slow, and expensive. What we need instead is high-trust collaboration, which is different from consensus. Instead, collaboration might mean you get involved only when it's really needed, because you trust your fellow collaborators. You delegate when it makes sense. You and other team members are free to take calculated risks.

With Command & Control, any innovation that occurs is nominal and incremental. It's lockstep. There's nothing inherently wrong with that, but a lot of value is left on the table. A gap exists between performance and potential because people have to work within constrictive parameters and prescribed methods. No one is willing to risk coloring outside the lines.

Command & Control cultures don't lead to sustained creativity, insight, and breakthroughs. Innovation expert Robert Porter Lynch asserts that innovation flourishes where there's a collision of differences in an environment of trust. The greater the contrast in those differences, the greater the potential in the innovation.

Innovation is a team sport. In Command & Control environments, differences often create suspicion or even divisiveness. By contrast, in Trust & Inspire cultures, differences become the primary source of creativity, synergy, and innovation. Innovation thrives, and even derives, from diversity.

Moreover, in order to produce ongoing innovation, people have to be willing to take risks, make mistakes, and learn from those mistakes. They have to fail fast, fail forward, fail often—and learn faster. None of that happens if people don't feel there's trust, if people don't feel like someone has their back. Bottom line, if we don't give people a chance to fail, we won't innovate.

The data on this from the renowned LRN consulting firm is overwhelming. It shows that in a high-trust culture, people are thirty-two times more likely to take a responsible risk than they are in a low-trust culture. They're also eleven times more likely to innovate and six times more likely to achieve higher performance. Trust is what enables all of this to happen.

We take risks knowing that risks will sometimes result in failure, but without the possibility of failure there is no possibility of success.

—TIM COOK, CEO OF APPLE

Creativity flows out of inspiration, and people are inspired when they are unleashed—and when they have purpose. Those are the hallmarks of a Trust & Inspire culture. So are the other conditions that are needed for creativity and innovation to flourish: openly sharing ideas, being willing to take risks and make mistakes, the ability for the entire team to collaborate creatively, and no concern with who gets credit. Great innovators such as 3M, Zappos, Netflix, and Zoom have built cultures that have become the enabling source of sustained collaboration and innovation.

An example of the second epic imperative—collaborating and innovating to win in the marketplace—is seen through the remarkable leadership of someone I've had the privilege to know and work with: Eric Yuan, the founder and CEO of Zoom Video Communications.

He started thinking innovatively at an early age. Ideas for what would eventually become Zoom, the videoconferencing tool that took over the world, started forming in his head at age seventeen. As a first-year university student in his native country of China, he had to take ten-hour train trips to visit his girlfriend, Sherry. Those odysseys over the rails were not only time-consuming but exhausting, and he wanted an easier way to "visit" her. As he thought about ways to make that happen, the seeds of video calls were planted. (Yuan ended up marrying Sherry five years later, which put a halt to the wearying train trips.)

After Yuan attended a technology conference in Japan in 1995, he was riveted by the dream of working in the tech industry. Even though he spoke very little English, Yuan immigrated from China to Silicon Valley in 1997—something that required not only innovation but persistence on his part. Over a period of a year and a half, his visa applications were denied eight times. He kept at it, coming up with different approaches to satisfy requirements. Finally, his ninth attempt was successful.

Fast-forward a decade. Yuan, who oversaw Webex for Cisco, was still thinking about the dilemma that started on those train trips, and he presented management there with his idea for a smartphone-friendly videoconferencing system. Management wasn't persuaded. So Yuan left Cisco in June 2011 and started his own business to make his dream a reality. In August 2012, Zoom Video Communications launched the first version of their product. And talk about winning in the marketplace, especially during the COVID-19 pandemic and its aftermath—Zoom technology is used by more than 13 million people every month. The Zoom mobile app was downloaded 485 million times in 2020 alone.

The innovation behind Zoom's evolution is a story in itself—but even more compelling is Yuan's remarkable dedication to trust as his primary currency. He is trusting, and in turn, he is trusted. In fact, he was recently ranked by Glassdoor, which relies on anonymous employee ratings, as the number one CEO in the nation to work for. He has an almost-unheard-of 99 percent approval rating from his own people.

But that's not all: his influence goes beyond his own company. Yuan was named the 2020 *Time* magazine Businessperson of the Year, and he was included in *Time*'s 100 Most Influential People.

Trust permeates every aspect of Yuan's innovative leadership. He is known for his commitment to speed, calling it the "primary weapon" entrepreneurial companies have. But to get speed, he says, the pivotal factor is trust. "Without trust, we have no speed," Yuan maintains. "With trust, we move fast. That's why trust is everything."

Yuan inspires his people to be fast, relevant, collaborative, and innovative—but don't think he's forgotten the inspirational element of contributing to society. As just a few examples, at the outset of the COVID epidemic, Zoom provided K–12 schools with free videoconferencing to help teachers meet the educational needs of their students. And on the holidays, it dropped the forty-minute time limit on free accounts so families could virtually spend time together regardless of quarantines or travel restrictions—a great example of Yuan's collaborative spirit and commitment to doing what is right.

Don't We Already Know This?

You may be asking yourself, *Don't we already know this?* Yes, we do. The growing irrelevance of Command & Control has been apparent in leadership circles for many years now. But here's the most interesting thing of all: for all the knowledge we've gained about this intellectually, *Enlightened* Command & Control remains the dominant leadership style for a majority of leaders in most organizations today. It's still the prevailing norm by a large margin.

I recently saw this demonstrated at a leadership conference where I was on a panel with some distinguished experts and thought leaders on leadership. That wasn't limited to the panel; the audience itself was also filled with leadership experts. As I prepared, I was somewhat intimidated. I was excited to be part of the panel, but really wanted to make sure I added value. As I reflected on my own experiences from years past—both as a leader and as someone being led—I felt strongly that the most important thing I could share was the need to distinguish between a *thing paradigm* and a *people paradigm*.

During the conference, I tried to highlight this idea by hitting on some leadership basics such as "Manage things, lead people"; "Be efficient with things, and effective with people"; and "We live in a world that is overmanaged and underled." I knew these ideas would not be groundbreaking, because they weren't new. But I felt passionately that the lack of novelty did not make them any less profound.

Somewhat to my surprise, most of the audience reacted as if these ideas were revolutionary. People took vigorous notes, and many of them wanted to discuss these ideas with me afterward. For some, these ideas may have been more of a reminder than a revelation, but there was enough excitement for me to see that what I'd shared really had an impact.

At the end of the conference, an attendee told me, "Of all the insights and things we've learned at this conference, for me they all boil down to and fall under one idea that you introduced—that we are overmanaged and underled. All the other things are just methods that fall under the style you choose: management of things and people, or management of things and leadership of people."

This experience reinforced what I know to be true: although we *know* these things and we even *say* these things, we are not yet *doing* these things. If we were, it would be the norm and not the exception to experience leaders and organizations that operated in those ways.

For as much progress as we've made, we haven't made much progress.

Whenever I speak to audiences and explain what I mean by Command & Control, there is an almost immediate collective understanding and identification with the term. We "get" the Command & Control idea almost instantly, because we see it in our everyday lives. It's why we are inspired when we hear about Trust & Inspire leadership. If we were practicing what we preach, the preaching wouldn't feel so relevant.

Command & Control runs along a continuum, represented by two broad categories, though most of the time we don't distinguish between the two. Authoritarian Command & Control operates out of fear: what I can *do to you*; Enlightened Command & Control operates out of transactional fairness and exchange: what I can *do for you* (and you for me); by contrast, Trust & Inspire operates out of inspiration and purpose: what I can *do with you*.

There is no shortage of data around the premise that Command & Control remains the prevailing norm. A groundbreaking study from LRN gathered data from more than sixteen thousand employees in seventeen countries to glean insights about both organizational and individual behavior and how they impact performance. They categorize three archetypes of governance, culture, and leadership based on a continuum: "Blind Obedience," "Informed Acquiescence," and "Self-Governance." The results showed a dominance of what I describe as Command & Control.

For the purposes of what we're exploring here, I submit that "Blind Obedience" is comparable to traditional or Authoritarian Command & Control, while "Informed Acquiescence" is comparable to Enlightened Command & Control, inclusive of the incremental progress that has been made. What the study refers to as "Self-Governance" contains what I call a Trust & Inspire style of leadership.

Only 8 percent of the organizations studied could be described as Self-Governing, or Trust & Inspire. The other 92 percent are some variation of Command & Control. This conforms to what I've experienced as I've worked with organizations and leaders all over the world. Thankfully, the trend is moving upward, with only 30 percent being Authoritarian Command & Control (Blind Obedience), while the other 62 percent have moved to the more Enlightened Command & Control (Informed Acquiescence). The report later describes the extraordinary economic performance that comes from the Trust & Inspire (Self-Governance) organizations.

Similarly, in my own surveys of thousands of leaders, including some of the top companies in the world, the vast majority of people still say that the primary leadership style in their organization would best be described as Command & Control rather than Trust & Inspire. So it's likely that instead of the exception to the rule, your workplace might be more Command & Control than you suspect.

As I work within a variety of industries, two seem further along the path toward Trust & Inspire: technology companies and professional services firms. The LRN study validates this premise. The two epic imperatives of our time couldn't be more critical for success in those particular industries. Both need to build Trust & Inspire cultures to win the war for talent, and they need to collaborate and innovate to stay relevant in an ever-changing marketplace.

Changes in Degree, Not Kind

We have made progress, even significant progress. For all this progress, however, all we've really done is move from Authoritarian Command &

Control to the more sophisticated, kinder, gentler Enlightened Command & Control. We're still operating within the same paradigm. Yes, many organizations have made significant movement from coercion to a more motivation-focused approach. Many organizations have also brought more human resource and talent management into the equation. But these changes have been changes in *degree*, not in *kind*.

Even with the push for better management, all the leadership theory out there, and the improvements we've made, control is still the primary name of the game, and most leaders—even good, well-intentioned, high-character leaders—have an extraordinarily difficult time letting go and releasing control to others.

Remember the story I told of Senior having a hard time letting go and passing the baton to his son Junior, even though Junior was prepared to take the reins? Contrast that story to another dynamic in a similar company I met with more recently. In a comparable situation, the company was founded and run by a family and headed by a father-daughter duo. In this case, however, the father was in his early sixties and the daughter in her early thirties. Similar to Senior, the father operated in a traditional Command & Control style. He was the executor of every decision. His daughter's style of leadership was different; she wanted to empower people by delegating more responsibilities to trusted team members. The father's style always won out.

When unexpected health issues forced the father to step down, his young daughter assumed the role of CEO far sooner than anyone had planned. I went into a meeting with the management team soon after this transition in leadership occurred, unsure what to expect. Would the team resist the daughter's new ideas and management style? Would they trust her even though she was the youngest and most inexperienced in the room? Could they form a cross-functional, high-performing team?

I was delighted to find that the team and the daughter came together with a mutual understanding of trust and respect. The daughter acknowledged how much she needed the experience of those around her and was open to ideas and suggestions. In return, the members of the group were willing to listen to her and to try new things. As the daughter delegated responsibilities and tasks, I could see a high-trust, collaborative team forming in front of my eyes. Although the father ceded control only because he *had* to, it gave his company and employees the chance to change and grow in new ways. The daughter was able to avoid micromanaging and experiencing undue stress as she extended trust to well-seasoned employees. Those employees were given new opportunities and were able to contribute in meaningful ways.

In both these cases, the fathers were not bad bosses. But they were operating in such a Command & Control style that their organizations were prevented from reaching their full potential. Imagine what could have been possible if they had tried.

As I've worked with organizations around the world, I hear leader after leader desiring to make this shift—to cross the chasm in terms of how they lead. Of the hundreds of illustrations I might give, here are two simple examples of what I frequently hear:

1. At a recent meeting with a major pharmaceutical company preparing for their annual conference, their executive team told me, "We're trying to move from what we're calling a '1990s style of leadership' that's based on managing and controlling people to something new, something more relevant for a new kind of engagement and collaboration we need from our people."

2. A CEO I worked with from a military contractor told me, "We've been trying to move people from Command & Control into more transparency, more collaboration, and more trusting of our people."

Command & Control is becoming increasingly irrelevant and ineffective in our dynamic, multigenerational, interconnected world. I would go so far as to say that Command & Control has been ineffective for much of the past—it was simply more culturally accepted and seemed to work only because less was required. That's no longer the case. We cannot simply make cosmetic fixes, hoping to mask our outdated style. It's time for change, and the kind required to move from Command & Control to Trust & Inspire is not incremental; rather, it's a sea change. It's not a change in degree, it's a change in kind.

Why Do We Still Operate from Command & Control?

We haven't moved out of the industrial-age style of management because we haven't yet shifted our paradigm. We continue to have an inaccurate map—a distorted view—of people and leadership. We don't have complete and accurate fundamental beliefs. Incremental behavior change is not the solution; rather, we need to change our paradigm in order to truly change our behavior.

Like someone who has been wearing the wrong prescription glasses, our vision is blurred and we're unable to see reality for what it is. We might not even realize our prescription is outdated; it's been that way for so long that our eyes have adjusted—we've gotten used to things as they are. Our perception has become our reality. And until we try on a new pair of glasses with the proper prescription, we will continue to operate at a lower capacity, because that's all we know. It's time to update our prescription!

Understanding *why* we haven't changed will help us change. As we put on new glasses, we get a clearer picture of the world. And as we change our mindset—our paradigm—it's easier to change our behavior.

While several underlying factors have slowed our shift away from Command & Control, three are fundamental to understand to be able to change.

1. "Fish Discover Water Last"

No one would classify today as primarily industrial. In fact, when people talk about the industrial age, they are often referring to the late 1800s, early 1900s—a *century* ago. So why do we still operate with an industrial-age style of leadership? I think it's because we do not realize how completely immersed we are in this old style, still trapped with various relics of the industrial age. This is made manifest in our language, systems, processes, and practices.

Consider language. Much of industrial-era language about work is taken from military terms. We use words every day such as *company* or *mission*, or we refer to *frontline* employees. When we hire people, we call it *recruitment*. We tell people to *fall in line*. We talk about *subordinates*, *span of control*, *chain of command*, and *silos*. It's no wonder that the term people naturally use to describe militaristic leadership is *Command & Control* (which is also a military term). We use these terms and many others without a second thought. This language and way of thinking is so ingrained into our way of life that we often don't even recognize it.

This phenomenon is aptly captured in the proverb "Fish discover water last." We are the fish, and Command & Control, the water. If you understood any of the terms I just shared and didn't make the military connection, you can relate to a fish who's just discovered water. We have been completely scripted to operate in a Command & Control fashion without ever consciously reading the script.

Sure, we've made progress over the years—but it has been incremental, and based on progressing *within* a Command & Control paradigm rather than crossing the chasm. This is the style that has been modeled and taught to us. It's the model we have practiced for years without even stopping to think about what we might be leaving on the table. It's the model we've used without considering how great the gap might be between performance and potential. Trapped in this paradigm, we know the cost of everything and the value of nothing, to paraphrase Oscar Wilde.

But just because we are immersed in something, it doesn't need to define how we operate. Once we see clearly how we are surrounded by relics of the industrial age, we can choose to operate differently.

Think about your own scripting. What elements of Command & Control show up in your organization? What about on your team? Does Command & Control show up in the way you lead in your home?

Did you experience Command & Control as a student? In addition to language, a few other places these relics pop up include in our:

- *structures* (hierarchical, top-down, managers and workers, deciders and doers, superiors and subordinates)

- *systems* (forced rankings, annual performance appraisal systems, accounting systems in which people are expenses while machines are assets)

- *practices* (carrot-and-stick reward systems, centralized budgeting, "sandwich technique" feedback)

- *style* (Command & Control, micromanagement, abdication, supervision)

- *paradigms* (things versus people paradigm, scarcity versus abundance paradigm, motivation versus inspiration paradigm, leadership as position versus leadership as choice paradigm)

2. To Know and Not to Do Is Not to Know

As you've read so far, you may have thought something like, *I've been saying this for years!* Many of these ideas have been discussed for decades, and our management thinking has certainly progressed since the advent of scientific management. The human relations movement started around the 1930s, then progressed to a focus on human resources in the 1950s and 1960s. The 1980s and 1990s ushered in a movement around quality, empowerment, and emotional intelligence, and shortly after the idea of strengths was added that continues to this day.

For all our progress in management thinking, however, little has changed for most people, teams, organizations, and families. As Goethe said, "To know and not to do is not to know."

While we understand much of this intellectually, putting it into consistent, deliberate practice is not the norm. You might say that common sense is not common practice. We all struggle to bridge the gap between "I get it" and "I'm doing it." But that struggle is the beginning of a great journey toward congruence between our thoughts and our actions—in matching our style to our intent. That's authenticity. When we don't address the gap between what we say and what we do, problems inevitably follow. People are slow to trust those who can't "walk the talk."

I knew of an educational leader who, while extremely educated and qualified, was untrusting and uninspiring. The principal of a large high school in a big school district on the West Coast, he had a doctorate in educational leadership, taught additional leadership classes, and trained others on how to become better leaders. You could say that leadership was his specialty, since he'd spent years studying and teaching leadership. It was how he defined himself. He even taught a leadership class at the university level as an adjunct professor.

Here's the irony: he knew a lot about leadership, but he was not a good leader. As principal, he ran the school somewhere between an authoritarian dictator and a control freak. Slow to trust, he micromanaged people around him, from the office staff to the football coach. Likewise, he led the students with heavy-handed practices, resulting in discontent and rebellion from both the students and their parents. Morale plummeted with all stakeholders—students, teachers, administrators, parents—and the turnover in the school increased at an astonishing rate, dramatically higher than under previous principals. Scores of veteran teachers who had been at the school for years suddenly retired, quit, or sought teaching positions at other schools.

This principal could not recognize the gap between what he knew and what he did. Despite his knowledge, training, and work to understand the principles of leadership, he was not a good leader. My colleague described him as "Intellectually, he knows *everything*, but in reality, he knows *nothing*."

There are miles and miles between "I get it" and "I'm doing it."

3. Inaccurate Paradigms Can Live on Indefinitely

Let's say you moved to a different country. You've now been there for years, and you've learned the language. One day you try to hang a picture on the wall. As you hammer in the nail, you slip and hit your thumb. What language do you think you'd use to yell out? More often than not, the expletive comes out in your native tongue.

In a sense, Command & Control is our native tongue. So many of us have been brought up under a Command & Control style of leadership that we're trained in it, scripted in it, and good at it. Often it is all we've ever known—the only model we've ever seen in our homes, in our schools, and at work.

Trust & Inspire is really an acquired tongue. It's not spoken around us very often, certainly not as often as Command & Control. We're not immersed in it. Just like learning a foreign language, it takes time and practice and a lot of repetition before Trust & Inspire becomes ingrained. And in moments of stress—when we hit our thumb, so to speak—we tend to revert to our native tongue. To the way we know best.

How many of us have had great intentions for a family trip, only to go full Command & Control two hours into the car ride when we can no longer take the kids arguing and taunting each other? When stress gets high, we tend to go on autopilot. We do what feels natural, whatever will lead to the most efficient, short-term solution. For most of us, Command & Control feels natural. It's the essence of "the ends justify the means," trading effectiveness for efficiency. The car ride becomes one of quiet compliance, but nobody is having fun.

Just as it takes time for us to adapt and rescript, it takes time for cultural shifts to happen. Even when we learn a better way, there is always resistance—from people who don't buy in, are afraid, have a lot to lose, or simply don't want to change. An incomplete or flawed paradigm can live on for decades, even centuries, even after a more complete or accurate paradigm has been discovered.

A great example from history is the longevity of the practice of bloodletting. Bloodletting was among the most common medical practices performed by physicians for a span of more than three thousand years, until as recently as the late nineteenth century. When it was developed, people believed that disease lived in the blood, so the only way to cure the disease was to let blood out. This belief began with the Egyptians, continued with the Romans and Greeks, lasted through the medieval ages of Europe, impacted early America, and peaked in Europe in the nineteenth century. Even George Washington was treated with bloodletting in the hours before his death.

However, as early as the sixteenth and seventeenth centuries, a growing number of doctors and researchers pushed back against the notion that bloodletting was healthy. Some had even proven the theory false. Yet the practice persisted for hundreds of years after many of these discoveries were made and shared. As medical researchers Kerridge and Lowe stated, the fact "that bloodletting survived for so long is not an intellectual anomaly—it resulted from the dynamic interaction of social, economic, and intellectual pressures, a process that continues to determine medical practice."

The way we lead families, companies, teams, and students is often influenced by similar pressures. Even when we know there might be a better way, it's hard to change while trying to meet all the demands of the modern world. Especially when everyone around us is doing it the same way.

My father often reminded me that most significant *breakthroughs* are really "break withs"—that is, a break with the traditional way of thinking. Trust & Inspire is a breakthrough because it's a break with traditional Command & Control thinking. While it takes time for something to become a part of society's psyche, it only comes about as individuals start to break with traditional approaches and implement new practices. Only when enough people act does a "break with" become accepted as common knowledge and practice.

In a sense, Command & Control is modern-day bloodletting. It's mind-boggling that it persists to this day. Trust & Inspire is the "break with" that can lead to the breakthrough.

Moving from Command & Control to Trust & Inspire

These factors work against our desire to change. They acknowledge real and inherent risk. They are rooted in the fear that we don't know *how* to change. However, we needn't use them as excuses for not changing. Risk and return go hand in hand, and the research is overwhelming that the return on being a Trust & Inspire leader is infinitely better than any return on Command & Control.

The return is measured not only in dramatically increased performance but also in significantly higher energy and joy—greater well-being. I've seen people, families, and organizations literally transform as they've let go of Command & Control and embraced Trust & Inspire. I've also seen them struggle, not knowing why they blindly cling to Command & Control, and end up with neither command nor control.

We can't solve a problem that we don't understand. Now that we've identified and understand some of the thoughts or attitudes that get in the way of making this change, we can focus on overcoming them. We will learn how to do this—how to overcome specific barriers that keep you clinging to Command & Control—to shed your old ways and become a Trust & Inspire leader as you journey through this book.

Think back to when you identified a Command & Control leader in your life. What would have been the impact if that leader had operated with a Trust & Inspire style? How different would your world have been? What could you have accomplished had you been truly inspired and given the trust needed to act on that inspiration? What if Trust & Inspire were the norm? What kind of results could you produce? What kind of results could others produce? What would it feel like to go to work? How might the gap narrow between performance and potential?

Command & Control will simply not equip you to succeed in today's world. Its expiration date has passed. Trust & Inspire is the new, relevant way to lead for our world today.

"Every Airman, Every Day, an Innovator"

Earlier I noted how many of our management terms, even Command & Control itself, come from the military. Even in a sector with an inherent need for both clear command and strong control, many military leaders are moving away from a style of Command & Control and toward one of Trust & Inspire.

I've had the privilege to work with many top leaders from all branches of the military, and I find them to be among the finest leaders: aware, prescient, and understanding of the new realities impacting the military and people everywhere. One such leader is three-star lieutenant general Dorothy Hogg.

General Hogg is the epitome of *military*. Entering the United States Air Force in 1984, she rose through the ranks to become an influential leader, receiving many awards and accolades along the way. Today, she's the surgeon general of the United States Air Force. When we sat down to talk, I immediately saw that she appreciated the relevance of the kind of leadership needed today—Trust & Inspire—especially in a military setting. We were on the same page. I was taken aback by the mantra she repeatedly shares with her airmen: "Every airman, every day, an innovator." She not only says it, she exemplifies it.

She extends an extraordinary amount of trust to her people, challenging them to think outside the box, try new things, and create and innovate—and they're inspired by it.

Talk about innovators! As just one example, consider how she and her teams responded to the COVID-19 challenge. While much of the rest of the United States and world was reeling, she and her teams immediately focused on coming up with new solutions. They figured out how to extend the use of personal protective equipment; created innovative ways to safely disinfect N-95 masks, such as using ultraviolet light; implemented a groundbreaking model of teleworking and pioneered new ways of transporting infected patients. They even put together a commander's toolkit that enabled leaders to safely stay in touch with and help airmen under their direction.

Those were some of the bigger initiatives, with lots of little ones, too. General Hogg continues to extend trust, and the people she leads continue to be inspired. As the world and the nature of its problems continue to change, General Hogg and her team will continue to change with it—to innovate and stay relevant in solving those problems.

This can happen for you, too. For your team. For your organization. For your family. For your community.

Great things happen when it does.

COMMAND & CONTROL	TRUST & INSPIRE
Industrial Age	Knowledge-Worker Age
Stability	Change & Disruption
To Know and Not to Do	To Know AND to Do
Informed Acquiescence	Self-Governance
Coercive	Persuasive
Native Tongue	Acquired Tongue

CHAPTER 3

Style Is Getting in the Way of Intent

A good intention, with a bad approach, often leads to a poor result.

—THOMAS EDISON

I'll never forget the day I was with the leadership team of a large Fortune 50 company. In a survey of their company, we found a gap between how the senior leaders saw themselves and how their employees saw those same senior leaders. It was a substantial gap. When the senior leaders were asked to rate themselves on how much they genuinely cared about their employees, 99 percent rated themselves at the highest possible level of caring on the scale. When employees were asked, "Does senior leadership care about you?" the employees rated those same leaders at only 31 percent. That's a staggering sixty-eight-point gap!

So who's right—the employees or the leaders? In reality, they could both be right. It could well be that the leaders genuinely *did* care about their people—in my experience, most leaders do. But if there's a sixty-eight-point gap between how much you care and how the people you care about are interpreting whether or not you care, you have a serious problem. And in the end, everyone will pay for it.

At Franklin Covey, we use an instrument to measure trust on teams and in organizations called a Team Trust Index. In the thousands of times we've used these surveys, revealing trends have emerged. Probably the most significant, and most surprising for the person or team getting the results, is the gap in how they see themselves and how others see them. One of the biggest areas people struggle with is how one's intent does—or, more often, *doesn't*—translate into behavior and experience.

I believe what eBay founder Pierre Omidyar believed—that "people are basically good." At the risk of sounding naive, I also believe that most (though not all) have positive intent and care about others. Indra Nooyi—who was consistently ranked as one of the most powerful women in business as chair and CEO of PepsiCo—said the best advice she'd ever received was this from her father:

> Always assume positive intent. Whatever anybody says or does, assume positive intent. You will be amazed at how your whole approach to a person or problem becomes very different.

If it's true that most people have positive intent, where does the breakdown happen? It's in the way we lead. Our style. How we do what we do. Our *style* is getting in the way of our intent.

Almost without exception, leaders struggle with this. This is true even in families. I love my children more than anything in the world, and yet there have been many times where the pressure has been on, or I've been stressed, or something's gone wrong, and I've slipped into heavy Command & Control. When that happens, I still feel genuine love and caring for my kids, but that's not what *they* experience. My caring takes a backseat to how I handle the situation.

One day my wife, Jeri, surprised me by cleaning my office. To an outside observer, and to Jeri, the place looked like a disaster. But for me, everything had its place—and I knew right where everything was. It was what I like to call an "organized mess." Jeri rolled up her sleeves and cleaned the whole thing, she consolidated files, folders, and papers. She cleared off surfaces, including the floor. The place was spotless!

You should have seen my face when I walked through the door. I was really upset. I couldn't find *anything*. I spent hours looking for things I could have immediately put my hands on just a day earlier.

Jeri's *intent* was one of love and consideration, but that's not what I experienced. But the bigger gap between style and intent was mine—let's just say I didn't react in the most graceful way, certainly not consistent with my deep love for Jeri or my appreciation for her efforts.

You know your own heart and your intent—but does your style match it? The reality is that most of us judge ourselves by our intent and others by their behavior. The problem is that others do the same— they judge themselves by their intent and they judge us by our behavior. If we want to avoid the pitfall of our style not matching our intent, we need to do reality checks now and then. We need to take a look in the mirror and ask ourselves, "Is what I intended coming through?"

Amazing things happen when our style matches our intent.

Style Flows from Paradigm

I want to differentiate between two kinds of leadership "style"—what I'll refer to as *meta-style*, or overarching style, and *sub-style*, or situational style.

Both Command & Control and Trust & Inspire are overarching *meta-styles*. Both of these represent the underlying mental framework we operate from—our paradigm and the fundamental beliefs guiding how we see people and leadership. All of us operate somewhere on the continuum between Command & Control and Trust & Inspire—and most people operate more from the Command & Control side of the spectrum.

A *sub-style* is what most people think of when they think of their "leadership style." An internet search of *leadership styles* returns results like "9 Common Leadership Styles" and "The 7 Primary Leadership Styles" and "The 8 Most Common Leadership Styles, and How to Find Your Own." This is what I mean by a sub-style. There are a lot of sub-styles, including authoritative, transactional, coaching, democratic, laissez-faire, visionary, and more. And each of these can be effective, depending on the situation or context. I'm not advocating for or against any of them, per se. My point is that above any sub-style is your overarching *meta-style*, which flows from your paradigm. And that meta-style—the way you primarily lead—is either Trust & Inspire or some iteration of Command & Control.

Yes, situation and context matter, but your paradigm matters more. No matter what role or situation you're in, your meta-style is the dominant lens through which you view the world.

The new way to lead is an overarching style rooted in a holistic paradigm, built upon timeless principles of human effectiveness. You will approach leadership with a more accurate, more complete, and more relevant mindset when your meta-style is Trust & Inspire.

Take a moment to reflect on who you truly want to be as a leader by considering the following questions:

Describe your intent as a leader: How do you hope others see you?
Is your style congruent with your intent? Why or why not?
Would your team/colleagues/family agree? Why or why not?

Style Is a Choice

You might be thinking, *You can't teach an old dog new tricks. My style is who I am!* Well, I suggest you get ready to learn a new trick right now, because style is a choice. You can adapt your style and change the way you lead.

A great example of someone who changed his style, as well as his fundamental leadership paradigm, is a good friend of mine, Art Barter. In fact, he didn't just change the way he led, he became an ambassador for it.

Art was CEO of a global communications equipment company for many years. His company worked predominantly with governmental organizations worldwide. In the early part of his career, Art employed a heavy Command & Control style, working in an extremely competitive environment where the stakes were always high.

While attending a leadership conference, he had a powerful personal experience that impacted his mindset. This led him to adopt "servant leadership"—the idea of turning the traditional power leadership model upside down, with the goal of the leader to serve. He made this shift when there was significant risk to making the change, when the company wasn't performing well, and his employees were disengaged. Rather than doubling down on his old style of leadership, Art jumped in with both feet with his new approach—and never looked back. His focus on servant leadership enabled him to change his paradigm and shift from Command & Control to Trust & Inspire.

The change that came from unleashing the potential and talent of his people had a dramatic impact on the company. Revenues grew from $10 million to $200 million in just six years, with customers in more than eighty countries.

Art has since started and runs the Servant Leadership Institute; its aim is to help people all over the world make the same change he did. Here's the thing: Art didn't just begin to care about people when he adopted servant leadership. He had always cared—but now he was able to match his style with his intent, becoming a Trust & Inspire servant leader. The results speak for themselves.

Each of us can make such a change. Each of us can shift our paradigm, which will help us change our behavior, aligning style with intent. Each of us can choose to adopt the meta-style of Trust & Inspire. Whatever sub-style we employ can operate from either a paradigm of Trust & Inspire or Command & Control. Even someone who espouses a Servant Leader sub-style might, in fact, still be operating from an Enlightened Command & Control paradigm. An example of this might be the humble, caring, even inspiring leader who has great integrity but still has a hard time letting go or extending trust to others.

The overarching paradigm we operate from can make the same action look and feel different, and have a vastly different impact. When we operate out of a Trust & Inspire paradigm, people around us are deeply impacted by our belief in them. It sends a ripple effect throughout our teams, organizations, and communities.

Whatever your role or situation, your impact is completely different when you approach it through the lens of Trust & Inspire rather than Command & Control.

Micromanagement Is the Ultimate Manifestation of Command & Control

I once worked with a pastor who was the ultimate micromanager. He was probably at the peak of Enlightened Command & Control but just couldn't quite progress any further. He lived his beliefs and was a kind and generous person. He even described himself as a servant leader.

But he wasn't a Trust & Inspire pastor. Why? Easy—he couldn't let go. He couldn't trust anybody. Even though he was trustworthy himself, he didn't see others that way. Even though he treated people with love and respect, he second-guessed their decisions constantly. This impacted not only the way people felt about him but also his ability to influence them. People who once felt inspired by his sermons suddenly felt a little bitter when he shot down another of their ideas. He would have been a great leader if he hadn't been such a terrible micromanager. His style constantly got in the way of his intent, and although people trusted and respected him, they didn't feel he trusted and respected them.

Think of how powerful this pastor could have been had he been willing to change his paradigm and view people with even a modicum of trust. He could have gone from micromanager to macro-leader. Instead, he got bogged down in his desire to control everything.

It's fine to be detail-oriented, but it's vital to always keep the focus on *efficiency with things* and on *effectiveness with people*. Sure, Trust & Inspire leaders might sometimes micromanage processes and procedures, but they never micromanage people. Remember, people don't want to be managed; they want to be led.

> *People follow leaders by choice. Without trust, at best you get compliance.*
>
> —JESSE LYN STONER, AUTHOR
> AND CONSULTANT

The Meta-Style Continuum

Enlightened Command & Control today looks a lot different from the almost "Neanderthal" Command & Control of the Dark Ages or the Authoritarian Command & Control from the advent of Frederick Winslow Taylor's scientific management. It has progressed considerably over the years, becoming better in numerous ways. That's why it's "enlightened." But it still falls far short of Trust & Inspire—it cannot bridge the divide until we shift our paradigm. However, it is worth exploring where someone might fall on this continuum.

Some people still operate with heavy-handed Authoritarian Command & Control. They demand compliance and try to control every aspect of every situation. They are sometimes unempathic, uncaring, and expedient, focusing primarily on profit and efficiency and not on people.

Fortunately, considerable progress has been made to move us toward Trust & Inspire. The first change was to bring in more trustworthiness with a focus on integrity and ethics. Then more kindness and benevolence was added in the concept of human relations. To use a farm metaphor, farmers discovered that if they played music in the barn, cows produced more milk. So managers added perks and other things to try to make people happy. We want people to be happier. But the problem is that farmers were not playing music because they wanted the cows to be happier; they were playing music in the dairy because they knew that happy cows produce more milk, and they wanted the cows to produce more milk.

So managers became more sophisticated about it. They added emotional intelligence to the mix. Then they added strengths and competencies to tap into people as assets, creating the concept of human resources. They even brought in mission statements and strengths. Collectively, this became "Enlightened" Command & Control.

People who exercise this kind of leadership are typically good, caring, and trustworthy people—but they often don't extend trust to others. They're uncomfortable about genuinely unleashing people's potential, so they end up containing people instead. They motivate people, but they don't inspire them. They tap into people's strengths but not into their passions.

More and more, managers are evolving their style in response to the Five Emerging Forces. But for all their progress, most have effectively just moved up the continuum to a "kinder, gentler" Enlightened Command & Control. They know that people want to be treated differently, and they want to treat people differently—but they still cannot cast off the fundamental paradigm of Command & Control. And most people don't even recognize it.

Who we choose to trust is perhaps our most powerful unconscious bias. No matter how good our intentions might be, no matter how skilled we might become, we will never be able to make the jump to Trust & Inspire if we operate from a lens of Command & Control. To make it over the chasm, we need to adopt the fundamental beliefs of a Trust & Inspire leader. We'll dive deep into these beliefs in the next chapter.

Wondering where you might fit? Take a few minutes for this short exercise.

Circle the number where you view yourself on the Meta-Style Con-

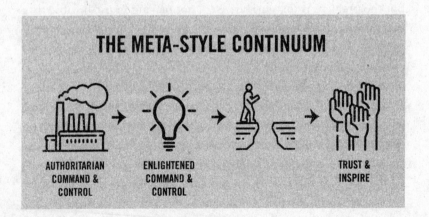

THE META-STYLE CONTINUUM

AUTHORITARIAN COMMAND & CONTROL → ENLIGHTENED COMMAND & CONTROL → → TRUST & INSPIRE

tinuum, and then take a stab where you think others might view you. (What's really interesting, of course, is when others actually rate you on this continuum—anonymously. Let's just say that most of us have some blind spots.)

COMMAND & CONTROL

	AUTHORITATIVE ←→				ENLIGHTENED ←→			TRUST & INSPIRE		
How I view myself:	1	2	3	4	5	6	7	8	9	10
How my boss views me:	1	2	3	4	5	6	7	8	9	10
How my peers view me:	1	2	3	4	5	6	7	8	9	10
How my direct reports view me:	1	2	3	4	5	6	7	8	9	10
How my family views me:	1	2	3	4	5	6	7	8	9	10

Principles Govern

Principles are universal, natural laws that apply at all times, in all cultures, and in all contexts. Power or position does not ultimately govern human effectiveness; principles do. Trust & Inspire is aligned with enduring principles, so it works in any context and relationship, at any time, amid any change. Not only is it the most relevant approach today, it will be the most relevant approach tomorrow. In a sense, this "new way to lead"—Trust & Inspire—isn't really new. Instead, it has been and always will be the most effective way to lead, regardless of the era, because it is based on the most accurate and complete paradigm of people and leadership.

Other leadership styles eventually fall flat or have their flaws exposed as society shifts and needs change. Enlightened Command & Control is already past its expiration date. The Five Emerging Forces are opening the doors to let in the style that has always worked best, regardless of whatever trend is in vogue.

How different might history have been if this Trust & Inspire style had been better understood and utilized?

COMMAND & CONTROL	TRUST & INSPIRE
Micro-management	Macro-leadership
Leadership is a Position	Leadership is a Choice

PART TWO

Becoming a Trust & Inspire Leader: The 5 Fundamental Beliefs and 3 Stewardships

Now let's look closely at how Trust & Inspire leaders think and what they do. The next section provides practical advice on how to make the change from a Command & Control style of leadership to Trust & Inspire. This part of the book is about rolling up your sleeves—the playbook, if you will. First, you'll be challenged to take a hard look at your paradigms about people and leadership and the actions that follow. And then I'll walk you through how to make the life-changing switch to Trust & Inspire.

The 5 Fundamental Beliefs of a Trust & Inspire Leader

In the last chapter, we briefly looked at how principles govern our leadership style. The fundamental beliefs of a Trust & Inspire leader are based on timeless and powerful principles. As with all principles, these beliefs are not surprising. In fact, you'll likely find that many you agree with, or at least hope for. What makes these beliefs powerful is that Trust & Inspire leaders don't simply agree with them intellectually— they consistently *live* them.

We'll go into each of these beliefs in the next chapter. You'll find they offer a mindset of how to think about and believe in people and leadership. This paradigm will guide your behavior and interactions with others in significant ways. These beliefs are to a Trust & Inspire leader what the principle of gravity is to a rock climber. Ignore these beliefs at your own peril; work with them, and they'll work for you.

The 3 Stewardships of a Trust & Inspire Leader

A fundamental belief of a Trust & Inspire leader is that *leadership is stewardship*. Put another way, leaders are stewards. Stewardship is a responsibility that implies the highest level of trust, or being entrusted. When we have a stewardship mindset, we have been given a job to do, and we've been entrusted to see it through. I like to describe stewardship as "a job with a trust."

The overarching framework for this book consists of 3 Stewardships that work together and build off each other. The 3 Stewardships of a Trust & Inspire leader are:

1. **Modeling**—*Who You Are*

2. **Trusting**—*How You Lead*

3. **Inspiring**—*Connect to Why*

Each of these 3 Stewardships—modeling, trusting, inspiring—is accompanied by a crucial descriptor. *Who You Are* refers to leaders' credibility and moral authority and to the behavioral virtues needed today. *How You Lead* is the way leaders extend trust to and grow the people around them. *Connect to Why* is how leaders connect with people and connect to purpose in inspiring others.

Many leaders are one-dimensional. They might do well on one of

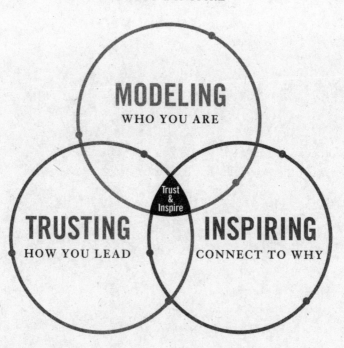

these stewardships but fall short on the others. Many good leaders are two-dimensional. They offer a more complete style or picture, but one that is nonetheless incomplete. People are looking for leaders who embody all 3 Stewardships: leaders who model, leaders who trust, and leaders who inspire.

This approach will powerfully enrich your life, but even more important, it will deeply enrich the lives of those you lead.

CHAPTER 4

The 5 Fundamental Beliefs of a Trust & Inspire Leader

I bring you the gift of these four words, "I believe in you."

—BLAISE PASCAL

When I first went to my publisher to talk about the idea for this book, I prepared heavily, hoping to articulate this concept in a way that would communicate how valuable I feel it is. I was scheduled to meet with my editor, Stephanie, who invited her boss, Jonathan, the head of the imprint under which my books are published.

I told Stephanie and Jonathan that I wanted to write a book on the new kind of leadership needed in our world today. I laid out the contrast between Command & Control and Trust & Inspire. I showed how even Enlightened Command & Control is a relic of the industrial age that still prevails almost everywhere.

They both "got it" instantly. Jonathan said that most of the publishing industry is built around Command & Control. (In fairness to the publishing industry, almost everyone I talk to about this concept tells me that "their" industry is primarily built around Command & Control.) Stephanie jumped in and said, "That's interesting, because I agree that the industry is very Command & Control, but, Jonathan, you're not. You're Trust & Inspire. In fact, the way you lead and trust and empower your people is the whole reason I came to work here."

Stephanie went on to describe the kind of enabling culture she had experienced both in her role and at their publishing house. Her assertion made a lot of sense to me. Publishing is an industry that is under pressure of constant change, and the very nature of the work demands a level of creativity, innovation, and flexibility that Command & Control simply doesn't accommodate and can't effectively produce. I wasn't especially surprised, then, that as I wrote this section of the book, Jonathan was appointed the new CEO of the entire publishing company. I believe his designation as CEO is due not just to the fact that he has delivered tremendous results over the years, but more specifically to *how* he goes about getting those results.

The 5 Fundamental Beliefs of a Trust & Inspire Leader

Trust & Inspire leaders like Jonathan stand out. We feel different around them than we do around other leaders. It is exciting and exhilarating to be led, taught, coached, parented, or helped by someone like this. Working with such a person isn't like working with other people. The difference is palpable.

Why do we *feel* differently? It is because leaders like this not only *think* differently; they *behave* differently. We want to be better because of the way they treat us, how they speak to us, what they expect of us, and what they see in us. They ask for our opinion and listen to what we say. They paint a picture of what could be—and we become eager to be a part of it. These actions stem from the fundamental beliefs of a Trust & Inspire leader.

Command & Control leaders have a narrow, restrictive view of people and of leadership. Their beliefs about others are limited, deficient, and outdated—relying instead upon labels—and their actions usually match those beliefs.

By contrast, Trust & Inspire leaders have an expansive view of people and of leadership. Their beliefs are rooted in enduring principles of human effectiveness—and their actions match those beliefs. Their behavior flows from a deep well of beliefs that are part of who they are as a person.

Collectively, these beliefs make up a more complete, accurate, and relevant paradigm through which we view people and leadership today. Like a pair of glasses, a paradigm is a lens through which we view and interpret the world. The power of an accurate paradigm is its ability to effectively explain, guide, and predict. But an inaccurate or incomplete paradigm is limited and limiting.

The beliefs of a Trust & Inspire leader are also like a lens; they enhance our vision. They bring people and things into focus. They help us see the world in a new way. And with that clear vision, we are better able to perform, serve, contribute, and learn. We see people not only as they truly are, but as what they could be.

The beliefs of a Command & Control leader, on the other hand, are like a pair of broken glasses with an outdated prescription that blur our vision and give us a false perception of reality.

Each of us can become a Trust & Inspire leader through understanding and acting on the following 5 Fundamental Beliefs:

- People have greatness inside them . . . so my job as a leader is to unleash their potential, not control them.

- People are whole people . . . so my job as a leader is to inspire, not merely motivate.

- There is enough for everyone . . . so my job as a leader is to elevate caring above competing.

- Leadership is stewardship . . . so my job as a leader is to put service above self-interest.

- Enduring influence is created from the inside out . . . so my job as a leader is to go first.

I BELIEVE...		SO MY JOB AS A LEADER IS TO...
People have greatness inside them	1	Unleash their potential, not control them
People are whole people	2	Inspire, not merely motivate
There is enough for everyone	3	Elevate caring above competing
Leadership is stewardship	4	Put service above self-interest
Enduring influence is created from the inside out	5	Go first

1. People have greatness inside them . . . so my job as a leader is to unleash their potential, not control them

A Trust & Inspire leader believes that there is greatness in everyone—every person on your team, every student in your class, every child in your home. Their intent is to develop and unleash that greatness while helping people see that greatness within themselves.

What sets Trust & Inspire leaders apart is the way that they view people as fountains of greatness, brimming with potential. Because of that, they actively *look* for the greatness in people. They see the world as a garden and themselves as gardeners. They know that the true power is in the seed. Gardeners need to make the conditions right for a seed to be able to grow, but the seed grows because it has the *capability* of growing. Gardeners can support a seed, but they cannot make it grow.

Like the wildflowers in Death Valley, greatness often lies dormant, simply waiting to be awakened by the right conditions. Just as the ability to grow is within the seed, the true power is within people. That's plain to see when you walk into a room full of kindergartners—there is so much potential and possibility in each little person! Remembering this helps us look for the greatness in those who are no longer children. Our desire to trust and inspire people increases when we see them from a paradigm that acknowledges their inherent worth, ability, and potential. When we believe in their potential—both seen and unseen.

> *Everyone is born a genius, but the process of living de-geniuses them.*
>
> —BUCKMINSTER FULLER

Command & Control leaders don't see power in people; rather, they see power in the position. Whether a parent, a coach, a teacher, or a boss, people with this mindset believe that they have the answers and can make or break every situation. They believe they have the power. Whether a micromanaging boss or helicopter parent, this type of person believes that if the people they were leading would just do what they were told, everything would be so much easier. They cannot cede control because they only trust themselves (or occasionally just a select few). Such an attitude may breed compliance, but it stifles potential and leaves little room for growth.

Compare that to the bloom of possibility that comes when you trust and believe in the greatness inside others. Think how differently you would approach your children, interact with your colleagues, speak to your friends from this vantage point. When you believe in people and see their inherent potential for greatness, it opens you up to a whole new world of possibilities. No skills you can master or tactics you can try will substitute for a belief in others. That belief is key to unlocking unlimited potential and achieving outcomes that are different in kind. It is also key to inspiring others.

While belief in others is fundamental to Trust & Inspire leadership, it's nearly as important to be able to communicate that belief. Trust & Inspire leaders do all they can to communicate people's worth and potential to them. Their expression of belief is a gift to others. Like giving someone a new pair of glasses, it enables them to see the greatness in themselves. They gain a new perception of the world and of their possibilities in the world. Their self-confidence and self-trust grow.

From there, a Trust & Inspire leader works to develop people's potential. It is not enough to see it or even to acknowledge it in words. True leaders unleash greatness by seeing it, communicating it, and developing it.

Command & Control leaders often don't see the greatness in others, let alone communicate or develop it. Consider the demoralizing impact this has on people, teams, and cultures. With such a mindset, a leader might maintain the status quo or even get some incremental improvement. But that leader will get coordination only between silos, at best, and will rarely achieve real collaboration and creative innovation. Apathy reigns, leading to subpar results and eventual burnout.

By contrast, I'll never forget the day I was working with the top management team at the largest public utility in a foreign country. At the conclusion of our session together, the CEO of the company stood up and addressed each of his direct reports, one by one. Calling them by name, he told each member of his executive team, "I trust you. And here's why I trust you." He then proceeded to share very specific reasons why he had confidence in that leader, and why that leader mattered to him and to the company. The feeling of mutual belief and respect was palpable.

How much more inspired would you feel about your boss, your parent, your colleagues if you *knew* they trusted you, if you *felt* they believed in you, if you *recognized* that they saw greatness in you—and if they then told you and others how they felt about you? How would this enhance how you saw yourself? How could things change if you discovered the greatness you have inside?

The pattern is a simple, iterative, virtuous, upward cycle: *see* the potential, *communicate* the potential, *develop* the potential, and then *unleash* the potential. *See, communicate, develop, unleash.* This is how Trust & Inspire leaders elicit and inspire the very best in the people they lead. The people, in turn, contribute their best—even volunteer it.

As we leaders engage in this upward cycle, we create an agile culture not only able to confront disruptions, but one that also embraces the opportunities such disruption creates. The end result is real collaboration and creative innovation as people are freed, put forth their best effort, and contribute their best thinking. People are inspired and invigorated as you work hand in hand with them to achieve results while enabling everyone to reach their full potential.

Don't treat people according to their behavior; treat them according to their potential.

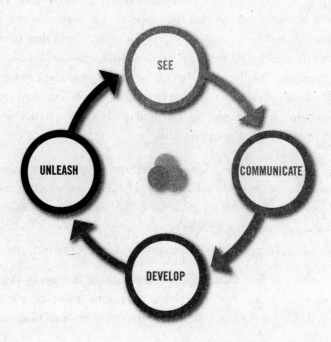

Treat people as they are, and they will remain as they are. Treat people as they can and should be, and they will become as they can and should be.

—GOETHE

2. People are whole people . . . so my job as a leader is to inspire, not merely motivate

Trust & Inspire leaders recognize that people have multiple layers that make up a whole person. In Command & Control organizations, many think about nothing more than people's physical needs, neglecting or even ignoring their emotional, mental, or spiritual needs (or merely giving them lip service with impersonal practices). At work, this means leaders give employees a paycheck. At home, it means that parents give children food, shelter, and clothing.

Trust & Inspire leaders know that this is a limited view of humanity and does not serve people well. For people to reach their highest potential, we must see and treat them as whole individuals. Trust & Inspire leaders focus on the four aspects that make up the whole person—body, heart, mind, and spirit. In other words, they recognize and address physical/economic needs (body), emotional/social needs (heart), mental/intellectual needs (mind), and spiritual/meaning needs (spirit). It's important to note that sequence matters. For example, you cannot help a student meet their mental needs if their physical or emotional needs have not been met first.

If we are to achieve a richer culture, rich in contrasting values, we must recognize the whole gamut of human potentialities, and so weave a less arbitrary social fabric, one in which each diverse human gift will find a fitting place.

—MARGARET MEAD, CULTURAL ANTHROPOLOGIST

For the last few decades, we've been making changes by degree— but in most cases, our underlying paradigm about people hasn't changed. That's why employees are still so often referred to as "assets."

Even a well-intentioned expression like *People are our most important asset* fundamentally reveals the need for a shift in mindset. Seeing people as assets is to see them as something to be managed, leveraged, controlled, and used. It's seeing only the part of a person we need or want, rather than their whole self.

With such a mindset, a coach would never understand why a physically capable player had a bad game. A professor would never understand why a bright student did poorly on a test. A parent would never understand why an obedient child made a poor decision. Things happen, but often not for the reasons we think. If there comes a time when the greatness in an individual is hard to see, it's often because we are blind to one or more of the four needs in that person's life. It's seldom effective to focus only on the part of the person we want, because people can't be compartmentalized.

When people come to work, they bring their whole selves, even if they try to go into "work mode." But that never truly changes who they fundamentally are. If that were the case, no health-care worker would ever feel the anguish of losing a patient. But health-care workers do feel that anguish—not just because of their compassion, but because the experience impacts their bodies, hearts, minds, and spirits.

Seeing others holistically—rather than as fragmented pieces or parts—is not just a strength but a necessity. It helps us connect with and understand the people we lead. We are no longer in the dark as to why people do what they do, because we understand them. We see them as people who are capable of giving far more than anyone could ever "manage" out of them. We are better able to tap into people's unique skills and gifts. We are better able to help them integrate the varying aspects of their lives, to support them in the areas where they need it, and to help them thrive and achieve total well-being.

We care about people's overall well-being, not just whether they can make their needs and lives fit into our work schedule in some sort of work-life balance formula. As a result, people are happier and produce better outcomes—whether at an office, in a nursing home, or simply on a car ride home from school.

In contrast, Command & Control leaders—either unaware or un-caring of the difference between inspiration and motivation—plow forward to try to "move" people. They employ different tactics and tricks, incentive programs, reward systems, spiffs. Many such leaders get decent results from this in the short term, so they think people are satisfied. They believe that motivation is all it takes—that people don't want more, that they don't yearn for a greater sense of purpose, mean-ing, and contribution.

You can command the body—but not the heart, mind, and spirit. The heart and spirit will go dormant, and the mind will figure out ways around the system in which it's confined. You can motivate hands and backs, but you can only inspire hearts and minds. External forces are insufficient—even if they get us the immediate result we want. We never truly get the best result, because extrinsic motivation has been proven to stifle innovation and creativity. It can lead people to feel like they need to do whatever it takes to get the reward or to avoid the pun-ishment. That's not inspiration.

> *The ultimate goal is to get to inclusion—where people's voices are heard and they bring their whole Selves To Work.*
>
> —JUDY MARKS, CEO OF OTIS WORLDWIDE

People not only want but need inspiration. We all have desires to give back, to have a cause, to find fulfillment. Motivation cannot answer this for us. It has to be something deeper—something from within.

I often hear feedback like this about leaders: *They motivate, but they don't inspire.* There's great value in the distinction. How would you feel if you were described that way by your team? Or your family?

I'll never forget the compelling motto of the 2002 Winter Olympics: "Light the Fire Within." That is what inspiration does. It lights what is already inside people—their greatness and their passions. Rather than trying to motivate from without, Trust & Inspire leaders look to ignite or fan the flames of the fires within.

Whenever I'm invited to speak or present at a conference or with a client organization, I always hope I won't be introduced as a "motivational speaker." I certainly want people to leave my presentation feeling motivated, but I know that will only serve them for an hour or two, a week at best. But if I can inspire, that fire can burn for years. I routinely have people come up to me after a presentation and tell me about a class they took from my father in 1983, or about a speech they heard him give in 2010. They tell me the experience has never left them and that it inspired them to make a significant and long-term change in their life.

Among countless others, my father's example has indeed inspired me. He encouraged me to adopt the following mantra whenever I have a speaking engagement:

"Seek to bless, not to impress."

Whatever the particular leadership role, we aren't in this to find people to work *for* us, but to find people to inspire to work *with* us. In turn, they will inspire us with their talent.

3. There is enough for everyone . . . so my job as a leader is to elevate caring above competing

When I was growing up, mealtime at my family home was like a full-contact sport. If you wanted food, you had to act quickly. By the time I was a teenager, I was one of nine kids. The problem was that my mom's muffin pan fit only eight muffins. Do the math: even though Mom and Dad both forewent a muffin, that still left only eight muffins for nine of us kids. If you wanted a muffin, you had to beat out one of your siblings. If my brother got a muffin, that means I didn't get one.

Command & Control leaders see the world that way. If you get some, I get less. If you succeed, my success is diminished. This scarcity mindset leads to jealousy and an unwillingness to even work with others, much less recognize their success. It can breed bitterness, dissension, and unhealthy competition and contention. It can lead to what my father called the five metastasizing emotional cancers: competing, contending, complaining, comparing, and criticizing. Command &

Control leaders don't look for the talents or positive attributes in others unless it serves them in some way—and even then, such leaders can feel threatened if the talents of their people exceed their own. Leaders with a scarcity mindset are never satisfied, because they feel a need to beat others to what they see as scarce resources.

On the flip side, Trust & Inspire leaders operate with an abundance mentality. Unlike the eight muffins at our dinner table, there *is* enough for everyone. We can share the muffins or just make more of them. Or get a bigger muffin pan. Another person's success doesn't diminish my own.

Competing against others externally in the marketplace is good. It tends to bring out the best in people and organizations, typically enabling us to improve, innovate, and perform at a higher level to stay relevant. That's usually not the case with internal competition. It often brings out the worst in us; it significantly diminishes collaboration and engagement; and it frequently leads to a toxic, even cutthroat, culture.

> *Keep competition on the outside, collaboration inside.*
> —STEPHANIE FRERICH, MY
> SIMON & SCHUSTER BOOK EDITOR

When we operate with an abundance mentality, jealousy dissipates. People become eager to work with others and applaud them when they succeed. Trust & Inspire leaders look for opportunities to celebrate and enhance the virtues of the people around them because they genuinely care for others and their well-being.

> *The way you achieve your own success is to be willing to help somebody else get it first.*
> —IYANLA VANZANT, SPEAKER AND
> AUTHOR OF *IN THE MEANTIME*

While an abundance mindset is all about caring for others, a scarcity mindset is about caring for yourself and competing with others.

Scarcity convinces you that there's only so much to go around, and if someone else gets it, you get less. That means you need to compete, and others do, too. But when you have an abundance mindset, you believe there is plenty—enough for everyone—and that you can all share things like respect, trust, prestige, recognition, profits, and decision making.

An abundance mentality flows out of a deep inner sense of personal worth and security. It leads to a natural desire to elevate caring above competing because that's simply being true to our beliefs. Of course, we want to win. But because we care about others, we want them to win, too. And rather than compete with each other, we *complete* each other—and together become a complementary team.

> *Good management is largely a matter of love or, if you're uncom-*
> *fortable with that word, call it caring because proper management*
> *involves caring for people, not manipulating them.*
>
> —JAMES AUTRY, AUTHOR AND
> FORMER FORTUNE 500 EXECUTIVE

4. Leadership is stewardship . . . so my job as a leader is to put service above self-interest

One of the quickest—and most enduring—ways to change our behavior is to change our name or change our role (or the way we see our role). Such an immediate change in name and role affects not only how we now see the world, but also impacts how we want to behave differently in it.

When my first child was born, my entire world changed in a matter of minutes. I became a father—an immediate change in name and role. A commensurate shift happens no matter in what situation a change in name or role occurs.

When we start with the fundamental belief that leadership is stewardship, we are doing both—changing our name and changing our role. Seeing leadership as stewardship will impact our behavior more powerfully and enduringly than perhaps anything else we might do.

A stewardship consists of inherent responsibilities implicit in leadership itself. When we have a stewardship paradigm, we have been given a job to do, and we've been entrusted to see it through. Viewing our roles through the lens of stewardship calls on the best in us and helps us release the best in everyone, including ourselves.

People who operate from a Trust & Inspire paradigm have a sense of stewardship about everything, including their time, talents, money, possessions, relationships, and family. Similarly, leaders who operate from this paradigm also have a distinctive sense of responsibility about their role as a leader, seeing themselves as stewards—as having a responsibility for the growth and well-being of those they serve and lead.

Uplifted by seeing others as whole people and fueled by an abundance mentality, a stewardship approach creates a genuineness in our lives that goes far beyond technique and recognizes the unlimited possibilities for positive interaction.

Stewardship is not about being the boss; it's about having a job with a trust. It's about responsibility and serving others in order to achieve a greater outcome. It's about leaving something in better shape than when we stepped into our role. That is what stewardship is about for everyone—whether it be an administrator, a parent, a member of a team, or even an individual leading his or her own life. And it is especially true for anyone leading others.

> *In a learning organization, leaders are designers, stewards and teachers.*
>
> —PETER SENGE, AUTHOR OF *THE FIFTH DISCIPLINE*

Above all, stewardship is about *putting service above self-interest.* Self-interest tells you that you have to put yourself and your needs first. It's a belief that serving others is for someone else, particularly the weak. Yet leaders who see themselves as stewards see it as the greatest strength. This doesn't mean they neglect themselves. But they don't feel the need to elevate their wants above the wants and needs of others, because they know that serving others is what enriches life.

This is why we are so inspired by those who dedicate their lives to helping others—the firefighter who runs into a burning building, the parent who sacrifices their dream for the dreams of their children, the doctor who dedicates part of their time each year to the health and healing of those struggling. These people inspire us because they are models of service above self. Serving a cause greater than ourselves brings us joy. To serve others and care for their well-being—even if doing so doesn't appear to benefit us in any way—is perhaps the highest form of humanity. Interestingly, it also happens to produce better outcomes.

Leadership is stewardship, and leaders are stewards.

> *We have lost the stewardship connection, at a leadership level, across society. As a leader, it's not about you. As a leader, it's about the people to whom you are in some way responsible . . . And that's what stewardship comes down to.*
>
> —JOHN TAFT, FORMER CEO OF
> RBC WEALTH MANAGEMENT

5. Enduring influence is created from the inside out . . . so my job as a leader is to go first

Leading is about intentional influence—an influence that endures, even when the leader is not present. Such enduring influence is created and sustained from the inside out.

> *Leadership is about empowering other people as a result of your presence—and making sure that impact continues into your absence.*
>
> —DR. FRANCES FREI AND ANNE MORRISS,
> AUTHORS OF *UNLEASHED*

When a drop of water drips into a larger body of water, the waves start at the inside and ripple outward. It's that way with people, too. The ripples—the enduring influence—always start with us. The influence then moves out to our relationships, then to our teams and organizations. And then to our stakeholders and the external marketplace. And then to all society. And the best way to create this kind of enduring influence from the inside out is to simply *go first*. That's what Trust & Inspire leaders do. They start with themselves. They look in the mirror. They model the behavior. They go first.

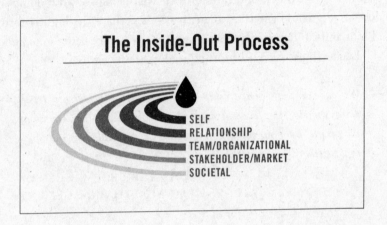

For decades, Fred Rogers was a model to people worldwide through his children's television show, *Mister Rogers' Neighborhood*. He was able to influence and change many lives through his love and vulnerability, both of which were seen and felt even over a television screen.

One of his best qualities was that he always "went first." As just one example, by 1969, laws had been passed in the United States to prevent racial segregation, but the country was still very much segregated. Mr. Rogers had already "gone first" by introducing the first recurring Black character on a children's show—Officer Clemmons. But that's not all. He took it a step further. During one episode in the summer of 1969, Mr. Rogers invited Officer Clemmons to join him in removing his shoes and socks and putting his feet into a wading pool so they could both cool off from the heat. At a time when swimming pools across the nation were still largely segregated, this could have been seen by some as controversial. And yet Mr. Rogers did it, modeling racial equality and love for your neighbor to children (and their parents) watching at home. He went first, modeling the way he hoped others would act. And the influence he had was profound—and enduring.

While it's true that Mr. Rogers was a great example, he had a platform unlike what most have. You may find yourself asking, "How do I become a Trust & Inspire person when I'm in a Command & Control culture, and I'm not in charge?"

One answer is simply to go first. All of us are part of something bigger than ourselves, and it can feel difficult to have influence, especially if you're not the formal leader. But if you want to influence other people, if you want to improve the communication within your team, if you want to change the culture of your family, don't wait on others. Just go first.

Be the first to:

... listen
... admit you were wrong
... be loyal to the absent
... affirm and praise a wayward child
... keep a commitment
... hold yourself accountable
... admit that you're unsure
... take responsibility for poor results
... create transparency when everyone else is operating from hidden agendas
... tell the truth instead of creating spin
... extend trust
... give someone the benefit of the doubt
... show respect
... share difficult information
... choose abundance
... be courageous
... clarify expectations
... assume positive intent

If you want to have enduring influence with others, lead by modeling the behavior.

I can't help but think of Nelson Mandela, the former president of South Africa and the country's first Black head of state. A man of incredible insight, Mandela understood and exemplified the principle that enduring influence is created from the inside out, something he consistently demonstrated. He once said, "You can never have an impact on society if you have not changed yourself."

He also understood the importance of leaders going first. One of the most inspiring indications of that came at his inaugural ceremony, when he put members of his party on one side of the aisle and his jailers—his *enemies*, those who had kept him prisoner for twenty-seven years—right up front on the other side. It was an extraordinary symbol of peace and forgiveness, and an illustration of his belief in going first.

> *We decided that in order to reinvent GM, each of us top leaders have to first get humble and reinvent ourselves. How can we expect to disrupt the auto industry until we disrupt our own leadership first?*
>
> —MARY BARRA, CHAIR AND CEO OF GM

Our Fundamental Beliefs Create Our Leadership Paradigm

The cumulative effect of these beliefs creates a Trust & Inspire leadership mindset—an expansive lens through which we view the world. Our paradigm matters enormously because it is difficult to act with integrity outside whatever paradigm we have. As we internalize these beliefs and act on them, we will find the strength—indeed, the humility and courage—we need to become Trust & Inspire leaders. Our actions will be guided by these beliefs. And in order to live with integrity and manifest our authenticity, we cannot act in ways that betray our beliefs.

It is difficult to raise children to reach their potential if we don't see that potential. It is difficult to help colleagues thrive when we don't view them as anything more than labor. It is difficult to meaningfully contribute to the world if we want to keep it all to ourselves.

COMMAND & CONTROL	TRUST & INSPIRE
Machinist	Gardener
Fragmented Person	Whole Person (Body, Heart, Mind, Spirit)
Scarcity Mentality	Abundance Mentality
Self-Interest	Caring
Compete	Complete

CHAPTER 5

The 1st Stewardship: Modeling, or *Who You Are*

Children have never been very good at listening to their elders, but they have never failed to imitate them.

—JAMES BALDWIN, AUTHOR AND POET

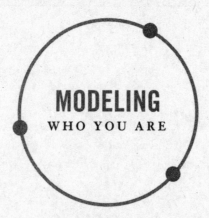

MODELING
WHO YOU ARE

I once worked with a leader who, a year into his job as the new CEO, wanted to make sure he was building the right culture at his company and that he had the confidence of his team. He decided to email a memo to the entire company—more than a thousand employees—that read:

Dear teammates,

True leaders are not chosen to lead by the Board of Directors and shareholders. True leaders are chosen by their teammates based on the respect they have earned, the results they have achieved, and the confidence the team has that the team will win with that leader in place. I was chosen by the shareholders and our Board to be your leader. I was not chosen by you. May 1st was my one-year anniversary as your CEO, and enough time has elapsed for you to decide whether you would like me to continue to lead this great team.

Please click on this link and tell me if you want me to remain the CEO, as well as any constructive comments you may have for our business or for my leadership. If I do not have your collective vote of confidence, I will move along.

This survey is anonymous, so please be honest. If you choose for me to remain, this will be your free choice, and I will be honored to lead with all my energy and ability.

Please respond on or before May 12th with your vote. Thanks.

The response rate was more than 95 percent, a rate that would be the envy of anyone conducting any kind of survey. And of those who responded, an amazing 97 percent said he should stay. I think I'd be lucky if I could get 50 percent of my own kids to vote for me on that basis! The 3 percent who voted against him staying were still somewhat positive, asking him to make improvements in certain areas.

What this leader did was simply remarkable. It was an extraordinary extension of trust to ask, "Do you want me to be your CEO?" What gave this leader the guts to do this?

He displayed humility and courage in his leadership. He was authentic and vulnerable—as demonstrated by his email to the company. He had shown empathy and understanding for others while at the same time he established a strong track record of performance—which gave people confidence in his leadership. And he was willing to "go first." In short, he *modeled the behavior*. It was who he was.

How do you think those people are going to respond to his leadership going forward?

How do people respond to your leadership?

Albert Schweitzer said, "Example is not the main thing in influencing others; it's the only thing." You may not consider yourself to be an example—but like it or not, if you are breathing, you're modeling. As a Trust & Inspire leader, modeling is your 1st stewardship. The people around you learn from you simply by being in your presence, either in person or virtually. The question is, what are they learning? Or, what are you modeling?

Modeling is *who you are*. It is the source of credibility and your moral authority as a leader. Modeling is built on the fundamental beliefs that enduring influence is created from the inside out and that leaders go first. When you are credible, that gives you influence. When you have moral authority, that also gives you influence. So at the heart of modeling is credibility and moral authority. Let's consider each in turn.

Modeling Is Credibility

Both character and competence are needed to have credibility. Each is necessary on its own, but neither is sufficient without the other.

On a recent trip to Ireland with my wife and daughter, I volunteered to rent a car and drive us around the countryside. They exchanged wary glances before my daughter said, "We love you, Dad. But we don't trust you to drive on the opposite side of the road." They weren't doubting my character—but they were definitely doubting my competence!

Many of us know someone who is a wonderful person but terrible at their job. No matter how honorable people might be, they need competence for us to fully trust them. On the flip side, you might have someone with high competence and low character. While you might trust them to deliver results, you might not trust how they do it. Such a person might accomplish a lot but run over people in the process or violate the values of the organization. You're afraid to turn your back on such a person because of what might end up in your back.

Your continued display of credibility not only helps others build confidence in you, it also helps you build confidence in yourself. Indeed, self-trust flows from credibility. And credibility is crucial to the kind of modeling needed in today's disruptive world. My friend and colleague, leadership development expert Barry Rellaford, put it this way: "Leadership is not a popularity contest; it's a credibility contest." It's better to be trusted than to be liked.

Modeling Is Moral Authority

Moral authority is not the same as formal authority, which comes with title or position. When you operate with care and consistently model uplifting behavior, you develop a moral authority that inspires others.

A study from LRN shows that this is not only important but necessary: 87 percent of people surveyed say that the need for moral leadership is higher today than ever. Those same people also reported that only 7 percent of their leaders consistently demonstrated behaviors that produce moral authority. There is obviously a disconnect, even if the leaders have good intent. But just because you hold the position of leader, parent, doctor, teacher, or coach, that doesn't mean that you are a good one. As LRN founder Dov Seidman put it, "Formal authority can be seized, won, or bestowed. Moral authority must be earned by who you are and how you lead."

> *I rent my title . . . I own my character.*
>
> —THASUNDA BROWN DUCKETT,
> PRESIDENT AND CEO OF TIAA

The players on any sports team know this to be true. A player doesn't gain a team's respect by simply being appointed the team captain, but by working harder than anyone else on the team. By running farther. By performing the best. In other words, by "going first." That inspires people. The same LRN study found that 95 percent of leaders who consistently demonstrate moral leadership behaviors are able to "inspire best efforts" from others.

When I think of moral authority, I immediately think of Kenneth I. Chenault, the former longtime chairman and CEO of American Express. Ken obviously had the *formal* authority at American Express because of his role and title, but his *real* influence came about because of who he is. There was so much confidence in his credibility and leadership that he didn't have to rely on his position or title for his influence.

A person's reputation precedes him or her and leaves a legacy in its wake. That's certainly the story of Ken Chenault. Whenever I present on Trust & Inspire leadership in public settings, I frequently speak of Ken. What's inspiring to me is what happens afterward. Perhaps more frequently than with any other leader I point to, people come up to me after my presentations and comment on Ken's leadership, on how they've been impacted by him, and especially on who he is as a person. Google chairman Eric Schmidt says Chenault "exemplifies the best leadership that I've ever worked with."

Chenault was so widely respected by his own people that they were in awe of him—not just his intellect and business talent, but his emotional qualities as well. His employees, even those who competed with him for the CEO spot, looked up to him and were inspired by him, a product of his moral authority and modeling. Louise Parent, the company's vice president and general counsel, remarked in *Black Enterprise*, "He is the kind of person who inspires you to want to do your best. Part of the reason is his example."

It's a privilege, not an entitlement, to lead.

—KEN CHENAULT, FORMER CEO
OF AMERICAN EXPRESS

When who we are speaks louder than what we say, people respond. Modeling is essential to inspiring people, helping us do our best work, and creating a positive, inclusive culture.

The Influence of Modeling

I'll never forget the time at a basketball game where, caught up in the moment, I stood up to yell at the referee for missing a call during the game, only to look down and see my young child stand up and yell at the same ref. It wasn't my best modeling moment. People close their ears to advice and open their eyes to example. So the best way to become a Trust & Inspire leader is to model the behavior that you would like to see. We must walk the walk before people will listen to our talk.

> *Leadership is a matter of how to be, not how to do.*
> —FRANCES HESSELBEIN, FORMER CEO
> OF THE GIRL SCOUTS

When we are intentional about the example we set, we accelerate the influence of our modeling. If a team leader ignores a demeaning remark from a member of his or her team, it cements the behavior as acceptable in the culture.

In a school setting, every teacher knows that he or she sets the tone for the classroom on day one. If a teacher snickers at a student's response, she has given tacit permission to the rest of the class to do the same. If a teacher doesn't correct inappropriate comments or behavior, he has marked those comments or behavior as acceptable. Regardless of whether students consciously think it, they'll justify their behavior because of the model they see. "If Mr. Johnson interrupts people, then why can't I?" Mr. Johnson might say all the right things, but if his words don't match his actions, they lose all meaning. And that makes him difficult to trust.

A great sequence and pattern for intentional modeling is found in following the Greek philosophy of influence, best represented by *Ethos*, *Pathos*, and *Logos*. *Ethos* is your personal credibility—how people view you, whether they believe what you say. *Pathos* is about feelings and relationships. It's being emotionally in tune with others and their needs. *Logos* is about logic—whether you are rational in the work you do with people.

Notice the sequence of these three ideas. You start by focusing first on your credibility and then on your relationships with others before focusing on the logical work. Too often, leaders make the mistake of starting with Logos—the rational work they're trying to help others accomplish—before they focus on their credibility and relationships with people. Doing so comes across as "telling" rather than "showing," as directive rather than instructive. Like the Greeks, we've learned that when it comes to people, it's more effective to start the opposite way, focusing first on credibility and relationships. Doing so comes across as "showing."

We are who we are in large part because of the models around us, whether good or bad. We learn by example, which is why we're so drawn to stories. We like to hear tales of bravery and to imagine that we would do the same. And although we often look to high-profile people for examples, our most impactful models are the everyday people around us—leaders, colleagues, teachers, coaches, parents, siblings, and friends. Even if we fail to recognize it, their modeling influences us for good or bad.

I've looked up to many people as models throughout my life, but nothing compares to the modeling of my parents, who taught me to contribute and to live a caring and hopefully generous life. Even though they weren't perfect parents (no one is), I trusted them because they spent their lives trying to be good people and good examples—and they taught me to try to be the same. Their modeling inspired me. It continues to inspire me even now that they're gone. Your experience may have been very different from mine, but no matter who the people are, our most influential models are the people who surround us day by day, not distant icons. And that's the opportunity in front of each of us—to be that kind of model for others.

What Trust & Inspire Leaders Model

While there are many important attributes to model, I've identified those with the greatest impact for the new way to lead. While I'll combine these "behavioral virtues" into pairs, each is independently important to model. The reason I've organized these behavioral virtues into pairs is that each is tremendously influenced by, and in some cases balanced by, the other. If you consider the leaders who have most influenced and inspired you, you'll likely find they have modeled these behavioral virtues:

- Humility and Courage

- Authenticity and Vulnerability

- Empathy and Performance

Humility and Courage

Two towering, seemingly paradoxical qualities—humility and courage—are especially vital for us to model.

Some people have high levels of humility but lack courage. These people care about relationships but often don't have the will to correct people when they're wrong or to give critical feedback. This may happen in parenting, when parents are humble enough to recognize that their child has issues, but they are too afraid to correct that child's misbehavior. Or it may happen on teams, when team leaders are humble enough to recognize their team has become dysfunctional, but they are too fearful of confronting team members about what needs to change. Such team leaders are often more concerned with being liked than in doing what is right. In the end, everyone suffers from this lack of courage.

It takes a lot of courage to take on tough issues, especially with people you care about and love. In the long run, it demonstrates more loyalty to and care for the person when you are loyal to principles first.

For example, you want your doctor to tell you the truth, not what you want to hear. Same with a leadership team. Doing so takes courage.

> *Without courage, we cannot practice any other virtue with consistency. We can't be kind, true, merciful, generous or honest.*
>
> —MAYA ANGELOU

Of course, the opposite can also be true. There's no shortage of Command & Control leaders who are high in courage but low in humility. It's probably why there is always that one person in your meetings who consistently speaks up, even without anything valuable to contribute. Such a person is not afraid to speak out and often seeks the spotlight. They have lots of courage, not as much humility.

Humility is a foundational virtue for all other virtues because it acknowledges that principles govern. The opposites of humility—arrogance, ego, and pride—teach us that we are in charge, so we put ego above principles. By contrast, humility teaches us that we should understand and live by principles, elevating service above self-interest.

We cannot make progress if we lack humility. Humility is the first step toward growth. It takes great strength to be able to admit that you failed or to apologize.

Humility is widely misunderstood today; it is often seen as weak, soft, timid, and passive—the opposite of what real leadership is. In truth, humility is enormously strong, firm, courageous, and active—the very essence of leadership. A humble person is more concerned about *what* is right than about *being* right, about *acting* on good ideas than *having* the ideas, and about *recognizing* contribution than *being recognized* for making it.

In terms of inspiring others, a study from LRN found that leaders who demonstrate humility are eighteen times more likely to inspire colleagues than leaders who don't.

It takes courage to have humility, but that act of vulnerability is what endears people to us. When we show how to be humble, people will be inspired to give their best efforts and to follow suit.

By practicing humility, we show others that credibility matters—enough to change our habits to align with principles. Enough to be vulnerable. Those who refuse to practice humility may think they are projecting strength when in reality they are exposing their weakness.

Courage is more commonly understood as a leadership virtue to model, but we often forget the foundation on which courage is based. Self-serving courage (standing up for yourself) can be appropriate, but that is not as powerful as service-oriented courage (standing up for others). The kind of courage most needed to model in our world today is the *courage to do the right thing*—even when it's hard or unrecognized. The ultimate test of courage is often when there's a cost in doing so.

Another test is when nobody will know about it—will we still do the right thing? To display such courage in doing the right thing, especially when difficult, is the highest manifestation of integrity.

Courage is a choice based on your values, while fear is a reaction based on your emotions.

In his landmark book, *Good to Great*, thought leader Jim Collins did research on what caused good companies to transform into great companies. The data showed that leadership mattered enormously. What really surprised Collins was the "the type of leadership required for turning a good company into a great one," because rather than a big-personality, high-profile, self-aggrandizing leader, it was a "Level 5 leader" who led these changes—the highest level of leader on his scale. Such a leader is characterized by having both deep personal humility and intense professional will (courage). As Collins says, "Level 5 leaders are a study in duality: modest and willful, shy and fearless . . . They are more like Lincoln and Socrates than Patton or Caesar." Humility, bolstered by courage, is a powerful force.

People will be inspired when you have the bravery and fortitude to be humble. They will care less about your status and position when they learn about your humility and courage. In the movie *Braveheart,* William Wallace said to the heir to the throne, Robert the Bruce, "Your title gives you claim to the throne of our country, but men don't follow titles; they follow courage."

To lead others, we must be humble and courageous enough to be authentic in every area of our lives. Humility and courage are the parents of authenticity. Together they inspire others to do as we do.

Authenticity and Vulnerability

Today social media and the internet have given a platform to an unprecedented and unlimited number of people. Voices that were never heard before have become influential in many different spheres of life.

A lot of that has been positive, but it has also introduced issues. We've probably all seen a well-meaning friend post a satirical news piece thinking it was real—maybe we've even done so ourselves! But in a world of "fake news" and Instagram influencers, authenticity can be hard to find. Everyone seems to have an agenda. Everyone is trying to sell something. Everyone wants the biggest platform they can get.

It raises the question *Is what you see really what you get?*

We are drawn to authenticity. We're inspired by people who are genuine, vulnerable, and growing. Who are flawed and human, just like we are.

Authenticity means *real*. If honesty means that our words match reality, authenticity means that our reality matches our words—we are who we say we are. This has a significant impact on how those we lead experience us.

In a real sense, authenticity is the highest manifestation of integrity—being whole, complete, integrated. There's no pretending, no putting on airs. I love the expression of authenticity found in the motto of North Carolina: *Essi Quam Videri.* For those of us who never learned Latin, it means, "To be rather than to seem."

Inauthenticity, on the other hand, means artificial or fake. Think of when you've been around someone who is not authentic. You often feel unimportant, and you are uninterested. You usually leave a conversation feeling frustrated or confused about the other person's motives. That person may have said the right things, but their actions don't line up. The audio doesn't match the video. And that is utterly uninspiring.

People will forgive leaders for not being as good as they should be,
but they won't forgive them for not being as good as they claim to be.

—DIANE SAWYER, ABC NEWS ANCHOR

Three Lives: Public, Private, Inner

We all lead three lives. Our *public life* is what everyone sees—what we put on social media, what we list on our résumés, what we present to the world. Our *private life* is how we act in our own homes with our family and closest friends. Our *inner life* is what we think and do when we are alone. To be truly authentic, we should try to make our three lives congruent.

In 1931, Mahatma Gandhi went to England to speak before the House of Commons, hoping to influence the British leaders in his quest for Indian independence. Many prominent people attended the conference, including members of Parliament. Gandhi arrived in his usual simple dress and humbly approached the stage. He then proceeded to speak powerfully for two hours straight, mesmerizing the crowd. And he did it all without notes.

People were astonished at the incredible speech he delivered. Afterward, members of the press asked Gandhi's secretary, Mahadev Desai, how Gandhi was able to speak so articulately for such a long time without using any notes. Desai responded, "You don't understand Gandhi. You see, what he thinks is what he feels. What he feels is what he says, and what he says is what he does. What Gandhi thinks, what he feels, and what he says and what he does are all the same. He does not need notes. You and I think things that sometimes may be different from what we feel. What we say depends on who's listening. What we do depends on who's watching. It is not so with him. He needs no notes."

Gandhi was so aligned in his three lives that he had ultimate integrity. His authenticity was strong because he had earned it through being consistent in his modeling. He was true to himself at all times, in any circumstance, with anybody. While he never had formal authority or position, his modeling of this kind of authenticity gave him extraordinary credibility and moral authority.

My life is an indivisible whole, and all my activities run into one another. . . . My life is my message.

—MAHATMA GANDHI

There is great personal power in the lifelong work of aligning our public, private, and inner lives. People gain confidence knowing that who we say we are *is* who we are—all of the time. That's real authenticity.

When my father passed away, I reflected a great deal on what I wanted to say at his funeral. What kept coming to mind was that as good as my father was in public, he was even better in private. He, too, had high integrity because he was always the same. He didn't turn it on for the camera. There was no switch he flipped to get into his "7 Habits" mode. He *was* the 7 Habits. He lived them on a daily basis. With him, what you saw was what you got. And he treated those he interacted with on a daily basis—his family and his work associates— as good as, or even better than, he treated the powerful people he met.

Vulnerability Is the Gateway to Authenticity

We've defined authenticity as being who you say you are. Vulnerability, then, is when you open yourself up for others to see for themselves who you really are. It is the act of being open and transparent. It creates real intimacy, because that is precisely what you are doing: *intimacy* means "into-me-see."

Counterintuitive to what many of us may have learned growing up, leaders who are vulnerable—who can admit wrongdoing, acknowledge inadequacies, ask for help—are not weak. We need to break with the idea that leaders never show weakness, that there is strength in hiding behind a façade. That doesn't mean we need to share all of our deepest fears or problems with everyone. But it also means we can stop being an inauthentic leader who hides behind a mask, or what we might call a "mechanical leader"—someone who goes through the motions but never truly emotionally invests. Trust & Inspire leaders are vulnerable by opening up their authentic selves.

Vulnerability is not weakness; it's our greatest measure of courage.
—BRENÉ BROWN, AUTHOR AND PROFESSOR

A great example of vulnerability being strength is the recently retired CEO of Intuit, Brad Smith. As shared by Jeffrey Cohn and Srinivasa Rangan in a *Harvard Business Review* article on modeling vulnerability, Brad told his board that he wanted to do a 360 assessment and share the results not only with the board, but also with his executive team and with the entire company. As CEO, he posted his feedback results outside his office for all to see. By doing so, he showed the company not only what he was working on but also that he wanted to be held accountable. He modeled authenticity, vulnerability, and openness. He modeled wanting to continuously improve. He modeled that weaknesses can become strengths. You can bet that people's trust in him rose and that they were inspired to similarly want to improve.

Charisma may motivate, but it is authenticity and vulnerability that truly inspire.

What does a vulnerable parent look like? Too often, parents feel a need to always be strong in front of their children, to be the authority at all times. Many parents demand a child apologize after doing something wrong, but has your child seen *you* apologize after making a mistake? If children haven't seen that apology modeled and haven't *felt* the ensuing impact, how will they know how to do it—or the power that comes from doing it? They won't. Too often children learn to say "sorry" without experiencing the power of a meaningful apology. Sometimes we need to subordinate our need to be right in favor of preserving, enhancing, and growing our relationships. When we are vulnerable, we communicate to our children that they are more important to us than our pride or ego.

I acknowledge that it's possible to go too far in being vulnerable—so far that it could backfire. In fact, *any* behavioral virtue, when pushed to the extreme, can become a weakness. For example, a leader might go too far in being vulnerable if they become so open and transparent about their fears and insecurities that people who are seeking leaders who have vision and clarity lose confidence in them. Vulnerability is not a one-size-fits-all approach in every situation but rather requires good judgment—even boundaries. Our bigger problem, though, is not that we are too vulnerable but that we are not nearly vulnerable enough.

"Declare Your Intent" . . . Even Better, "Declare Yourself"

My brother David is famous for the way he runs meetings at work. At the start, he frequently stands at the whiteboard and says, "Let's write up our agenda for this meeting." Everyone shares what they'd like to accomplish while he writes it on the board.

After they finish building the agenda, he usually looks around and says, "Okay, now let's write up our *hidden* agendas!" Everyone gets a good laugh out of this, but the point he makes is valid. Are all of them always honest about what they want to get out of the meeting? Are they being transparent about their goals at work? Are some people hoping to gain an advantage over another person or department?

People are wary of those who seem to have hidden agendas—and unfortunately, many people or organizations do have them.

Even in relationships, people often have hidden agendas. When you sit down to have a discussion with your child about her grades, is your real agenda to help her or is it to fix the problem? When you get into a political discussion with a friend, is your real agenda to listen and understand or is it to come up with the best retort possible? Authenticity is critical to building a relationship of trust. And that means you need to "declare your intent."

Declaring your intent involves opening your agenda, giving the *why* behind the what. It is a great practice in using vulnerability to operationalize authenticity.

One of the best examples of this practice comes from Doug Conant, the former president of Nabisco Foods and former CEO of the Campbell Soup Company. When Doug became the CEO at Campbell's, the company had one of the lowest employee engagement scores in the country. It also had near rock-bottom financial performance among global food companies. Doug was able to lead the transformation of the company during his ten-year tenure—employee engagement scores skyrocketed from abysmal to world class, and its financial performance rose from the bottom to the top tier.

There were many factors behind this transformation, but Doug told me that a huge part of their success came from his practice of what he called "declaring himself," which included declaring his intent. He told me that whenever he met with new people he worked with at Campbell's—typically employees but sometimes even partners or customers—he always tried to start off by "declaring himself." That meant he told them who he was, what mattered to him, and how he approached leadership and work. He told them about his goals for the company and for the relationship. He explained not only his *what* but especially his *why*.

Those Doug talked to felt trusted. They also had clarity about who he was, what he believed in, and why he did the things he did. The "mystery" had been taken out of the relationship.

Doug was vulnerable as he modeled this level of intimacy and authenticity, and that set the tone. He not only declared his intent, he declared himself. And he invited others to reciprocate and declare themselves if they would like.

Imagine if your next staff meeting could start with "declaring your intent." Imagine if your next meeting with a direct report could start with "declaring yourself." Imagine if your next discussion with your spouse about finances could involve that same level of authenticity and vulnerability. How would it change things? What kind of results could you achieve? How much time could you save when you no longer had to worry about reading body language and understanding subtext?

When we are real about why we do the things we do, we will find that others are willing to do the same. In fact, modeling authenticity and vulnerability is a powerful enabler in creating and unlocking psychological safety for our team. These two behavioral virtues greatly accelerate building trust. And as understanding and trust increase, our ability to achieve great outcomes skyrockets.

It's easy to regard those who inspire us as nearly superhuman. We might say, "Sure, they can be vulnerable because they've got so much going for them already." The people I know who are authentic and vulnerable didn't start those practices only after achieving a certain level of success or notoriety. I would argue that their authenticity and vulnerability are vital components in what helped them achieve that level of success in the first place. They *behaved* their way into greater authenticity and success.

In my book *The Speed of Trust*, I identify thirteen specific "authentic behaviors" that help leaders build trust along with corresponding "opposite behaviors" and "counterfeit behaviors." I won't go into those here, but the point is that many leaders lose their authenticity when they fall into traps of counterfeit behaviors that look real on the surface but are not actually real. But if those leaders consistently seek to model the authentic behaviors, they can intentionally behave their way into greater trust and success.

All of us, even our heroes, fall short at times in matching our words and our actions. It's the big things *and* the little things. The best way to build trust as a leader is to be who we say we are. To let our actions speak louder than our words. If we want to inspire others, then we strive to be inspirational.

This doesn't mean we have to be perfect. We should try to live the way we want our employees, our colleagues, our nieces and nephews to live. We should try to live by and be true to enduring principles. Even trying, in and of itself, models something worthwhile. We can model the behavior we want to see.

We cannot teach that which we are not any more than we can return from a place we haven't been.

Empathy and Performance

Empathy and performance are two virtues that feel completely independent of each other—and in many ways, they are. Yet they are amazingly and remarkably interdependent.

One of the greatest needs for humans is to be understood. What oxygen is to the body, understanding is to the heart. It gives people emotional and psychological air.

In a world increasingly divided and polarized, with everyone talking but so few listening, no one feels truly understood. Some may pause to listen a little, yet most people don't listen with the intent to understand; rather, most listen with the intent to *reply*. Simply waiting your turn to reply isn't empathy. Empathy is understanding. It's understanding another person's thoughts, feelings, experience, and point of view. It's not evaluating or interpreting; it's not agreeing or disagreeing. It's simply understanding. It's being able to get into and see things from the other person's frame of reference rather than only from your own.

Years ago, Princess Diana provided a simple yet profound example of empathy. In the midst of the AIDS epidemic in the 1980s, many prejudices and misunderstandings about people with AIDS circulated worldwide. People with AIDS not only suffered physically, but they also felt marginalized and misunderstood. Many people thought AIDS could be contracted simply by touching someone with the disease.

To help combat these myths, Princess Diana visited a hospital with AIDS patients. There she intentionally and very publicly shook the hands of all the patients, making sure the hand-shaking—the physical contact—was filmed and documented for everyone to see. At the time, many thought doing so put her at risk—both physically and in terms of reputation—but she did what she knew was right. She not only modeled compassion, she modeled empathy as well. Her empathic approach helped create greater understanding. Going first inspired the world to follow.

When I came in as the new CEO of Covey Leadership Center many years ago, we were addressing eight legal disputes. Some of these disputes had dragged on for many months, even years. They had consumed enormous amounts of time and energy of our entire team, including me. Dealing with them was both exhausting and enormously frustrating because I felt that we should be focusing our efforts on clients. I was also disappointed that we had such disagreements in the first place, so I made up my mind that I'd seek to resolve all eight of them within two months. No more dragging on indefinitely.

My basic strategy was to listen to each party first with the intent to understand their viewpoint—their "side." I didn't want to merely be able to repeat it back to them, but to understand it deeply enough that each party felt understood. I wanted to model empathy. I paid the price to do so—and it was difficult, because I didn't agree with much of what I heard. But my first goal wasn't to evaluate, it was to empathize—so I stayed deeply engaged in the process until the other party felt understood. The true test of understanding is not when you feel like you understand, but when they say they feel understood.

Once others felt understood, it was remarkable how they became far more open to hearing my side. More significantly, they became far more willing to find creative, synergistic solutions to solve our disputes. We resolved seven of the eight cases within the two-month goal, and the eighth took just a few months longer.

While it can take time to truly empathize with another person, once we've achieved understanding, we can move fast and produce extraordinary results. What's really slow is how long things take when people don't feel listened to or understood. Remember again that with people, fast is slow and slow is fast.

The power of empathy is unsurpassed. It's a gift, not only because of what it does to people, but because of how it enables us to elevate performance. Habit 5 from my father's 7 Habits is, "Seek First to Understand, Then to Be Understood." In other words, listen or model empathy first. When people feel understood first, we can get a lot more done together and we can get it done faster. So the key to influence is to first *be influenced*. Then others respond openly, creatively, and productively. It helps each of us perform better.

Empathy is a missing piece in many, if not most, relationships—at work and at home. It's also missing in many, if not most, teams and organizations. And that limits our effectiveness and impact. Modeling empathy with others dramatically increases not only well-being, but also the performance of all involved.

> *[Empathy] is the human desire in all of us to want to make life better for somebody else. It makes you feel larger. It makes you feel part of the whole human race . . . It's a much better source of ambition than just for self.*
>
> —DORIS KEARNS GOODWIN, HISTORIAN AND
> AUTHOR OF *TEAM OF RIVALS*

Modeling Performance by Delivering Results

Performance is *the* vital behavioral virtue we need to deliver on as Trust & Inspire leaders. Not at the expense of the other behavioral virtues, but in conjunction with them. The truth is that we could have all the other virtues, but not having performance would profoundly diminish our leadership.

Results matter, to our credibility and effectiveness as a leader. They matter to the kind of modeling needed today. Producing results gives us clout and latitude—it gives us options. If you want flexibility and choices—freedom—you've got to perform.

I'll never forget that on the ninth day on my job as the new CEO of Covey Leadership Center, I had to win over our bankers, who were intending to pull our line of credit because we had come to be seen as too much of a credit risk. While we were creating value for our clients, we were not doing well ourselves; we hadn't yet figured out a good business model that enabled us to be profitable. So while we had high growth, we also had extremely low (or no) margins. We had had eleven straight years of negative cash flow, no outside capital, and huge debt. You finance people out there, do the math—we were going to grow ourselves right out of business!

This lack of performance had also put us in violation of ten of our seventeen bank covenants. The bankers had become cynics. The bank didn't care that we were good people who tried to model the behaviors, or that we cared about our clients. Performance was what mattered to them. Without performance, they didn't trust us.

We were fortunate to be able to negotiate a path forward that included benchmarks of performance to keep the credit line open. As we improved the business and delivered on each benchmark month by month, the bank's trust and confidence in us grew. Over the next couple of years, we delivered on all the benchmarks. At the conclusion of our credit term, the bank told us that they not only wanted to renew our line of credit, they wanted to double it! Results converted the cynics.

Similarly, I remember working with a team that, because they hadn't produced a single product or service for several years, was viewed skeptically within the business. Based on the lack of performance, cynics believed the team was being carried because of favoritism. I told the team that the only way they could change that perception was to perform. And to do it quickly.

To their credit, they finished in six months what was scheduled to take another two years—and the new product they developed produced millions of dollars right out of the gate. What a shift—people now saw this team as performers, and that influenced every other interaction they had.

If we do everything else well, but don't deliver results, it's insufficient in the end. Again, performance is not the only thing that matters; we've all seen leaders who get results while violating ethical norms, while exploiting people in the process, or while operating with self-serving agendas—none of which is acceptable. But it's also not acceptable to be a good person who doesn't perform, who doesn't deliver. Bottom line, we need to do both.

Leadership is getting results in a way that inspires trust. How we do what we do matters enormously. But it also matters that we deliver. It's not *either/or*—it's *and*.

The better our track record of results, the greater our credibility and influence. The smaller our track record of results, the more our constructive criticism comes off as whining.

Empathy and performance may seem like odd companions, but they go hand in hand. When we deeply listen to others, only then can we truly learn what things are most important to them—and only then can we commit to do those things. And keeping those commitments is performing.

Performance without empathy for others—whether teammates, partners, or customers—can be hollow, shallow, and incomplete. While empathy is empowering for everyone involved, without performance it falls far short of the mark.

Thankfully, there is synergy between the two: strong empathy can propel us to greater influence, which in turn can lead to better performance. We need to model both of these behavioral virtues—separately and in combination.

Modeling the Behavioral Virtues—A Leader's Story

Someone who has modeled the behavioral virtues brilliantly is my friend Cheryl Bachelder. When she took over as the new CEO of Popeyes Louisiana Kitchen, the fast-food restaurant chain, she walked into the middle of a mess. And I don't say that lightly. Cheryl herself said, "I walked into a burning building."

The CEO office had been a revolving door—the company had blown through four CEOs in just seven years. Cheryl was the fifth and bets were out on how long she'd stick around. (Three candidates before her all turned the position down before she was hired to fill the spot.) As she describes in her book, *Dare to Serve*, sales were down. The number of customers had declined. Profits had fallen to dangerously low levels, and product development was flagging. The stock price had slid from its peak of $34 per share to $11 on the day Cheryl walked through the door.

Not only was performance down, so was morale. Trust and inspiration were at an all-time low. The relationship between the company and its franchisees was, as Cheryl described it, "on the rocks." As she took over the top spot, Cheryl faced what I call an "inheritance tax" with her franchisees. They didn't trust the company, and the company didn't trust them. No one had trust, and no one was thriving.

Fast-forward eight years. Financials—the hard numbers that are easy to measure—told the story. Unit sales per restaurant grew by 45 percent. Restaurant profitability soared, doubling in terms of real dollars. Popeyes' market share overall grew from 14 to 27 percent. The stock price went from $11 to a remarkable $79 at the end of Cheryl's ten years as CEO, when the company was acquired by Restaurant Brands International.

If you think that kind of growth and profitability stoked the franchisees, you're right. As Cheryl put it, "The franchisees were so delighted with the business results that they rapidly remodeled existing restaurants and began feverishly building new Popeyes, with excellent returns on their investment." More than six hundred new restaurants opened around the globe.

Summing it up, Cheryl said, "During this time, the company was the darling of the industry . . . a favorite of the franchisees . . . a favorite of lenders . . . a favorite of investors . . . and a case study in serving up superior performance results. The secret to Popeyes' turnaround performance? We dared to serve."

Cheryl and her team became Trust & Inspire leaders. Going into the challenge of her life, Cheryl asked herself, *What if a purpose and a set of principles could guide us to industry-leading performance?*

No more need to wonder what-if. The results are in.

When she became CEO, Cheryl was facing an uphill battle. She knew it, and so did everybody else. She later told me that her top priority—and number one success measure—was to establish trust with franchisees, modeling the belief that *leaders go first*. She asked her team to think about whether they were partners the franchisees could trust.

With that, Cheryl was off and running, focusing on her relationship with her franchisees. She and her team demonstrated humility, courage, and vulnerability by listening deeply to and empathizing with the needs and concerns of their franchisees. In her first thirty days, she recalls, "the most important thing I did was keep my mouth shut, and I went on the road for a listening tour." She met with and listened to franchise owners, restaurant general managers, and Popeyes customers. And she let them all tell her what was wrong. The answers, she said, "were usually in the room; everybody knew what was wrong. Nobody was fixing it."

Cheryl listened and responded with authenticity, showing her character and desire to help franchisees succeed. Then *she* fixed it. She implemented solutions to every problem she heard. She recognized that in addition to building a high-trust relationship with the home office, what the franchisees needed to see from her and the company were results. She needed to demonstrate to everyone a way forward—which she did. She performed.

Through it all, she focused on serving the needs of all stakeholders, especially franchisees, employees, and customers, and not just shareholders. Demonstrating her authenticity, she even told Wall Street the exact thing she had told her board: that her franchisees, not shareholders, were her first priority, which was quite a courageous statement from a CEO to her investors and board. And in the end, she abundantly met the needs of all stakeholders, including shareholders.

Cheryl refused to make excuses. She says that sometimes it's hard to own your mistakes and throw your plans overboard, but it's critical to fix whatever you did wrong. Once her team made a decision without any franchisee input or involvement—and it completely backfired. When angry franchisees approached her with their concerns, Cheryl took a step back. She showed humility by listening and then recognizing the wrong that had been done. She didn't make excuses. She had the humility to admit what happened and then the courage to make it right. The blowup in the relationship with the franchisees calmed down within a few weeks because she defused it and worked to rebuild trust.

Cheryl says that most people "conclude that it is the leader in the spotlight who delivers results. Because, of course, nice guys finish last. Have you worked for a leader who loves the spotlight? Were you served well? My message is simple, but unconventional. If you move yourself out of the spotlight and dare to serve others, you will deliver superior performance results."

Cheryl is an example of modeling all the behavioral virtues. She demonstrated humility and courage, modeling authenticity and vulnerability. Perhaps most important, she demonstrated empathy, listening to *everybody*. And her performance was nothing short of remarkable. Because she went first in modeling the behavior she wanted throughout her company, her team and franchisees did the same. And you can see what happened as a result.

> *Leadership is not about your ambition. It is about bringing out the ambitions of your team . . . The leader must have both the courage to take people to a daring destination and the humility to selflessly serve others on the journey.*
>
> —CHERYL BACHELDER, CEO OF POPEYES

Would I Follow Me?

How do you evaluate your modeling? Take a minute and think about yourself as a leader. Ask yourself the following questions:

If I were my leader (boss/teacher/parent/guardian, etc.):				
	DEFINITELY NO ←→ SOMEWHAT ←→ DEFINITELY YES			
Would I want to follow me?	1	2	3	4	5
Would I trust me?	1	2	3	4	5
Would I be inspired by me?	1	2	3	4	5
Would I choose me as my leader?	1	2	3	4	5

When those around me (work colleagues/family/friends/community) think of someone who is credible and has moral authority, do they think of me?

_____

When they think of someone who models humility and courage, do they think of me?

_____

When they think of someone who models authenticity and vulnerability, do they think of me?

_____

When they think of someone who models empathy and performance, do they think of me?

_____

When they think of someone who goes first, do they think of me?

_____

Why or why not?

_____

By looking inward, we sometimes find that we have been operating in a way that doesn't help those around us reach their highest potential. We might even find that we have unintentionally become something we do not want to be, or that we have modeled behavior we wouldn't want in return. While we might see ourselves as credible, others may not. Our style might be getting in the way of our intent.

Becoming a Trust & Inspire leader requires continual self-evaluation because it begins with you. Just as an airline asks you to put on your own oxygen mask first before helping others, you cannot be effective in raising those around you if you don't work on yourself first.

> *One of the things I learned when I was negotiating was that until I changed myself, I could not change others.*
>
> —NELSON MANDELA

"First who, then what," Jim Collins smartly advised. Truly, *who you are* matters. You can't fake being something you're not. People will eventually see through it. The longer that takes, the bigger hit you'll take when they do. "Fake it till you make it" might be an understandable starting point for some, but it's not sustainable over time. It is also not enough to focus on improving your outward skills or trying new tactics to increase engagement. Skills cannot replace character. Tactics cannot replace competence. You don't have to be perfect, but you do need to try.

Regardless of where you might be as a leader, take heart in knowing that you can start working on any of these behavioral virtues today.

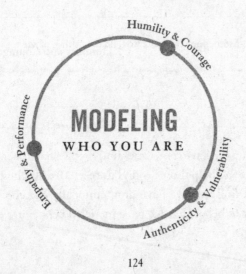

Part of the beauty of modeling is that it doesn't require anyone besides yourself to start. You can choose to model humility and courage, authenticity and vulnerability, empathy and performance. None of this is dependent on another person. Everyone is a model; it's up to you what you are modeling.

> *For there is always light, if only we're brave enough to see it. If only we're brave enough to be it.*
> —AMANDA GORMAN, FIRST NATIONAL YOUTH POET LAUREATE IN THE U.S.

COMMAND & CONTROL	TRUST & INSPIRE
Formal Authority	Moral Authority
Position	Influence
What You Do	Who You Are
Tell	Show
Directive	Instructive
Courage	Humility and Courage
Seeming	Being
Hidden Agenda	Open Agenda
Give the What	Give the Why Behind the What
Shareholders	All Stakeholders

CHAPTER 6

The 2nd Stewardship:
Trusting, or *How You Lead*

Just remember that your real job is that if you are free, you need to free somebody else. If you have power, then your job is to empower somebody else.

—TONI MORRISON

TRUSTING

HOW YOU LEAD

Who Trusted You?

Think about a person who trusted you. Someone in your life who believed in you, maybe even more than you believed in yourself. Someone who showed confidence in you, who took a chance on you, who extended trust to you.

This could be anyone: a boss, coworker, coach, teacher. It could be a parent, family member, clergy person, or just a friend. Anyone. Maybe this happened when you were six or seven, or maybe it happened when you were sixty-seven. It doesn't matter who or when—it'll be different for everyone. What matters is remembering this person and what he or she did and how they made you feel.

I'll never forget my first job coming out of college and the person who trusted me. That person is John Walsh, who was then a partner at the real estate development firm Trammell Crow Company. I had been hired directly by the managing partner of the firm rather than by one of the regional partners who traditionally made all the hires. The managing partner thought that surely at least one, if not several, of his regional partners would be excited to work with me, so he hired me on his own. I then interviewed with numerous partners to find a specific regional office that might be the best fit for me.

Problem was, *nobody* wanted me. Over a six-week period of time, I interviewed with thirteen different partners to see if I was a good fit for them—and not a single one had any interest.

I was fresh out of college trying to find my first real job. Having faced rejection after rejection—thirteen of them!—by the offices, I was feeling as down as I had ever felt. My confidence was at an all-time low. I was sure the managing partner who hired me in the first place was saying to himself, *What have I done? I must have made a big mistake.*

But the next person I interviewed with was John Walsh. I felt like I really connected with him. He came out of the interview and said to the other partners, "I like Stephen. He's raw, but I believe in him. I think he can do something here. I see his potential. I'm going to take a chance on him. I want him on my team."

John believed in me more than I believed in myself. He extended trust to me. This belief and trust did something extraordinary for me, and I did not want to let John down. I worked harder than ever before, and I focused on delivering for him. I wanted to prove that trust was justified. I wanted to pay it back to him.

Inspired by that kind of confidence in me, I was able to rise to the

127

occasion. I did pay it back by becoming someone John could count on and who delivered results for him—even great results. That helped him look good, too.

The impact of this experience was profound. I'm overwhelmed when I think back on what it did for me and my life, how it instilled confidence in me, and how it inspired me to grow and do even better than I thought I was capable of.

So back to you: Who was such a person for you? My guess is that there's probably more than one for most of us. I can think of several people who have inspired me by showing this kind of belief in me. So, think about it. In your life, who has believed in you? Who trusted and inspired you?

Once you identify such a person, consider three questions:

First, *what was the situation?* For me with John Walsh, no one wanted to hire me, but John did.

Second, *how did it make you feel when someone took a chance on you—trusted you?* I felt inspired. And I wanted to show gratitude to that person and work harder than anyone could ever imagine to pay it back. I wanted to prove that trust justified.

And third, *how did it impact you and your life?* For me, it profoundly changed the whole trajectory of my life.

How about for you?

Trustworthiness versus Trust

I recently spoke at a conference for leaders running businesses in more than a hundred and fifty countries. After speaking on trust in more than fifty-five countries on-site—and in even more virtually—I noticed that as beautifully different as every culture is, one common thread that runs through them all is trust. Every functioning society, organization, and family functions only inasmuch as there is trust. Indeed, trust makes our world go round.

Trust as a noun is complex. Because I wanted to give this international audience something to think about as we started our discussion, I put up a slide on screen that read:

> It is possible to have two trustworthy people working together and to have no trust between them.

I read those words slowly aloud, pausing before telling the audience they had the next five minutes to discuss the significance of this statement at their tables. I wanted them to talk over why it might be true. Then I walked off the stage.

Before you go any further in this book, I invite you to do the same. Take a few moments to ponder the significance of that statement, because in all my years of teaching trust, this is perhaps one of the most profound insights I've learned.

What hits you?

The idea that you can have two trustworthy people working together and no trust between them continues to be one of the biggest challenges I run into when working with people—whether it be on a team, between teams, in an organization, with partners and customers, or even on a personal level.

Back to my international audience. After giving them time to discuss, I finished the sentence:

> It is possible to have two trustworthy people working together and to have no trust between them . . . if neither person is willing to extend trust to the other.

When most people think about trust, they simply think about *trustworthiness*. That's not necessarily a bad thing—rather, it's not a bad start. It's difficult to have real, meaningful trust between people when one or both parties isn't worthy of it.

I'll offer another insight: most Command & Control leaders are trustworthy. That's right. Particularly those in the Enlightened Command & Control category. Here's the kicker: in my experience, our most significant challenge is *not* a lack of trust*worthy* people—the biggest challenge is trustworthy people who do not extend trust to other trustworthy people.

I can't tell you how many leaders I've worked with who are credible and authentic, who care deeply about both their work and their people, and yet who just can't seem to extend trust, or who won't extend enough trust for it to really matter.

As much or more than any other question I get asked about trust is, "Is trust earned or given?" Many younger generations tend to see trust as *given*; after all, "Why hire me if you're not going to trust me?" Many traditionalists, on the other hand, tend to see trust as *earned*, but often lean on that paradigm as a reason to withhold trust.

So is trust earned or given? I always smile and say, "Yes!"

The answer really is both—trust is earned *and* given. I would not advocate for trusting someone who is clearly untrustworthy. That isn't sustainable nor is it smart—in fact, I wrote a whole book about what I refer to as *smart trust*. You earn trust by being trustworthy. But trust is more than just being trustworthy. It also has to be given. It has to be extended to others. You could capture it in this simple formula:

Trust*worthiness* x Trust*ing* = Trust

Trust is only achieved when someone is willing to *extend* it to the other—to be *trusting*. The sense of satisfaction, the results, the speed with which things get done really come into play when you begin to extend trust to others.

I prefer to give my trust a hundred times and risk being disappointed two or three times than to live perpetually in an atmosphere of distrust.

—CARL FREUDENBERG, FOUNDER OF
THE FREUDENBERG GROUP

The 2nd Stewardship—Trusting: How You Lead

As we discussed in the previous chapter, the 1st stewardship for a Trust & Inspire leader is modeling. The 2nd stewardship is trusting. Trusting is all about *how we lead*. Do we lead by withholding trust or by giving it?

In fact, the word *trust* in *Trust & Inspire* is all about trust*ing*. You see, "trust the noun" (what we get) is the fruit of "trust the verb" (what we do). Trusting—how we lead—flows out of the fundamental beliefs of greatness being inside people and that our job as a leader is to unleash people's potential, not control them. We unleash the greatness inside people through trusting them. Not blindly or indiscriminately trusting them, but smartly—with clear expectations and accountability.

Most of us tend to think we're pretty good at trusting others. But we're proven wrong by the data, which unequivocally shows otherwise. My team and I have been measuring trust with individuals, inside teams, and across organizations for more than fifteen years, assessing how trusting leaders believe themselves to be, and how trusting others perceive them to be. One of the questions asks leaders to gauge how frequently they themselves extend trust, and most think they do so frequently and routinely.

When we ask those who work with the leaders how frequently their leaders extend trust, however, they rated them *277 percent lower* than the leaders rate themselves. That's a difference of nearly three times—a pretty big drop-off! While leaders want to say, "I'm pretty trusting," everyone else who works with them says, "No, no you're not. You think you are, but you're not."

You may identify with this when thinking of managers you've had who thought they were pretty trusting but you didn't feel that way. There are exceptions of course—leaders who actually extend trust as much as they think they do. We want those exceptions to become the norm. But we must address the gap, because that gap, that lack of trusting, leads the same people to identify their leaders as Command & Control in the same data points.

Back to my earlier point, one of the primary reasons for this trend is that most people, no matter how trust*worthy* they are, truly struggle with the ability and skill of extending trust. Their style is getting in the way of their intent. A leader—no matter how enlightened and trustworthy they might be—will never become a Trust & Inspire leader without learning to extend trust frequently, naturally, smartly, and even abundantly.

The "What" of Trusting: A Better Way to Live

Extending trust to others is a better way to live. This is true in all walks of life. By trusting others, leaders build the capability and confidence of those who are trusted. They unleash human potential and multiply performance. They not only produce better results, they also build a better culture with more energy and joy. Indeed, extending trust is the essence of what great leadership entails. The very first job of a leader is to inspire trust, and the second job of a leader is to extend trust.

With many reasons why trusting is a better way to live, I think the strongest is its impact on well-being. Research shows that people who are trusting are happier, healthier, and live longer. According to Canadian economist John Helliwell, the number one factor linked to happiness—even more than income and good health—is relationships of trust. Indeed, the most stressful part of the workday for 75 percent of people is their boss! High-trust relationships and teams are so much more pleasant, fun, and joyful than low-trust ones.

Think about it from a personal standpoint: for most of us, the happiest relationships are those in which we trust each other. Without trust, it's exhausting—and no fun.

I'm reminded of the *Star Wars* anthology movie *Solo*. The informal leader of a group of criminals, Tobias Beckett (played by Woody Harrelson), becomes a sort of mentor to young Han Solo. There's a scene where Beckett advises Solo, "You want to know how I've survived as long as I have? I trust no one. Assume everyone will betray you, and you will never be disappointed."

The young Han Solo replies, "Sounds like a lonely way to live."

Indeed, not trusting *is* a very lonely way to live. It's also stressful, exhausting, and no fun.

The How of Trusting: Clarify Expectations and Practice Accountability

When my first book, *The Speed of Trust*, published, the idea that trust was a competency—an actual skill that you could deliberately focus on and improve—was a paradigm shift for most people. In that book, I laid out a comprehensive and practical framework for deliberately growing trust. While people are pretty clear that we tend to lose trust because of our behavior—and that you can definitely behave your way *out of* trust—I proposed that in the same way, you can also intentionally behave your way *into* trust.

Perhaps the most practical part of the book is where I introduce specific, high-leveraged behaviors for being a high-trust leader and building a high-trust culture. While there's not a rigid sequence to these behaviors, the first twelve position us well for the final thirteenth, which is "extend trust." The behaviors most critical to being able to extend trust and operationalize trusting are clarifying expectations and practicing accountability.

There is a reason people struggle with extending trust—so let's be very clear here: there *is* risk in trusting people (if there were no risk, you wouldn't need to have trust). But—*and this is vital*—there is also risk in *not* trusting people. I believe not trusting is often the greater risk. As organizations and as a society, we've become very good at measuring the cost of trusting too much, but we're not very good at all at measuring the cost of not trusting enough.

I'll never forget an experience that taught me how trusting can quickly and powerfully impact a culture. In August 2019, Jim Gash was promoted from being an associate dean at Pepperdine University's law school to becoming the new president of the university. Just a few days into his new administration, Jim invited me to come and work with him and his new team. While Jim knew most of the people in his cabinet, there were a few people he didn't really know yet—at least not very well.

Right about the time he was named president, tension arose surrounding a controversial decision that came up in the school that Michael, one of the deans, oversaw. Michael wanted to talk to Jim about the situation and explain how he had handled it. Michael didn't really know Jim, and was not sure how he would respond. Michael prepared to walk Jim through the situation and asked for an hour of his time so he could give him the background and all the details.

On the spot, Jim told Michael, "Let me ask you a couple of questions before scheduling time to meet. First, does this decision represent your best thinking and that of your team?"

"Yes, it does," Michael responded.

Jim then asked, "Was the process you utilized in making the decision fair to all parties?" Again, Michael responded that it was. Jim then said, "Michael, I trust you. Just move ahead. We don't need to meet."

Again, Jim didn't know Michael. But Jim knew from other colleagues that Michael was well respected and had a strong reputation as someone who could be trusted. What makes this all the more interesting is that Michael was actually in the room when Jim told me this story.

I asked Michael what this experience did for him. He said it inspired him like nothing else, and that he wanted to prove the trust justified. Jim's decision to begin this new relationship by trusting established a tone with Michael and then with all of Jim's team, faculty, and staff—a tone of trust, openness, and collaboration. Michael expressed how Jim trusting him made him feel valued and how, in turn, he reciprocated the trust to Jim from that moment on—even though they had no previous relationship.

If Jim had withheld that trust, Michael might have left that meeting more cautious, perhaps even suspicious of Jim—and it might have taken a much longer time to build that relationship. It also would have set a very different tone for the rest of the team as they took time feeling out each situation and relationship with Jim as the new leader. A Trust & Inspire leader can build trust fast.

Because of this experience, imagine the next time a member of Jim's cabinet encounters a problem or tough scenario. They will be willing to turn to him, knowing that if they've done their best work and if they've been fair, he will be trusting and will support them. When you build trust with one, you build trust with many.

The Importance of Clarifying Expectations

One of the things Jim did so well came in his first response to Michael. He clarified his expectations right up front. He asked if the decision represented his best thinking and whether it was fair to all parties. This clarity mitigated the risk inherent in trusting. Had Jim accepted Michael's thinking without clear expectations, the extension of trust could have been viewed as irresponsible. Michael could have walked away thinking Jim was a pushover.

Clarify expectations is based on the principles of clarity, responsibility, and accountability. The opposite of clarifying expectations is to leave expectations undefined and assume they're already known or to fail to disclose them. As a result, there is no shared vision of desired outcomes.

A counterfeit manifestation of clarifying expectations is to create "smoke and mirrors"—to give lip service to clarifying expectations, but to fail to pin down specifics like results, deadlines, or dollars that facilitate meaningful accountability. Another counterfeit manifestation is going with the ebb and flow of situational expectations that shift based on people's memories or interpretations or on what is expedient or convenient at the time.

When you clarify expectations, you create a shared vision and agreement up front about what is to be done. This is the behavior of prevention. Do this well up front, and you will avoid headaches and heartaches later on. In contrast, if you don't pay the price with this behavior in the beginning, you *will* have trust issues later.

Some people push back on clarifying expectations, often stating that they simply don't have the time to do it. But consider the converse: How much time and energy are wasted when you don't take time to clarify expectations and then have to unravel something after the fact?

Also, keep in mind that clarifying expectations effectively is always a two-way street. Mutually agreed-upon expectations are far more valuable to trust than dictated expectations. People need to have the opportunity to push back, to help come to an expectation that is realistic and that can work from both points of view. This is a great source of power and flows out of a desire to understand and feel understood. When the source of power is positional, legitimate questions of expectations are often met with some variation of "Because I said so"—or, in effect, "I expect you to trust me while I withhold trust from you."

From customers and colleagues to a partner or child, everyone wants to be trusted and to deliver. When we as leaders are trusting, we tap into that innate desire inside people. When we as leaders mutually establish clear expectations around the trust being given, it sets everyone up to win.

The global company Siemens recently demonstrated this when they released their new remote work approach—what they called "mobile working"—developed in the midst of the COVID-19 pandemic. A major point from their "New Normal Working Model" policy read, "We trust our employees and empower them to shape their work themselves so that they can achieve the best results possible."

Right when some companies began to crack down on workers they couldn't monitor in the office anymore, Siemens took the opposite route. They extended *more* trust to their employees. They trusted in the greatness and potential within the seed. This is especially notable, since companies as large as Siemens with more than four hundred thousand employees typically respond to disruption by exerting more control rather than by extending more trust.

Consider also the explicit declaration of trust in this policy. When we trust others, it is important that we *communicate* the trust we extend—both what and why. This sets a powerful expectation about the importance of trust. Too often we have unexpressed extensions of trust with the people around us. There is power in communicating our trust to people. We need to tell them *why* we trust them. One of the outcomes we're seeking is for people to *feel* trusted. People will be inspired when they do.

What are the expectations for this trust from Siemens? To quote from the policy:

> Under the permanent plan, and effective immediately . . . employees in more than 125 locations in 43 countries will be able to work from wherever they are most productive for an average of two to three days a week.

This communicates both the intent of the trust (for employees to be most productive) and provides parameters for those employees to make their own decisions. These are clear expectations that mitigate risk and enable the organization to tap into the best their people have to offer.

Similarly, Mary Barra, chair and CEO of General Motors, described her company's "Work Appropriately" remote work policy with clear expectations around the trust being given as follows: "Where work permits, employees have the flexibility to work where they can have the greatest impact on achieving our goals."

She also laid out the *why* behind this trusting policy: "Our employees are capable of making smart decisions without overly prescriptive guidance."

How much more attractive does this make Siemens or GM to a young employee looking for a place to take his or her talents? Such trusting policies—based on the fundamental beliefs of a Trust & Inspire leader—are differentiators, especially when contrasted to the excessive verification and surveillance-style practices of some organizations where their people, who are now working from home, often feel they're just being "micromanaged from a distance."

The Significance of Practicing Accountability

This behavior is built on the principles of accountability, responsibility, stewardship, and ownership. The opposite is not to take responsibility, to say, "It's not my fault." Its counterfeit is to point fingers and blame others, saying, "It's their fault."

You first need to clarify expectations so that you can practice accountability.

There are two key dimensions to practicing accountability, and the sequence matters. As a Trust & Inspire leader, you hold *yourself* accountable first, and you hold *others* accountable second. Interestingly, when most people think of accountability from the perspective of a leader, they tend to gravitate to the second dimension. The Enlightened Command & Control leader is often quick to say, "I hold people accountable!" and to wear that value as a badge of honor. Don't get me wrong; there *is* value in holding others accountable, but you'll do it far more effectively when you hold yourself accountable first. At the end of the day, you can't sustain trust without accountability. Holding yourself accountable first, in and of itself, models the behavior you'd like to see. You're showing the way. It aligns beautifully with authenticity and vulnerability. It also takes humility and courage. When people—particularly leaders—hold themselves accountable, it encourages others to do the same.

This is also true in a marriage or a family. When someone says, "I'm sorry I spent that money impulsively; that wasn't in harmony with our agreement," or, "I shouldn't have yelled at you; that didn't show respect," such self-accountability encourages others to do likewise. On the other hand, when someone says, "I committed to you that I'd be there, and I was," that acknowledgment of self-accountability similarly shows other people that they can trust you, which makes your extension of trust to them all the more meaningful.

If you haven't held yourself accountable first, your attempts to hold others accountable will be undercut. Such attempts might be viewed as unfair, blaming, or micromanaging. Remember that a fundamental belief of a Trust & Inspire leader is that enduring influence is created from the inside out, so your job as a leader is to go first. This is especially important when it comes to accountability.

Still, holding others accountable can be tricky. People often have strong feelings about their own performance. Plus, sometimes attempts to hold someone else accountable can feel like a lack of trust.

In fact, I've heard people ask, "Are you going to trust me, or are you going to hold me accountable?" as if the two were mutually exclusive when they're not. In reality they're hand in glove. People actually respond to accountability. It's why sports teams keep score. It helps us know how we're doing and what to work toward. How difficult—or fun—would it be to play a game where you don't know how you were doing until the very end?

Like clarifying expectations, the key with practicing accountability is to develop a mutually agreed-upon process of accountability wherever possible. It's very easy to unilaterally lay out accountability *for* someone. But that is not nearly as effective as doing it together when possible. A lack of involvement from the other person often leads to an equal lack of commitment. Have you ever tried to hold someone accountable to something to which they're not committed? It's more work for you—and it's exhausting for both of you.

The involvement of others tends to create far greater commitment. A mutually agreed-upon process of accountability with others who are involved requires an extension of trust. That mutual agreement is essential. If you've agreed to touch base on a project weekly, your checking in will be viewed as honoring your commitment. If you haven't agreed, it may feel like micromanagement.

The Why of Trusting: Grow People

Perhaps the most significant dimension of trusting is the reason for doing it in the first place—the *why*. The overarching responsibility of any Trust & Inspire leader is to grow people. By contrast, the Command & Control leader focuses on fixing people.

Growing people through trusting them is a better way to lead. Great leaders grow people, and nothing grows people better—or faster—than an extension of trust. There's nothing soft about this idea. When people grow and get better, performance improves.

That's certainly true of my John Walsh story, and I bet it's true of your stories as well. The most significant growth I've experienced and that I've seen in others comes from a meaningful extension of trust. And it works in any stage of life.

Consider the "green and clean" story I shared at the beginning of this book. My dad's way of leading was very much Trust & Inspire. Think how easy it would have been for him to go Command & Control—or, as he always put it, "win-lose"—when I didn't follow through on taking care of the lawn. He could have taken away the responsibility. He could have done the work himself. Or worse, and perhaps most common in today's world, he could have micromanaged me into getting the job done.

But you know what? My dad lived true to his own words. He began "with the end in mind," and while a green and clean yard was certainly part of his intended outcome, his bigger "end in mind" was not the yard—it was *me*. My dad was more concerned about and committed to my potential. He was more concerned about and committed to what I could become. As he said at the time, his larger purpose was to "raise kids, not grass."

I felt this. It inspired me, I embraced it, and I grew immensely because of it.

The simple but profound impact of my father's Trust & Inspire style with me as a seven-year-old boy has stayed with me my whole life. I've seen the application of this same style of leadership ignite passion, creativity, ownership, and commitment—both in others as well as in myself—throughout my entire career. This way of leading works, and it's particularly relevant to the new kinds of challenges we're facing today. Trusting others changes how leaders see others, and being trusted changes the way people respond to leaders. In short, trusting creates trust. And trust, in turn, changes everything. A study from the leadership consultancy firm Zenger Folkman showed that "the combination of trust and virtually every other leadership behavior brings dramatic improvement." They analyzed data from more than four hundred thousand people, looking at sixteen different leadership competencies, and found that when the impact of adding high trust to each competency was calculated, the average increase in engagement went up 23 percentage points.

The implications of this study are clear: "Whatever skills or capabilities might be your strengths, if you can increase trust, then that skill will be enhanced, and the outcome improved."

Trusting is a vital dimension in becoming a Trust & Inspire leader, especially when compared to the nontrusting tenets of Command & Control, where the oft-repeated maxim of "trust but verify" more often feels like "all verify and no trust."

Why is extending trust such a better way to lead? Simply put, because of what it does for people. Specifically, how it helps grow people. While the impact of trusting is profound and far-reaching, there are three growth outcomes from extending trust that I'd like to call out specifically.

1. People Rise to the Occasion and Perform Better

If micromanaging people stifles their creativity and commitment to the work (and it does), trusting people does the opposite. When you extend trust, you're telling people that you believe in them. You believe they'll make rational decisions and good judgments. When given that level of belief and responsibility, people suddenly want to live up to it—they want to prove the trust justified. They go beyond their normal level of effort and tap into something deeper within, giving them access to greater energy, creativity, commitment, and, ultimately, results. This is true even in settings with long-held and widely accepted "best practices."

Consider a traditional corporate call center. If you want to see a relic of the industrial age that's still going strong today, look at the way many call centers operate. Most are highly Command & Control. Calls are heavily scripted and robotic, so much so that many could be easily outsourced. Everything is timed and analyzed down to the second to maximize efficiency.

In stark contrast to the industry norms, the customer service reps for online retailer Zappos operate without scripts, and their calls are not timed for efficiency. Rather than seeing this as a cost, Zappos sees it as an opportunity to build a relationship, deliver a "wow" experience, and simply make the customer happy. As the late, former Zappos CEO Tony Hsieh put it, "We don't have scripts because we trust our employees to use their best judgment when dealing with each and every customer . . . [W]e trust that they want to provide great service . . . because they actually do."

Talk about trusting! As a result, customer service reps perform better at Zappos. They respond to that extension of trust; they don't want to let their trusting leaders—or their customers—down, but instead want to make them happy. They create more loyal customers who return more, buy more, and tell their friends. The net result is both world-class customer service and industry-leading productivity.

Similarly, I recently worked with the CEO and top leadership team of a major global financial nongovernmental organization (NGO). The CEO clearly stated that in order for their organization to grow and impact their stakeholders more powerfully and more in alignment with their mission and vision, they all had to "trust more" at every level—starting with her as CEO. Her entire summary of what was needed to trigger their growth and impact hinged entirely around trusting—what she called "trust more."

I think she got it right. While other things need to happen as well, it is only through trusting that we transform, multiply, and accelerate both our growth and impact.

One of my favorite examples of how trusting transforms people comes from Muppets creator Jim Henson. After *The Muppet Show* had been a successful comedy television series for years, Jim and his team were working on producing their first Muppets movie. He asked the renowned composer Paul Williams to write the songs for the film.

Here's how Paul described his experience of Jim trusting him—and what it did for him:

> Jim had to be the easiest and most trusting man I ever had the opportunity to work with. When we met for the first time as a team in my den to discuss the basic outline of the story, I was given a gift I would always treasure. Walking Jim to his car, I told him I'd "keep him in the loop" as Kenny [Ascher] and I wrote the songs for the film. He responded with, "Oh, that's all right, Paul. I'll hear them in the studio when we record them. I'm sure they'll be terrific."
>
> Never in decades of writing songs for a living have I encountered such trust. Been given so much freedom. Jim gave us his trust. We gave him "The Rainbow Connection."

To be trusted is the most inspiring form of human motivation. It brings out the best in us all.

2. People Develop New Capabilities

As leaders, we naturally tend to be more trusting toward people who are already competent and capable. This is generally part of smart trust. And yet one of the remarkable things about trusting is that often people develop new capabilities and competencies *after* and specifically *because* we've extended trust to them.

For example, Julia Hartz, CEO of the global online ticketing company Eventbrite, acknowledged not feeling prepared or capable as she transitioned to the role of CEO. She said, "It was like I was in Candy Land, and then I stepped into Tron." Her career path hadn't equipped her with many of the capabilities she would need to operate as a leading tech CEO; in fact, she never planned on working in the technology industry—and certainly never planned on becoming a CEO once she did enter the industry.

Julia studied broadcast journalism in college and spent the early years of her career working for cable networks, beginning at MTV and ending at FX. After five years in the cable network industry, she was offered a job at a new network. The offer was exciting, but the pay was lower than what she was making at the time. Her now-husband, serial entrepreneur Kevin Hartz, suggested that she join him instead and that together they start a new company. They founded Eventbrite in 2006 and haven't looked back.

Eventbrite has seen extraordinary growth since its founding. By 2016, Kevin had been CEO for ten years, and in true entrepreneurial spirit, he was ready to move on to start a new project. He proposed that Julia succeed him as CEO. The board agreed, and she was entrusted with the stewardship of CEO—something she had never wanted or intended.

"When you become CEO, there's something in that title that changes everything mentally," Julia says. "I had to quickly figure out how to center myself and focus on the mission and not let the bigness of it get in my way or slow me down or render me paralyzed."

The trust she had been given by the board, and even more by Kevin, inspired her to develop the new capabilities she would need to support and lead a billion-dollar company. She says Kevin "believes I can do anything," and suggests that "if you have that person who just constantly says 'you can do anything,' you start to believe it."

The trust Julia was given has come full circle, as she has developed a Trust & Inspire culture and helped others develop new and extraordinary capabilities through the power of extending trust. "I didn't want to dictate the culture. I didn't want to get in the way of brilliance happening. If you want to build a sustainable culture, you have to have a strong philosophy and then let people do with it what they will and be okay with that."

And they have. Under Julia's leadership, Eventbrite has received numerous accolades for the company's culture, including being named to the Great Place to Work Institute's "100 Best Workplaces" and Glass Door's "Employees' Choice Best Places to Work."

Extending trust, being trusting as a leader, and building a Trust & Inspire culture are vital elements for developing the kind of capabilities needed to stay relevant in today's changing world.

3. People Reciprocate and Return the Trust

When people receive trust, they are inspired to reciprocate by returning the trust, creating a virtuous, upward cycle of trust and confidence that creates even more trust and confidence. Trusted people will reciprocate not only by trusting you back, but also by following your example and extending trust to others—resulting in growth of both people and performance.

I recently spoke at the Novak Leadership Institute at the University of Missouri. The organization was named for David Novak, who in 1999 became CEO of YUM! Brands, which housed Kentucky Fried Chicken (KFC), Pizza Hut, and Taco Bell. David's first opportunity had arisen five years prior, when he was offered the chance to revitalize the KFC business. At the time David stepped in, the company was struggling, particularly with franchisees where resentment, distrust, and even bitterness had built up between the company's leaders and the franchisees. David was told by several people not to accept the position because he would be going to a "management graveyard."

He decided to take the job anyway, but he knew things needed to change, starting with how to treat franchisees. He knew that success depended on building trust with them, which meant not just being trust*worthy*. He needed to actually be *trusting* of the franchisees, and they needed to believe and feel it.

Instead of viewing them as problematic, he chose to view them as true partners—and he treated them as such. He declared to his team, "I love working with franchisees!" when the reality at the time was that everybody else hated working with franchisees. Many at the company were worried and told David that his approach would never work—that the franchisees were the problem.

On the contrary, the franchisees responded to being trusted. They worked harder and gave trust back in return. The trust they were given enabled them to feel a sense of partnership, which inspired them to operate better. David worked with them to create a Chef's Council of franchisees who created and improved product offerings. Franchisees welcomed this change since under previous leadership, any attempt they made to innovate was seen as coloring outside the lines. They were required to follow the plan.

The old model was very much Command & Control. It managed for compliance, which, in fairness, is vital to maintain consistency for an internationally franchised brand. But compliance alone can't produce the kind of agility to operate successfully in the ever-evolving land-scape of today's marketplace. And that approach ignores the team's cre-ativity. After all, these franchisees are all entrepreneurs, many of whom invested their entire life savings to grow a business! They got into the business because they're passionate. They want to succeed, and, like anyone, they want to be able to contribute meaningfully to that success.

Trusting the franchisees dramatically revitalized the business: a franchisee invented KFC's Crispy Strips, which became the most successful product since the Original Recipe. Through the Chef's Council, they created another hugely successful product, Chicken Pot Pie. KFC started growing again, and they nearly doubled their profit in just three years' time.

When asked about his success at KFC, David replied, "It all started with one simple decision: *to trust franchisees.* That opened the way for them to trust me and the corporation in return, and together we un-leashed the power of our people to succeed."

Building upon his success at KFC, David then became CEO of YUM! Brands, when the company grew from $4 billion to $32 billion in revenue, and the number of restaurants around the world doubled. Trusting his people—and recognizing them for their achievements—helped David build a high-trust culture that helped people grow and produce remarkable results. David told me the best summary of his leadership style was the title of his book, *Taking People with You.*

Leadership coach Marshall Goldsmith operates in a similar way. When he meets with prospective clients, he tells them his fee up front. But then he says, "You only pay me if you feel like I met your expectations. I don't get paid unless *you* decide it was worth it." He offers no contracts or written agreements.

Leading by trusting, Marshall immediately establishes a feeling of mutual trust between both parties. Marshall is then better able to inspire and help his clients grow and make the changes they want to because they reciprocate his extension of trust and give it back to him. Because they know he has their best interests at heart instead of just looking to make money, they are more willing to listen and trust him, both of which are essential ingredients for growth and a successful coaching relationship.

Go for more trust because trust is the ultimate human currency.

—BILL MCDERMOTT, CEO OF SERVICE NOW

The When of Trusting: A Better Way to Begin

Trusting starts with the belief that there's greatness inside each person and that our job as a leader is to unleash that potential. Trusting also acknowledges that the life and power is in the seed, not in the gardener. As with a seed, we don't create the potential; we merely nurture what is already there by creating the right conditions for the seed to flourish. For the potential to be developed. For the results to be realized.

Trusting creates the right conditions. Trusting ignites people by waking them up and inspiring them to be better than before. It helps the team, the organization, the family. How much more willing will children be to help with chores if they help design how chores are shared? Giving trust to people, even to children, gives them the opportunity to grow while resulting in better ideas and outcomes than you could have produced on your own. Nothing is as inspiring as an offering of trust!

When you start with trust, you're able to go so much further, faster. And leaders need to go first. Think of it as the "First-Truster Advantage": when we are the first to extend trust, we are also the first to reap the benefits of doing so. We also transform the nature of our interactions, relationships, and teams by being the first to extend trust to others—something that is typically recognized, appreciated, and valued.

*How wonderful it is that nobody need wait a single moment before
starting to improve the world.*

—ANNE FRANK

Again, there is risk in trusting people, but not trusting people is
more often the greater risk. When we address the common barriers
that impede a Trust & Inspire leader, in upcoming chapters, we will
further develop the *how* of trusting—how to skillfully and appropriately extend trust in various situations and settings. This will be yet
another practical way of operationalizing trusting.

My daughter McKinlee experienced this firsthand when she
coached a boys' high school volleyball team a few years ago. It was her
first year teaching at the school, and she didn't know any of the students
yet, so when they had tryouts the second day of school, she didn't know
what to expect. Into the gym strutted Leo, a lanky six-foot-three with a
full beard at age sixteen. He was loud and mouthy. During tryouts, he
goofed off and showed a bit of attitude. Even though he was skilled and
the team needed the height, McKinlee decided that he wasn't the right
fit for the team based on his inappropriate behavior during tryouts.

When the final team roster was posted, Leo was disappointed that
he wasn't on it. He later asked for a meeting with McKinlee. He explained how much volleyball meant to him and how he would be willing to work harder than anyone else. She laid out clear expectations of
him and the team. "If you can agree to these expectations, I'm willing
to trust you and give you a chance," she said. "Can you do it?"

Leo agreed. Little did she know that Leo would eventually turn into
not only one of her best players but also one of the best leaders and most
respected members of the team. Leo rose to the occasion and performed
better. He became the team hype man, lifting others and pulling the
team through tough moments. He became McKinlee's go-to when she
needed someone to help with something, both on and off the court.

Leo developed new capabilities. Every day after practice ended, he
stayed in the gym for an additional hour, working on his individual
skills. He took the initiative to record and analyze stats for the whole

team, watching countless hours of game film. He helped lead the team to a regional championship and their best season ever.

Leo not only reciprocated the trust, he paid it forward. When a nervous six-foot-three freshman walked into tryouts Leo's senior year, McKinlee didn't have to say a word. Leo took him under his wing and mentored him, helping the freshman gain skills and confidence.

But Leo didn't stop there. He carried this leadership over into the other sports he played, becoming a founding member of the school's athletic council. Two years after McKinlee met Leo, he was given the "Athlete of the Year" award by the school—an award my daughter was lucky enough to present.

When asked about this, McKinlee said, "I didn't do anything. All I did was give Leo a chance, and he ran with it. He had that greatness inside him all along—and I think he knew it. He just needed a chance to let it shine. I can't imagine how different his or my life would have been if he hadn't been a part of our team."

Leo met the challenge given to him. He grew and became better than he was before. And he reciprocated the trust to McKinlee and extended it to his younger classmates. Sure, it may have been a small risk to trust Leo—but the returns for doing so were astounding.

> *I think we may safely trust a good deal more than we do.*
>
> —HENRY DAVID THOREAU

Call to Action

Remember the exercise we did at the very beginning of the chapter in which you considered someone who'd extended trust to you? I invite you to flip it around and ask yourself:

To whom might I extend trust?

Who is the "Leo" in your personal life? In your professional life? For whom can you be the kind of person McKinlee was for Leo, or that John Walsh was for me professionally, or that my father was for me personally?

In other words, pay it forward. For which people can you be that kind of person? A person who believes in them. Who has confidence in them. Who sees the best in them. Who inspires them. Who extends trust to them. Always remember this: no extension of trust is ever wasted, because its value does not lie in reciprocity but rather in the very decision to trust.

We need more trust in our world, not less. We need to be more trusting, not less. We need more Trust & Inspire leaders, not fewer. And while it takes two or more people to have trust, it only takes one to start—someone who is willing to lead in trusting others.

COMMAND & CONTROL	TRUST & INSPIRE
Trustworthy	Trustworthy and Trusting
The Power Is in the Gardener	The Life—and Power—Is in the Seed
Verify	Trust
Dictate Expectations	Mutually Clarify Expectations
Dictate Accountability	Mutually Agree to a Process of Accountability
Fix People	Grow People

CHAPTER 7

The 3rd Stewardship: Inspiring, or *Connecting to Why*

Great leaders . . . are able to inspire people to act. Those who are able to inspire give people a sense of purpose, or belonging . . . are able to create a following of people who act not because they were swayed, but because they were inspired.

—SIMON SINEK, AUTHOR OF *START WITH WHY*

One of the greatest hockey players of all time, Wayne Gretzky, was once asked how he rose to the top of his sport. He replied, "I skate to where the puck is going to be, not to where it has been."

Without hesitation, I can see that the puck is going toward inspirational leadership. Our world has changed, but we continue to aim at where leadership has been. We need to move to where it is going. We need to move toward inspiration.

In the next few years, we will see a significant, much-needed movement toward inspiring others as a strategic imperative. Simply attempting to motivate people, or even engage people, will no longer be enough.

All of us want to be inspired. This flows out of the belief that people are whole people—made up of body, heart, mind, and spirit—and that the job of a leader is to inspire others from within rather than merely trying to motivate them from without. This also flows out of the belief that leadership is stewardship, therefore the job of a leader is to put service above self-interest. These beliefs, combined with the desire of people everywhere to be inspired, are why for a Trust & Inspire leader, *inspiring* is the 3rd and final stewardship.

People Don't Leave Organizations, They Leave Bad Bosses

A recent Gallup study showed that 50 percent of employees "have left their job to get away from their manager at some point in their career." No matter how much they might enjoy their work, nobody wants to work with a bad boss.

I'm among those 50 percent. I've left a job not because of the work, which I loved, but because of the person I worked for. And I'm guessing a lot of you might be with me on that. Similarly, while 80 percent of employees are stressed about work, the vast majority—75 percent— said that the most stressful aspect of their job is their immediate boss. Bad bosses not only sap productivity, they sap energy and joy—in other words, they destroy well-being.

That doesn't happen just in the workplace. Research shows that in schools, the single most important factor in student outcome and achievement is the teacher. While students may not have the option of quitting like someone at a job does, they can choose to "leave" by becoming disengaged, belligerent, or, if all else fails, truant. The same could even be true in a family. How many of you know someone who, at best, has a deeply strained relationship with certain family members or has cut ties altogether because of what they've experienced?

Regardless of the situation, the lesson is that "things" like money, luxuries, or lifestyle don't matter nearly as much as people and relationships. That's why our Trust & Inspire mantra is *manage things, lead people*. If people don't feel they are treated with respect, if they're not valued for their worth and potential, if they're not inspired by their parent or boss or colleagues, they will leave or simply check out. It doesn't matter how many perks or conveniences might be open to them if they stay—if the relationship is bad, people won't stay. A disengaged person stays but has mentally and emotionally quit.

Remember that regardless of your role or whether people report to you, you *are* a leader. And your job as a leader is not just to keep people around, but to lead them in a way so they consciously and enthusiastically choose to stay, so they thrive and contribute meaningfully. You should not be satisfied with the premise of merely retaining people on your team, in your company, or at your volunteer organization.

How do we do this? Research from Zenger Folkman looked at sixteen different competencies of leadership to see which competency would be the most powerful predictor of "being seen as an extraordinary leader." These competencies included qualities such as taking initiative, championing change, communicating powerfully, and fostering innovation. From that field of sixteen qualities, the one that "clearly stood out" involved inspiration—the ability to "inspire to high performance."

Moreover, when the direct reports were asked to rank the competencies they most wanted to have in their leader, the ability to inspire came in first from among the sixteen. Not only was this ranked as the most important quality people wanted in a leader, it was done so by a strong margin. It was a "resounding first choice," as the report noted.

This study demonstrated that what people want most from their leaders—more than any other attribute—is to be inspired. And yet in multiple studies, including one of our own, most leaders rank low in the ability to inspire. The disconnect between what people want and what leaders give is staggering, and it results in a massive tax on well-being and productivity at both the personal and organizational levels.

We're not suggesting that there is a single "silver bullet" for leadership. But the ability of leaders to inspire those about them comes the closest to being that all-powerful solution. We simply cannot overemphasize how robust and dominant it is.

—JACK ZENGER AND JOE FOLKMAN,
AUTHORS AND RESEARCHERS

Everyone Can Inspire

We live in a time of "influencers," with more media than ever. We occasionally like to be mindlessly entertained, but we frequently gravitate toward people and stories that inspire us—the band we like, the actor we admire, the thought leader we respect.

But what makes people inspirational? Is it their stature or status? Their personality or good looks? Their sense of humor? Their charm? As interesting as it is to feel inspired by some of the things we see and experience, it can also be really stifling. Of course Usain Bolt inspires—he runs twenty-seven miles per hour! Of course Steve Jobs inspired many—he revolutionized six entire industries! It's easy to see others who inspire from the perspective of our ordinary, seemingly unremarkable lives, and it's easy for us to ask, "How am *I* supposed to inspire someone else?"

The problem is that far too often, we equate being inspirational with being charismatic. Many people believe that to inspire others—to be inspirational—you have to have that "it" quality. Sociologist Max Weber said, "Charisma is a certain quality of an individual personality by virtue of which he is set apart from ordinary men and treated as endowed with supernatural, superhuman, or at least specifically exceptional powers or qualities."

If to inspire is to be charismatic, then it's for only the rare few—the superhuman or the exceptionally gifted. Most people don't see themselves in that category—including me. We need to disconnect charisma from inspiration, because here's the truth: anyone can be inspiring!

Some people are both charismatic and inspiring. There are also many people who are charismatic but who don't inspire. But you know what? I know far more people who are *not* charismatic but who absolutely do inspire. That second-grade teacher who inspired you wasn't necessarily full of charm or personality. But he cared about and connected with you. That neighbor who inspired you might not have been powerful or wealthy. But she believed in you and supported you. The reality is, for all the charismatic, superhuman people out there who inspire, there are far more completely normal people who are inspiring their friends, neighbors, colleagues, and family every day.

You do not have to be charismatic to be inspiring. You don't need thousands of Instagram followers. You don't need to meet a certain standard of beauty. You don't need to be highly credentialed. Inspiration does not depend on any physical or even emotional quality or attribute. Rather, it is simply who you are and how you lead that inspires. While charisma may motivate, it is authenticity that inspires.

Someone who might think they mean nothing to the world may very well mean the world to someone.

Best of all, inspiring others is a learnable skill.

Connecting with People and Connecting to Purpose

Since everyone wants to be inspired, the big question is: *How do we inspire?*

The first two stewardships, modeling and trusting, are a great start. An authentic, vulnerable leader who models the behavior absolutely inspires us. When someone extends trust to us, that also inspires us.

In this "inspiring" stewardship, we next practice the principle of *connection*—specifically, connecting *with people* and connecting *to purpose*. When we genuinely connect with people—when they feel like we "see them" and have real interest in them—that's inspiring. It's also inspiring when people feel connected to purpose, meaning, and contribution—to why what they're doing matters.

A Trust & Inspire leader does both. First, they connect with the people around them. They have a strong understanding of why they matter. Second, they also know how to connect to purpose, meaning, and contribution—to why the work matters.

3 Levels of Connecting with People: Self, Relationships, Team

In connecting with the people around us, we can increase our ability to inspire by focusing on three different levels of connection with:

1. Ourselves
2. Our relationships
3. Our team

After we connect with people at all three of these levels, we can then powerfully connect to the work itself and seek to embed it with a sense of purpose, meaning, and contribution.

The important thing to understand is that *any kind* of work can become meaningful and significant, and *any* leader can become inspiring. Let's explore these three levels of connecting with the people around us, starting with ourselves.

1. Self Level: Find Your "Why"

Before you can help anyone else connect to purpose, first do it for yourself. Finding your "why" is as much a process of discovery as it is creation. It begins by being authentic, so start with honest self-reflection:

• What matters to me?

- Who matters to me?

- What makes me want to get up in the morning?

- What about my work makes me happy?

- What do I do at work that brings me a sense of meaning and purpose?

- When do I feel most alive?

- Why do I do what I do?

- What's my "why"?

Everyone's *why* will be different. For you, it might be related to your family, your work, or to your overall goals. Regardless, as you discover and connect to your own *why*, you will be able to meaningfully help others do so as well. They will sense your authenticity and that you have purpose. It is difficult to inspire others if you yourself don't feel inspired. As you become clearer about what really matters to you, others will be inspired to do the same, and they will want to connect with you in meaningful ways.

> *May you live long enough to know why you were born.*
> —CHEROKEE BIRTH BLESSING

Quite a few years ago, I was faced with a big career choice. I could continue my work at the terrific commercial real estate development firm Trammell Crow Company, or accept the invitation to begin working at the company my father had founded, Covey Leadership Center. While trying to decide what was the right life choice for me, I felt a bit confused and somewhat disconnected from purpose. My father helped me remember my *why* in a conversation when he asked me a simple question: "Do you want to build buildings or build people?"

This question reminded me why I had gone into business in the first place—because I loved developing people, and I wanted to maximize human potential. This helped redirect my focus and my energy and helped me recognize the right path *for me*. Another person's *why* might have been to build buildings, which also improves the lives of people. That is a valuable and important *why*. It just wasn't mine. The whole point is that everyone's *why* is personal. But connecting to it brings renewed energy, passion, and excitement. And when you feel inspired, that helps inspire others. Inspiration is contagious.

> *We're all called. If you're here breathing, you have a contribution to make to our human community. The real work of your life is to figure out your function—your part in the whole—as soon as possible, and then get about the business of fulfilling it as only you can.*
>
> —OPRAH WINFREY

2. Relationship Level: Caring

There is enough for everyone. Our job as a leader is to elevate caring above competing. These beliefs help create an abundance mentality, which inspires us to care about others. The predominant motive of Command & Control is self-interest, whereas the prevailing motive of Trust & Inspire is caring for others. Some might call it love.

The reality is that people want to connect. They want to know that you care about them. As the expression goes, "people don't care how much you know until they know how much you care." How different does work feel when your boss asks you about your family—and does so sincerely? What about when your team members remember that you have an important community commitment over the weekend and sincerely wish you the best, or offer thoughtful suggestions, or even offer help? When you feel that others are interested in what is important to you, you want to respond in the same way: with caring.

Rather than viewing your direct reports through a traditional lens of "span of control," do as Bob Chapman, CEO of Barry-Wehmiller, advised and see them instead through a transformative and expansive lens of "span of care." As you do so, your caring will not only connect you with your direct reports, it will increasingly connect you with *all* those you come in contact with.

Instead of asking "What's in it for me?" about a relationship, adopt the mindset "How can I best serve?" As you genuinely seek to learn about and connect with the people around you, your caring will grow. And so will your love.

Similar to the questions you asked yourself in discovering your own *why*, you should also ask your colleagues, partner, and your children, "What is *your why*? What matters to you?" If you've first figured out your *why* and have shared it with others by declaring yourself, others will be far more likely to reciprocate—to figure theirs out and share with you.

In a work environment, try to discover what matters to others beyond work. Why do they come to work? Is it so they can provide for their family? So they can earn enough money to buy a new gaming system? Because they love the field they're working in? No matter what their *why*, knowing it will help you understand them—and when you understand them, you can connect with them.

There are people who work for companies that have important missions, yet their only goal at work might be to stay employed so they can pay their rent. They do the minimum to accomplish that—to stay on the payroll. This doesn't mean they don't have more meaningful pursuits or passions. But maybe they need help connecting those interests to their work.

The two key attributes that demonstrate caring are empathy and compassion. When we empathize with people, we go out of our way to try to understand them. Not to judge, evaluate, or interpret them—just to understand them. When people feel we truly understand them, they tend to trust us and feel inspired by us—or at least, become open to it.

When we show compassion, we go beyond understanding by taking action to help them. We're moved to help those around us when we understand what they need. Compassion literally means "to go with someone in their experience." This is why a nurse is often the most trusted person in a hospital room. The health-care data shows that the greatest impact on the patient experience is caring through empathy and compassion. And nurses are some of the best there are when it comes to caring. When patients feel looked after, cared for, and understood—empathy and compassion—the patient experience improves.

> *We should consider the virtues of love and care in all of our leadership promotion decisions. We shouldn't just promote the most competent, but also the most loving and caring.*
>
> —JOHN MACKEY, FOUNDER AND
> CEO OF WHOLE FOODS

What's your mindset? If you say to your direct reports, "My passion is your potential"—and you mean it—that communicates volumes to them and to others.

Once my team and I were working with Great Clips, and had a discussion with Linda, one of the key leaders at a salon where she had worked for more than twenty years. My colleague asked her why she had chosen to stay at Great Clips for so long. She replied, "I stay for the people. I like cutting hair, but I could probably cut hair at almost any salon. My true passion and the reason I've stayed is because I love working with people and seeing them grow." You can probably guess how her employees feel about her.

As a leader, what if one of your *whys* was to help your people grow and to help them realize their potential? That is one of the most rewarding things you can experience in life. And it's a great demonstration of caring.

I recently caught up with a colleague I had hired thirty years ago at Covey Leadership Center. I was a young executive at the time, and she was recently out of college. As we reflected on that first interview, I was moved by what she remembered. She told me that what has stuck with her after all this time wasn't any of the interview questions or concerns she had about the position. What affected her most was that before the interview even started, I asked her for her personal opinion on a particular issue I was dealing with in the organization. As she tells it, I outlined my predicament candidly and asked if she would share her thoughts. She reported being sincerely struck by the genuine care I showed her as a person and by my interest in her opinion.

Neither of us remembers what the issue was, but she said that to this day, she has never forgotten how my care for her as an individual— demonstrated by my valuing her opinion—made her feel. I had no idea.

I've learned that people will forget what you said, people will forget what you did, but people will never forget how you made them feel.

—MAYA ANGELOU

3. Team Level: Belonging

If you've built a strong connection with the individuals around you through caring, you've set the stage to build a great sense of *belonging* when they come together to form a team. Belonging is what turns a group of people into a team. It's what turns acquaintances into real friends and neighborhoods into communities. It's what binds families together and how tribes work. Even stronger than the common work shared by members of a team are the bonds and relationships within it.

To build a strong team, we need to understand how to bring connection to everyone and create a sense of belonging and inclusion for all. We need to find out what's important to each individual and to the team as a whole. People need to see and feel how *their* being part of the team is important to the team. If the people around us feel like they are an important part of something bigger than themselves, they will become energized, and they will be inspired to contribute in new and different ways.

When this happens, the team finds meaning and runs with it. Sometimes the leader won't even need to direct anyone, because the team culture is so strong that team members direct themselves. This feels galvanizing, not manipulative. People will achieve better results when they are connected to each other and united around a common purpose. It becomes a co-creation process, because everyone on the team feels ownership. That's why self-directed teams can be so powerful.

> *Our development team doesn't look for stories. Their job is to create teams of people that work well together.*
>
> —ED CATMULL, CEO OF PIXAR

Similarly, a parent could create this kind of feeling within a family. A coach could create this feeling in a sports team. A surgeon could create this feeling in an operating room. And a military leader could create this feeling in a battalion. I've always loved the St. Crispin's Day speech by Henry V in Shakespeare's play, where he inspires his hugely undermanned fighting forces before an epic battle, leading them to victory: "We few, we happy few, we band of brothers; For he to-day that sheds his blood with me Shall be my brother."

People who even once experience this feeling of connection and belonging want to experience it again and again. It raises the bar and sets the standard of what's possible. I think organizational learning expert Peter Senge captured it perfectly:

> When you ask people about what it is like being part of a great team, what is most striking is the meaningfulness of the experience. People talk about being part of something larger than themselves, of being connected, of being generative. It becomes quite clear that, for many, their experiences as part of truly great teams stand out as singular periods of life lived to the fullest. Some spend the rest of their lives looking for ways to recapture that spirit.

This bond of belonging and inclusion creates something special. It can't be found everywhere. That is why people go looking for it.

People not only leave bad bosses, they'll also leave bad teams, even if they enjoy the work. But the inverse is also true. Even if the work itself is not especially significant to the person, the connection with the boss and/or other members of the team can often make up for it. So while in many cases the nature of our work may not be that exciting, being part of a team—and having a sense of belonging—can be inspiring in and of itself.

I know a young woman who has worked at a coffee shop for the last few years to support herself during school. She doesn't really care that much about serving people coffee. And she could probably find a different job closer to campus. But she loves her boss. And she loves her team. Her boss has created a sense of camaraderie and friendship between everyone. It makes going to work meaningful and enjoyable for her.

A Trust & Inspire leader is someone who fosters connections that benefit everyone. Those connections lead to inspiration, and inspiration drives incredible performance—56 percent higher than engagement and 125 percent higher than satisfaction, per the aforementioned Bain study.

Inspiring through Connecting to Purpose

We can intentionally seek to connect with ourselves, with people around us, and with our team. With ourselves, the connection is a sense of *authenticity* as we find our *why*. With those around us, the connection is a sense of *caring* as we build relationships. With our team, the connection is a sense of *belonging* as we create inclusion. Independent from the actual work we do, we can inspire through these connections alone.

Once these connections are in place, we are then able to make connections to the work itself. With our work, the connection is a sense of *contribution*—connecting to purpose and meaning and to why what we do matters.

From Success to Significance

People spend their whole careers, and some their entire lives, chasing what they define as success. For many, success is simply getting to a point where you don't have to work so hard to fulfill your basic needs. It could be the absence of worry over material things, or it might be a strong sense of status.

Some have loftier goals. Some want to amass a certain amount of financial wealth. Some chase Olympic gold or want to become the top competitor in their field. Some want to rise to the top in their organization while others seek to be recognized and acknowledged for their achievements.

Most people, however, find that success is not enough. People need something more. Maslow himself in his later years amended his hierarchy of needs. It was commonly represented as a pyramid with self-actualization at the top—what we might call *success*. Maslow later recognized self-transcendence—what we might call *significance*—as "the very highest and most inclusive or holistic level."

Think about it this way: How much would you need to be paid to dig a hole every day and then to fill the hole back up at the end of every day, with no other purpose? How long would you be willing to do it? You might be willing to do it for a while if it meant getting a big payout.

But at some point, money wouldn't matter. Because what truly matters, in the end, is *mattering*—making a difference. People want to know that their life and their work mattered, that they were significant. They want to find meaning in how they spend their time, not just a way to pay for it. They don't want to just go through the motions and feel like the work they're doing, or the reason they're doing it, doesn't matter. Of course, people want to be paid, and they want to be paid fairly, but sooner or later everyone realizes that money is just one part of the journey, not the final destination. Anyone who thinks otherwise is in for disappointment. That is the difference between success and significance.

Money motivates neither the best people, nor the best in people. Purpose does.

—NILOFER MERCHANT, AUTHOR
OF *THE POWER OF ONLYNESS*

In many parts of the world, our ability to meet our physiological and safety needs is ever increasing, giving us more time and energy to focus instead not just on self-actualization but on self-transcendence. As our options for work opportunities increase in a world of infinite choice, mere success does not carry the same weight it did in the past. People today increasingly want to use their talents, skills, and time to make meaningful contributions—to lead a life of significance.

A study from Achieve Consulting showed that "97 percent of millennials prefer using their individual skills to help a cause." While this is commonly understood to be true of Millennials, who are sometimes referred to as "the purpose generation," it really is true of all generations. In fact, a study from Imperative and LinkedIn showed that the "purpose-orientation" of people actually goes up as we move across the generations—with Baby Boomers being the highest. The point is, all generations and all people have a longing for significance.

A lot is written about how millennials want purpose. What I've come to believe is that everybody wants purpose. That's the secret sauce.

—KATHLEEN HOGAN, CHIEF PEOPLE
OFFICER OF MICROSOFT

Simon Sinek got it right when he said, "Start with Why." Every person, team, and organization needs to have a *why*, a meaningful, compelling reason to do what they do. But having a *why* alone is not enough. A Trust & Inspire leader starts with *why* but goes a step further and helps people *connect* the work they do to that *why*—in other words, they "Connect to Why."

People want more than a paycheck; people want meaning. They want to make a difference, to matter, to leave a legacy. Connecting with people and connecting to purpose are essential to this stewardship of inspiring. In a world of infinite choice, and with people everywhere having a growing desire for significance, it is a game changer for a leader to be able to inspire others.

Mission, Vision, and Values versus Purpose, Meaning, and Contribution

A person might be good at reciting the organization's written *why* but may not be really connected to it. Many organizations dedicate a lot of time, training, and resources to making sure their employees know about their mission, vision, and values. I'm clearly in favor of these things, since they can give an organization a strong compass, a "true north," and could very well represent an organization's *why*. But unless people are meaningfully connected to them, they're sometimes just words on a wall.

I've worked with many organizations where people can quote their values, for example, but where those things don't drive people's actions or decisions. Beyond these statements, what people really want is to be connected to a deep sense of purpose, meaning, and contribution. It's a deeper dive, a more practical application, of a similar idea—connecting to why it matters. I've also worked with organizations that have nailed this, and the difference in both culture and performance is night and day.

To what end, and to whose benefit, are our employees being asked to give of themselves? Have we committed ourselves to a purpose that is truly deserving of their initiative, imagination, and passion?

—GARY HAMEL, AUTHOR AND PROFESSOR

Education is a great example of this phenomenon. Few professions have as noble a mission as teaching. The vision of education is to help young people mature and become responsible citizens. By all accounts, people who believe in that vision and who commit their lives to that profession should be thriving in their role as educators. Yet 44 percent of teachers leave the profession within the first five years, 50 percent are considering quitting at any given time, and Gallup's research on teacher engagement shows that only slightly more than 30 percent are fully engaged.

In my experience, this has nothing to do with the inherent nobility of the profession or the quality of the teachers, and everything to do with the uphill challenges teachers face while not feeling connected to its mission. Overflowing classrooms, understaffed schools, and lack of resources, support, and appreciation are real barriers teachers regularly face. But, like most industries, perhaps the biggest barrier tends to be a predominantly Command & Control leadership style among many educational administrators, a style that simply doesn't trust or inspire teachers.

And if teachers don't feel trusted or inspired, how are they going to inspire their students? While systemic changes and more resources are clearly needed, creating genuine connection to purpose, meaning, and contribution can be an inspiring pathway to help teachers navigate through many of these challenges.

If such a disconnect can happen in a profession like education, where the mission, vision, and values are both clear and inherent to the profession, just imagine how greater a chasm can happen in a profession where they aren't.

One time I presented at the World Business Forum right after Harvard Business School professor Michael Porter spoke. He made the point that forward-thinking businesses and leaders will recognize that Corporate Social Responsibility (CSR), while good, is insufficient in today's world. People don't merely want a company to "do no harm"; people want companies to "create shared value"—to embed serving society into the actual business model itself, not just as an offshoot. People want businesses not just to be responsible but also to be meaningful, to have a purpose beyond profits, and to contribute to the communities that support them.

Corporate Social Responsibility is a good thing, but many businesses engage in it rotely, often because it is expected or simply to avoid being irresponsible. They are being compliant. This is Command & Control—perhaps Enlightened Command & Control, but Command & Control nonetheless. Now contrast CSR with more of a Trust & Inspire approach—Porter's concept of "creating shared value"—where contributing socially is not just a box to be checked, but an explicit purpose of the business, as important as profit. The contrast is not only striking, it also proves inspiring.

I once did a double take when I saw a person wearing a T-shirt that said, *Will work for meaning*. It's not enough to just have mission, vision, and value statements or to merely intellectually accept them. We have to explicitly create a connection to them, not just for ourselves but also for others. We have to tap into real purpose, meaning, and contribution, because inspiration flows from these sources. And more than any other competency, people today want to be inspired by their leaders, and they will use that inspiration to fuel the accomplishment of something good, something worthy.

Life is about contribution, not accumulation. It doesn't inspire anyone to say, "We need your very best thinking and your highest effort because if we can solve this problem, we will satisfy the shareholders." Satisfying shareholders is necessary, but by itself it is uninspiring.

In contrast, consider Veterans United Home Loans, a lender who focuses specifically on military service members. Their values aren't just words to them—they're what they genuinely believe and how they really operate: "Be Passionate and Have Fun," "Deliver Results with Integrity," and "Enhance Lives Every Day." They say, "As a team, we proudly serve those who have served our country. We find purpose in knowing what we do matters."

And they do. It's no surprise that they consistently show up on *Fortune* magazine's "100 Best Companies to Work For" year after year. I can tell you firsthand from working with them over the last few years that as an organization, they have tapped into extraordinary purpose.

The result is inspiration, which translates not only into enhanced lives but also into enhanced performance.

Work: A Sense of Contribution

The reason we sometimes get stuck at mission, vision, and values and don't get to purpose, meaning, and contribution is that too often we try to leapfrog the first and most important connection at any level—building a sense of authenticity within ourselves, a sense of caring with others, and a sense of belonging on the team. Without strong relationships and community feeling, it doesn't matter how compelling the work is. It can become hollow and feel forced or artificial.

People can work in a field that saves lives, but if they don't feel cared for or that they belong, they won't stay. If you try to manufacture meaning when it's not inherently there for people, not only will it not work, but it will likely backfire. The converse, however, is equally true. When you tap into real meaning and purpose, you can create extraordinary value on all levels. Consider the following from the consulting firm McKinsey & Co. in an article entitled "Igniting Individual Purpose in Times of Crisis":

> Purpose can be an important contributor to employee experience, which in turn is linked to higher levels of employee engagement, stronger organizational commitment, and increased feelings of well-being. People who find their individual purpose congruent with their jobs tend to get more meaning from their roles, making them more productive and more likely to outperform their peers. Our own research finds a positive correlation between the purposefulness of employees and their company's profit margin.

In short, we need to earn the right to create and tap into meaning and purpose by making the personal connections first. If we do this, people give us permission to influence and inspire them in their work. Our results can be far better than we ever could have imagined, because our up-front work in connecting with people leads to more inspired people. Our people will want to contribute their best, and they will want to create. And when you as a leader step up with a new initiative, your team will be much more likely to get onboard. Why? They know you, they trust you—and they know your *why*. They know you don't want hollow compliance but instead seek heartfelt commitment—and they are inspired to give it.

Build Trust with One, Inspire Many

All of this connects back to the idea of being efficient with things and effective with people. Some people might believe that it's far too inefficient to connect one-on-one, to build relationships one person at a time. That it takes too much time. And while it is true that it is not efficient, it is extremely effective and will lead to long-term gains—which is ultimately far more efficient, as we're playing a long-term game. Perhaps the single highest-leveraged activity we can do as leaders is to have one-on-ones with our direct reports because of the profound and inspiring impact those one-on-one meetings can have on both of us.

Another high-leveraged activity was modeled by Doug Conant, who, as mentioned previously, transformed the Campbell Soup Company. He was able to do so at least partly because he first put in the time with his people, as evidenced by the more than thirty thousand individualized handwritten notes he sent out to colleagues in the company over the years. He understood that with people, fast is slow and slow is fast. By going slow, note by note, eventually he was able to move exceptionally fast. When we attempt to go fast with people and skip those first steps, not only will we get slowed down, we may even come to a grinding halt.

What If My Organization, or My Role, Isn't Naturally Inspiring?

For some organizations, the inspiring aspects of their purpose are naturally more obvious; examples would be a hospital that saves patients' lives or a crisis center that provides safety and protection. Other organizations are able to take what might seem mundane and transform it into something extraordinary by imbuing it with purpose.

For example, I'll always remember how powerfully impacted I was—and continue to be—when I visited the Pepperdine Graziadio Business School. Consistent with the university's ideals of purpose, service, and leadership, their team shared with me their idea of not focusing on producing leaders who become the best *in* the world but rather focusing on producing leaders who become the best *for* the world. In their words: "Best for the World Leaders strive to do their best—not just be the best. We believe there is a world of difference between the two concepts of best *for* the world and best *in* the world."

What an inspiring vision and contribution! It's not hard to believe that the students and faculty at the university feel a sense of connection to this transforming and inspiring purpose, not only while they study and teach at Pepperdine but well beyond their time there. That kind of influence becomes enduring. And one of our Fundamental Beliefs is that enduring influence is created from the inside out—similar to what they are doing at Pepperdine.

However, for many jobs, a sense of purpose may not come as easily. How do you create meaning when you're sweeping floors? The reality is that you can bring purpose, meaning and contribution to every person and to almost any job or situation.

An illustration of this is when President John F. Kennedy visited NASA sometime after having given the United States his charge of "landing a man on the moon and returning him safely" by the end of the decade. The story goes that President Kennedy ran into a janitor during his visit and asked what he was doing. The janitor replied, "I'm helping put a man on the moon." The sense of purpose within NASA was so strong that it had made its way to the janitor. He, like everyone else in that building, understood that his contribution was connected to the overall purpose, and he was inspired by it.

How differently do you think he does his job being connected to that perspective? It may seem like there is a big gap between sweeping floors and getting a person on the moon, but every job contributes to the overarching purpose. Anybody can take pride in their job, no matter what the job is—and anybody can do any job without pride. Connecting to purpose can make all the difference.

Similarly, consider the apocryphal parable of the three bricklayers. While working, the bricklayers were asked what they were doing. The first bricklayer responded, "I'm a bricklayer. I'm working hard laying bricks to feed my family." The second bricklayer replied, "I'm a builder. I'm building a wall." The third bricklayer said, "I'm a cathedral builder. I'm building a great cathedral to Almighty God." Same work, three completely different perspectives. The first had a job, the second had a career, and the third had a calling. Indeed, purpose can turn a job into a calling.

> *You can go from job to career to calling—all without changing your occupation.*
>
> —ANGELA DUCKWORTH, PROFESSOR
> AND AUTHOR OF *GRIT*

For a great organization like St. Jude Children's Research Hospital that focuses on treating and curing childhood cancer, the very nature of their organization's purpose is inherently inspiring. For other organizations, a sense of purpose might require a little more creativity to see. However, you can bring a sense of contribution to nearly any organization or industry. Some do it by adopting good social causes such as "buy one, give one" as part of how they operate. Others are thoughtful and creative around seeing and articulating their purpose in a way that inspires.

Here are a few illustrations of companies that operate in a variety of industries where you might think there's not as much natural, inherent meaning in their work. Yet each of these companies has been able to create a statement of purpose that provides a sense of meaning and that can help inspire people by connecting what they do to why it matters.

Nike: Athletic apparel
"To bring inspiration and innovation to every athlete* in the world.
If you have a body, you are an athlete."

Starbucks: Coffee shop retail chain
"To inspire and nurture the human spirit—one person, one cup, and one neighborhood at a time."

Disney: Media and entertainment
"Creating happiness through magical experiences."

Patagonia: Outdoor equipment
"We're in business to save our home planet."

Harley-Davidson: Motorcycle manufacturer
"More than building machines, we stand for the timeless pursuit of adventure. Freedom for the soul."

How much more might you feel compelled to contribute when you believe your work serves something larger than yourself? How much more committed, engaged, and inspired might you be? What's the difference? Connecting to purpose, connecting to why it matters! The potential for meaning is there all along; people just have to see it and then connect to it. Once they do, inspiration follows.

Here's the extraordinary opportunity—and challenge—for us as leaders: we can create and embed purpose, meaning, and contribution into almost any role in almost any organization. The essence of any organization is relationships with a purpose.

Motivates, but Doesn't Inspire

Do you have a boss who truly inspires you? A coworker? A friend? On the flip side, do you have others who merely motivate . . . but don't inspire? By most accounts, Andrall (Andy) Pearson was a very motivating leader who was able to drive amazing results. Andy Pearson ran PepsiCo from 1971 to 1985, driving revenues from $1.1 billion to nearly $8 billion. He demanded performance, and his way of getting it worked.

Pearson's primary tools for motivation at the time were fear, surprise, and a fanatical devotion to the numbers. Every year, without hesitation, he fired the least productive 10 to 20 percent of his workforce to send a message to everyone else. This rank-and-yank, motivate-by-fear style worked. His approach raised the bar for even the most outstanding performers. Pearson was singled out for the relentless demands he put on his people. As one employee put it, Pearson's talents were often "brutally abrasive." In fact, *Fortune* named him one of the ten toughest bosses in the United States.

If you were an employee at PepsiCo in those days and someone asked, "How is he as a leader?" you might have replied, "He motivates, but he doesn't inspire." I'm happy to say that Andy's story doesn't end there. Later in his career, he came out of retirement for another shot and took a vastly different approach. We'll come back to the rest of his story later in the book.

Greatest Compliment You Can Receive

Consider this: perhaps the single greatest compliment another person can give you is to tell you, "You inspire me." That compliment inherently has all the other compliments within it. If you inspire people, it also means they respect you, they value your life and experience. They trust you. There's something you've done that they are reaching for, whether you've accomplished some great task or simply demonstrated some important quality they feel drawn to. They might feel you connected them to a sense of purpose—or they simply might feel you connected to them. In some way, you've brought greater meaning to their life.

> *To be inspired is great, but to be an inspiration is an honor.*
> —JULIETTE GORDON LOW, FOUNDER
> OF THE GIRL SCOUTS

When people tell you that you inspire them, it gives you a sense of stewardship to see them succeed. You want to help fuel their success; in fact, you begin to want nothing more than to see them become the best version of themselves. Not because of a reward, or a bonus, but because to help another person improve his or her life brings meaning to your own. This motive of caring—this ethic of service—is what drives a Trust & Inspire leader.

Inspiring Others Is Your Job . . . So Get Good at It!

As we discussed earlier, *everyone can inspire*. And as a Trust & Inspire leader, your very job *is* to inspire people. You inspire naturally through the first two stewardships of modeling and trusting. You inspire intentionally when you connect with people and in turn connect them to a sense of purpose, meaning, and contribution at work, helping them reach new levels.

The process of overlapping individual and organizational purposes is what I call "co-purposing." For some people, their personal purpose will align abundantly with their organization's purpose. For others, the two may only partially overlap. And yet for others, the two may not match at all. The key is that no matter how naturally it fits, everyone has a purpose, something inside them that drives them. Your job as a leader is to help others connect to it. Once you do, they'll be committed and engaged with new energy and understanding. And the more you

can help overlap people's individual purpose with the work's organizational purpose, the greater the possibilities of inspiration.

Always look in the mirror and start with yourself first. Work from the inside out. Find your own *why*. Then get good at building relationships with people and caring about their lives. Then help teams gain a sense of belonging. Finally, connect people with why the work they do matters. We need leaders who inspire. It's your job, and you can get good at this! Inspiring others is a learnable skill.

Whatever you do—whether you're a janitor or the CEO—you can continually look at what you do and ask how it connects to other people, how it connects to the bigger picture, how it can be an expression of your deepest values.

—AMY WRZESNIEWSKI, YALE BUSINESS PROFESSOR

Consider the following four statements. Circle the number that best describes how you are connecting with people and connecting to purpose.

	DEFINITELY NO ←→	SOMEWHAT	←→ DEFINITELY YES	
I have clarified my why. My own sense of purpose, meaning, and contribution is clear.	1	2	3	4	5
I have a personal connection with each member of my team. My people know I genuinely care about them.	1	2	3	4	5
I have cultivated a true sense of belonging and inclusion within my team. Each person feels safe to bring his or her whole self to work.	1	2	3	4	5
I have embedded purpose, meaning, and contribution into the work we do, individually and as a team.	1	2	3	4	5

A Summary of the 3 Stewardships

Over the last three chapters, we've covered the 3 Stewardships of a Trust & Inspire leader: modeling, trusting, and inspiring. When viewed independently, each of these stewardships is significant, but the true power comes when we strive to live and fulfill all three simultaneously. As we do, we can become an incredible catalyst for both transformation and performance.

One of the best examples of someone who has exemplified all 3 Stewardships of a Trust & Inspire leader is CEO Satya Nadella, who, as you read about at the beginning of the book, reinvented Microsoft. His remarkable feat is due to his leadership style—the fact that he models, he trusts, and he inspires.

Inheriting a situation from which many would flee, Nadella modeled humility and courage. Saying that "our ambitions are bold and so must be our desire to change and evolve our culture," he fearlessly transformed an ailing corporate culture and turned around an increasingly irrelevant company that was losing marketability, building both in ways no one could have expected or anticipated.

Nadella also modeled humility and gratitude. Assuming the top leadership position, he came into the job quietly, thoughtfully, and without even a hint of arrogance. No patting himself on the back or taking credit for one of the most remarkable transformations in corporate history. Instead, he credited the people he inspired, telling them, "Thank you. Without that tenacity, resilience, and the work of each of you . . . I even shudder to think where we would be. I'm deeply, deeply grateful, and I thank you."

Among a number of other inspiring leadership traits, Nadella modeled teamwork and camaraderie, overhauling the company's cutthroat atmosphere and completely changing the trajectory of Microsoft. In a few short years, he and his team created a "growth mindset culture" that brought about undeniable results. He also modeled empathy through his listening, which became foundational for the leadership he would provide. As he put it, "Listening was the most important thing I accomplished each day because it would build the foundation of leadership for years to come."

The revival of Microsoft hinged on Nadella's trust of his employees. He knew success depended on helping the world not only adapt but innovate—and he trusted his people to make that possible. He trusted his people to become more agile and to create in unprecedented ways. He trusted them to collaborate at a level that enabled everyone to create. He trusted them to restore Microsoft's relevance. And they did. They did all of that and more.

Nadella inspired. "My approach is to lead with a sense of purpose," he stated. He knew that astonishing things would happen when a "family of individuals united by a single, shared mission" became a team of more than a hundred thousand strong who were inspired—and then unleashed—through finding purpose and meaning. And that's exactly what happened. As Nadella put it, "I truly believe that each of us must find meaning in our work. The best work happens when you know that it's not just work, but something that will improve people's lives."

In just a few short years, Nadella and the people he leads created extraordinary value not just for shareholders but for all stakeholders, generating more growth in value over that time than Uber, Airbnb, Netflix, Spotify, Snapchat, and WeWork *combined*. Here's another way to see it: when Nadella took over as CEO, the stock price was $37; at the time of this writing, it's $301. To say that he exceeded expectations would be an understatement.

Before Nadella arrived with his Trust & Inspire leadership style and his commitment to the 3 Stewardships, Microsoft was dying. Today, it is one of only a few companies in history to be valued at more than $2 trillion. That remarkable achievement illustrates the power of a Trust & Inspire leader—one who models, trusts, and inspires people to give their best. As he put it, "The number one thing that you have to do as a leader: to bolster the confidence of the people you lead."

When we model, trust, and inspire as Nadella has done, we will

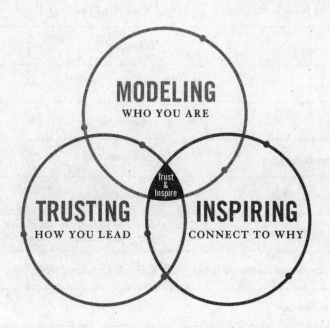

bolster the confidence of those we lead, people will be drawn to us, and people will be inspired to grow and give their very best—regardless of the situation.

If we could get our colleagues, our partners, our students, our friends, our children, and our family to feel that way, we could help unleash the greatness inside them.

Everyone has the power for greatness—not for fame but greatness—because greatness is determined by service.

—DR. MARTIN LUTHER KING JR.

COMMAND & CONTROL	TRUST & INSPIRE
Self-Interest	Caring for Others
Span of Control	Span of Care
"What's In It For Me?"	"How Can I Best Serve?"
Association	Belonging
Exclusion	Inclusion
Success	Significance
Start with What	Start with Why
Connect to What	Connect to Why
Mission, Vision, and Values	Mission, Vision, and Values *and* Purpose, Meaning, and Contribution
Corporate Social Responsibility (CSR)	CSR *and* Creating Shared Value
Accumulation	Contribution

CHAPTER 8

Stewardship Agreements

I never think of myself as being a woman CEO of this company. I think of myself as a steward of this great institution.

—VIRGINIA "GINNI" ROMETTY, FORMER
CHAIRMAN AND CEO OF IBM

Solving the False Dichotomy

As we discussed in the 1st stewardship of modeling, leaders need to perform—to get results. Getting results is a prerequisite for leadership. It is results that convert the cynics. Leaders know they are responsible for their own performance as well as for the results their team produces. And they are responsible for the *outcomes*, not just the activities.

The very best leaders know they need *both* to get results *and* to build the relationship. Unwittingly, too many leaders get trapped in the following false dichotomy:

Do I complete the task . . . or build the relationship?

We often hear expressions like, "this person is more 'task oriented,'" or "that person is more 'people oriented.'" Most people frame it as an either/or dichotomy.

The ongoing issue is, "I have to get the job done, but I know I also need to build relationships with people." As leaders, we want to be both *tough-minded* and *kindhearted*, as leadership authorities

181

Doug Conant and Mette Norgaard suggest. For too many, these seem like two separate responsibilities, and they can sometimes even manifest as competing priorities. The insufficiency of this false dichotomy sits squarely within an Enlightened Command & Control paradigm.

By contrast, Trust & Inspire leaders know it's their job to "get results in a way that inspires trust." Trust & Inspire transcends either/or, dichotomous thinking. It's *and*. And the key to the *and* is that it's all about the *how*. Indeed, *how you do what you do* will both help you get the job done *and* build the relationship as part of the process—not as a separate, compartmentalized task. It's not a dichotomy.

How you go about achieving the task will determine the outcome of both the task and the relationship.

The Imprint of Stewardship

We start with the fundamental belief that leadership *is* stewardship, and that leaders are stewards. Too often, stewardship gets narrowly defined as only applying in a spiritual context or pertaining to environmental matters of sustainability. In reality, Trust & Inspire leaders have a sense of stewardship about everything, especially their role as a leader for the people they lead. When we see ourselves as stewards, it brings out the best in us—and in others. We rise to the occasion and become more responsible, more committed, more inspired, and more inspiring.

This sense of stewardship flows out of an abundance mentality, which is based on a deep inner sense of personal integrity, authenticity, and security. We subscribe to the fundamental beliefs that people have greatness inside them, that people are whole people, and that there is enough for everyone. This accurate map or paradigm of viewing people and leadership changes everything. When you add to this paradigm the belief that leaders are stewards, it transforms us even further. It inspires us. Indeed, stewardship itself inspires.

The Tool: Stewardship Agreements

A stewardship agreement is a tool for mutually extending trust from one to another with clear expectations and mutually agreed-upon accountability. The simplest manifestation of a stewardship agreement I could give you is in the "green and clean" story of my father and me when I was seven. The job or stewardship I was given was to take care of the yard. The expectation for my stewardship was that I would keep the yard green and clean (both words expressing results). For guidelines and resources, I could do it any way I wanted as long as the lawn was green and clean. (Oh, there was one exception: I couldn't paint the grass green!) My father agreed to help me if I asked him—and if he had time. In terms of accountability, we would walk around the yard together once a week. I would assess and judge myself against the results my father and I had agreed on—green and clean.

I use this simple example because if it can work with a seven-year-old, it can work in almost any setting with almost any person.

The same elements my father used in that example provide the simple structure for stewardship agreements. They can be applied in nearly every imaginable situation—between employers and employees, between a leader and an immediate direct report, between teams from different departments, or between a parent and a child. Basically, a stewardship agreement can be used between any two people or groups of people who need to work together to accomplish a common goal.

Stewardship agreements become the Trust & Inspire tool or methodology to clarify expectations and practice accountability between people involved in any interdependent endeavor.

The purpose of a stewardship agreement is to get results in a way that grows people.

My father began teaching the concept of stewardship agreements more than fifty years ago. The principles were the same, but he called them by different names: Performance Agreements, Win-Win Agreements, or Win-Win Performance Agreements. He also called the process "stewardship delegation." The concept for all of these is the same.

While the principles haven't changed, the practices and applications of stewardship agreements have never been more relevant or vital than they are today in our era of remote work and dispersed workforces. Given the new world we're operating in, I submit that the ability to establish effective stewardship agreements with others is among the most crucial leadership skills of our time.

The basic idea is that a stewardship agreement shifts the paradigm of interaction from vertical positioning to horizontal partnering. From hovering over and checking up on people to self-supervision and accountability. From micromanagement to self-governance. From top-down posturing to becoming partners in success. From leaders judging others to people judging themselves. In short, it shifts the paradigm from *manager* to *coach*.

This is in line with how the nature of work has changed, and the shift to partnering, coaching, and self-accountability. Consider how many people are engaged in remote or hybrid work. The concept of "work from anywhere" had slowly been on the rise for years; up to 8 percent of days worked were done outside the formal office. But when COVID-19 hit in the spring of 2020, remote work went from being the exception to being the rule—overnight! More than 60 percent of days worked were remote.

For many people, if the job could be done from home, they no longer came to the office. This made hovering over and checking up on people a lot more difficult. The all-too-common refrain among bosses was, "How do we know if they're really working?" A stewardship agreement is a tool that is perfectly suited to remote/hybrid work, to a dispersed workforce, and more broadly, to the new way of working.

Unfortunately, rather than looking for ways to help their employees succeed in this new environment, many organizations responded to this challenge by investing in new and creative ways to "micromanage from a distance." Some employed tools such as "productivity software" and other practices that often look and feel to people like nothing more than forms of employee surveillance. That inspires no one.

Conversely, many people and organizations are thriving in this new environment. Organizations that have responded to this challenge by seeking ways to help their people succeed were pleasantly surprised to find how well people responded to the greater latitude and freedom associated with remote work. They have seen improved performance as well.

So what's the difference? I submit that if you look at the most successful remote work arrangements, you will find the makings of a solid stewardship agreement. You'll see clear expectations and a mutually agreed-upon process of accountability.

And here's the most important part: this same process is equally as applicable and effective in on-site or in-person work situations as it is in virtual, hybrid, or dispersed work situations.

> *The need to manage oneself is creating a revolution in human affairs . . . It requires new tools and far-reaching changes in traditional thinking and practices.*
>
> —PETER DRUCKER

As my father said, a stewardship agreement "is not a formal job description, neither is it a legal contract. It's an open-ended, psychological/social contract that explicitly defines expectations. It is written first into the hearts and minds of people, and then put on paper *in pencil* rather than in ink so that easy erasing can take place. When both sense it is appropriate and wise, you can discuss and negotiate it at will, based on changing circumstances."

Or, as with green and clean, it might never be put on paper, but it can still be clear and mutually understood. Using the language "stewardship agreement" is not the point. Rather, the point is that you have a common understanding and commitment toward your highest mutual priorities. If it feels easier, safer, or less formal or legal to avoid using the word *agreement*, that's fine; just call it a "stewardship plan" or a "stewardship understanding."

Stewardship agreements can be surprisingly simple and are liberating for all involved. They don't emerge from isolated techniques but rather from enduring principles. It is difficult to use them without first building a relationship of trust, and it's difficult to maintain them without personal credibility.

An effective stewardship agreement is the product of a Trust & Inspire paradigm. Strong trust relationships precede effective stewardship agreements. But it can work the other way as well: a good stewardship agreement can also help build a relationship of trust and can even help shift a paradigm. An example would be adopting a fundamental belief such as unleashing greatness rather than controlling it.

You can approach a stewardship agreement with a Command & Control paradigm, which is exactly what we've been doing since the industrial age. But at the end of the day, this doesn't work well. By contrast, from a Trust & Inspire paradigm, stewardship agreements can become effective, empowering tools that will help us overcome the common barriers that so often get in the way of trusting and inspiring others—of unleashing people's potential.

As a leader . . . your principal job is to create an operating environment where others can do great things.

—RICHARD TEERLINK, FORMER
CEO OF HARLEY-DAVIDSON

Stewardship agreements operationalize a *skill set* by giving us a *tool set* we can use to adopt a Trust & Inspire style, which in turn helps us meet the two imperatives of our time—winning in the workplace (culture) and winning in the marketplace (innovation). However, our ability to effectively implement a stewardship agreement hinges on having the right mindset flowing from the five fundamental beliefs of a Trust & Inspire leader we've already discussed. Since this mindset is where it all begins, below is a quick reminder of these fundamental beliefs before diving into the elements of a stewardship agreement.

THE 5 FUNDAMENTAL BELIEFS OF A TRUST & INSPIRE LEADER

I BELIEVE...	SO MY JOB AS A LEADER IS TO...
People have greatness inside them	Unleash their potential, not control them
People are whole people	Inspire, not merely motivate
There is enough for everyone	Elevate caring above competing
Leadership is stewardship	Put service above self-interest
Enduring influence is created from the inside out	Go first

The Five Elements of a Stewardship Agreement

There are five important elements that should be included when creating a stewardship agreement. The first three help clarify expectations. The final two establish practicing accountability.

1. **Desired Results** ⎫
2. **Guidelines**   ⎬ *Clarify Expectations*
3. **Resources**   ⎭
4. **Accountability** ⎫ *Practice Accountability*
5. **Consequences**   ⎭

Let's look at each of the five elements in turn.

1. Desired Results: *What do we want to accomplish—and why?*

A good stewardship agreement begins by specifying desired results up front—what is it we are after? Put another way, what is your "green and clean"?

The agreement needs to be as specific as possible so that people know exactly what we seek to achieve. It's not enough to tell our kids to "do a good job" while cleaning their room. We need to be clearer, show examples, provide modeling. Set dates or timelines for accomplishing the objectives, and be specific about quantity and quality. Commit people to getting the results, but then let them determine the best methods for accomplishing the results. People are more committed and produce better outcomes when they are allowed to decide on how to achieve the results. As we discussed, there is a risk in doing that, but we also have the possibility of even greater return—and certainly of greater commitment. The more clarity we can have around the desired results, the better.

The concept of a mutual stewardship agreement suggests that we clarify expectations together, not just top-down, and that we mutually commit to getting desired results. Remember, though, that we need to get the job done *and* build the relationship. So as leaders, we'll want to ask the question "What do *we* (both of us) want?" Yes, we know we need to get the job done, but what else matters to us and to the other person? We have to become clear not only on their stewardship, but also on what is important to them. By doing this, we'll work together to build the agreement on a much stronger foundation of mutual understanding and trust, which will enable us to both achieve the result and build the relationship.

I remember many times creating stewardship agreements with other leaders where in addition to hitting their team's sales and profitability numbers, it was equally important to both for them to build a high-trust culture of inspired team members. We measured both—the hard numbers and the soft numbers—with equal passion.

2. Guidelines: *Within what boundaries?*

Guidelines specify the parameters, principles, and policies within which results are to be accomplished. Guidelines might also identify the possible failure paths or watchouts that could get in the way of accomplishing the results. Guidelines also include maintaining organizational or family values, such as operating with integrity or operating within ethical standards. They can also help us identify guardrails that define appropriate boundaries, such as "don't paint the grass" in green and clean. Milestones should be included to help everyone know where they should be and when. Guidelines and guardrails help establish a clear path to success. Guidelines are established collaboratively, but recognize that the person carrying out the task has ultimate ownership for how it is to be accomplished. It's autonomy over task. At the end of the day, you can't hold people accountable for results if you dictate their methods.

3. Resources: *What do we have to work with?*

Once results and guidelines are established, it's important that people understand all of the resources at their disposal to help them achieve the desired results. These resources could include human, financial, technical, or organizational resources as well as support that is available. Be specific. Identify if and how each resource is available. For example, in green and clean, my father agreed to help me—be a resource—if he had time.

When people are aware of what resources they have access to, they can better plan how to use the resources to achieve optimal results. By mutually assessing resources up front, all involved better know what it's going to take to accomplish the desired results. It's important that both parties feel set up to win.

I remember one time after I'd set up a stewardship agreement with a direct report, it became clear to both of us that we had not allocated anywhere near the level of organizational resources needed for my direct report to succeed. Rather than sticking with the original misaligned agreement, we adjusted the agreement midstream and increased the resources available so my team member was set up to succeed.

4. Accountability: *How will we know how we're doing?*

As we've discussed, an agreed-upon process for accountability is crucial to a good stewardship agreement. Define accountability at the start against the desired results. It sends a message that you care not only about the results, but also about the relationship.

Accountability makes stewardship agreements real. Without accountability, people might begin to lose their sense of responsibility, or they might start blaming circumstances or other people for poor performance. But when people are involved in setting the standards of acceptable performance, they become even more committed to achieving the desired results.

Always tie accountability to the desired results and the agreed-upon expectations, like my father did with me in "green and clean." The truth is that results can be evaluated in many ways. The most common of these is measurement. Another way is through observation. Often the highest measure of accountability can be discernment—not just ours, but especially theirs.

Agree together, as clearly as possible, how performance will be evaluated so that there is no guessing. If needed, specify when and how progress reports are to be made and when accountability sessions will be held (like my father and me "walking the yard" every week). Are there milestones that will help people know where they should be, and when? These check-in sessions will also provide the opportunity to address potentially changing conditions or unforeseen circumstances.

When I was in a team leader position once, one of my team members asked me how he was doing in his role. We had previously set up a stewardship agreement, so I flipped this around and asked him instead, "You tell me, how do you think you're doing? I think you know better than I do." And he did. He acknowledged that he knew he wasn't performing as well as he should have been but was simply wondering whether I had noticed.

There are two big ideas relating to accountability:

First, when you have clear expectations in the form of desired results, guidelines, and resources coupled with a mutually agreed-upon process for accountability, you can shift from needing to evaluate others to them evaluating themselves against the agreement. That is a monumental paradigm shift, and it works with a straightforward stewardship agreement. It changes everything.

Second, people don't feel micromanaged if you're checking in when they asked you to or when you're coming to provide the help you offered in the first place. Most importantly, when the trust level is high, people will be much tougher on themselves than an outside evaluator or manager would ever dare be.

Also, when trust is high, discernment is more accurate than so-called objective measurement. That's because people know in their hearts much more than the measurement system can reveal about their performance. This is where the ideas of "you judge yourself" and "walk the yard" come into play. It is much more ennobling to the human spirit to let people judge themselves than to judge them—and it will produce more commitments and better outcomes in the end (both for the task and for the relationship).

I've seen this happen in great schools where rather than traditional "parent-teacher conferences," in which the teacher reports to the parent on the student, the school implemented "student-led conferences." In these, the students report on themselves to their parents *with* the teacher but led by the student. This shift in accountability from teacher to student—allowing students to judge themselves—is remarkable. It still gives the parent and teacher the opportunity to explore areas for improvement, but the student is actively leading this dialogue rather than feeling like a suspect being judged by superiors.

5. Consequences: *What are the implications if we do or don't achieve the desired results?*

Discuss consequences. Clearly understand together what will happen when the desired results are achieved—or not achieved. The consequences you discuss in the agreement could be both positive and negative. Positive or negative consequences might include opportunity, growth, development, contribution, or financial implications. The consequences will feel different if they're natural and logical and flow out of a Trust & Inspire paradigm rather than if they're artificial and arbitrary and flow out of a Command & Control paradigm.

In my green and clean example, I was too young to be concerned with an allowance, so the consequences were natural ones centered around contribution, growth, development, and opportunity. I felt pride in taking care of the lawn, I developed new skills, I grew in learning how to do things, and my parents gave me more and more responsibility going forward—all of which made me feel really good about myself.

People should go in with their eyes wide open to the consequences before they agree to be accountable to them. The agreement governs the outcome and actions to be taken, and both parties must be clear about it.

Our rule for clarity around accountability and consequences is simple: *no guessing*.

"Walk the Yard": Agreements Govern

I recently worked with a dental billing company called eAssist that, inspired by the "green and clean" story, began to implement stewardship agreements. One of the key things that made these work for them was coming together around the shorthand phrase of "walk the yard," referring to my father "walking the yard" with me weekly to give me an opportunity to report on my part of the agreement—in other words, to hold myself accountable to the agreement. The people at eAssist were inspired by this method of self-led accountability.

As they started implementing mutual stewardship agreements, they made sure to clarify expectations of how they would "walk the yard." They made this such a common phrase that being mutually accountable became built into their culture. Instead of something to be feared, a "walk the yard" is something positive. It wasn't arbitrary; people knew when to plan for it.

The key is that the agreement governed. And it included some guardrails to keep people from "painting the yard." They used the agreement to evaluate how things were going together—where they were making progress and where improvements needed to be made. Because of the mutual agreement, there was no guessing. The agreement governed.

As mentioned, as you consider creating a stewardship agreement, you will come to realize that some situations might call for creating a formal document together where ideas are written down, as they were for eAssist. For others, it might mean having a less formal agreement and more of a mutual understanding, such as with my father and me on "green and clean." Regardless of the form, if done well, stewardship agreements are empowering, ennobling, and inspiring—and they help us produce better results, both for the task and for the relationship.

Many years ago, I set up a stewardship agreement with a direct report of mine who was a rare and phenomenal talent, yet he was very quirky about when, where, and how he worked. This was back when working remotely from home (or from anywhere other than the office) was almost unheard of. In setting up the agreement together, I put a heavy emphasis on clarity around desired results, but I had to learn to completely back off on the ways I thought were proven best practices, on how to achieve them, and on when and where to work. He wanted his autonomy—and my trust. I gave it to him.

He produced like no one else had! We built a great relationship, and I saw firsthand how powerful and flexible stewardship agreements could be, especially with someone who had the kind of entrepreneurial bent he had. He stayed with me for many years before finally leaving to launch numerous successful entrepreneurial ventures. He told me later that had I tried to "manage" him in a Command & Control manner, he wouldn't have stayed the year.

A stewardship agreement can be a powerful tool for overcoming the common barriers to becoming a Trust & Inspire leader. It can provide great clarity and serve as a safe way to overcome fears and "what-if" scenarios. It provides a path for you to become part of the solution, to be a programmer, to balance risk, and to build on the strengths of those around you.

What If People Let You Down?

A stewardship agreement is not a guarantee that things will go the way you planned. What are you going to do when one of you violates the agreement? Because it happens. Change takes time, and it frequently takes more than a few honest attempts.

Consider my experience with my father. I absolutely violated the agreement when I did nothing at first, and the lawn started turning yellow. My father was tempted to go Command & Control on me and take back the responsibility. Do you remember what he had to remind himself of? "Raise kids, not grass." He brought us both back to our agreement and didn't give up on me.

When people let us down, the key is not to attack people but instead to address behavior. We do this well when we come back to the agreement. Agreements govern.

Don't lose sight of the fact that in at least some situations, the relationship you're building may well be worth far more than the task the agreement was intended to accomplish.

> *The real opportunity for success lies within the person and not in the job.*
>
> —ZIG ZIGLAR

Projects come and go, but people contain almost limitless potential. Your job is to develop and unleash their potential.

You might look at the "green and clean" example and think, *That's fine if you're a parent and can focus only on raising kids. I'm a leader, and I have to deliver the "grass"!* You know what? The stewardship agreement wasn't just a better way to raise kids, it was also a better way to raise grass! The lawn *was* green and clean! Even a seven-year-old boy could tell for himself how well he was doing on delivering the result because the leader built a clear agreement with him.

This experience influenced me profoundly. Interestingly, it equally influenced my father. How he saw me—as a person with greatness inside and capable of self-governing, even as a seven-year-old—was validated. Moreover, it shifted his leadership role from one of being a boss who was judging me to one of being a coach who was helping me. This is the profound shift taking place today—*from boss to coach*—and stewardship agreements can help us get there.

> *The role of the manager, in short, is becoming that of a coach.*
>
> —HERMINIA IBARRA, PROFESSOR AND AUTHOR OF *ACT LIKE A LEADER, THINK LIKE A LEADER*

As I noted at the beginning of this chapter, the false dichotomy leaders often face is believing that getting the job done and building the relationship are two separate tasks. They're not. A Trust & Inspire leader embraces stewardship and accomplishes both—by seeing, communicating, developing, and unleashing tremendous individual human potential.

COMMAND & CONTROL	TRUST & INSPIRE
Get the Job Done	Get the Job Done *and* Build the Relationship
Vertical Positioning	Horizontal Partnering
Micromanagement	Self-Governance
Dictate Methods	Establish Helpful Boundaries
"You're on Your Own"	"I Want to Set You Up to Succeed"
"I Hold You Accountable"	"You Hold Yourself Accountable to the Mutually-Established Agreement"
"I Judge You"	"You Judge Yourself"
Artificial and Arbitrary Consequences	Natural and Logical Consequences
Manage/Manager	Coach

CHAPTER 9

What Trust & Inspire Is *Not*

Real power has to do with one's ability to influence the hearts and minds of others.

—THE DALAI LAMA

Have you ever tried to argue the other side of a viewpoint that you didn't believe in?

I was on the debate team in high school, so this used to happen to me quite regularly. My teacher assigned me to argue the opposite side of my case; I rolled my eyes and let out a groan, frustrated that I couldn't argue the side I wanted to. But once I began, I found that exploring the other side gave me new understanding and perspective. In many cases, it made my own stance stronger and more nuanced; sometimes I ended up changing my stance altogether. I know that good attorneys will typically look exhaustively at the other side of their case in order to better understand their own side.

By now, hopefully you're on the side of Trust & Inspire. You get it, you see its importance, and you're ready to try it. Or maybe you're still a little skeptical. As you think about the implications of Trust & Inspire in your own life, you may have identified with one or more barriers. You might be saying, "There's no way this could work at my job—we'd never get anything done" or "There's no way I could do this with my kids—they'd walk all over me." Or you might see Trust & Inspire as antithetical to your environment, especially if it's highly regulated, such as is the case in a school or a hospital or the government.

I hear you. But like my debate teacher, I invite you to explore the other side with me in this chapter. Having just deeply explored what Trust & Inspire is, I'd now like to go into what it is *not*. I think you'll find, just like I did on my debate team, that your understanding and excitement about Trust & Inspire will grow as we dig into what it's not.

Trust & Inspire leadership is *not* weak, soft, cowardly, wishy-washy, mild-mannered, consensus paralysis, feelings-focused, indecisive, without controls, without structure, without vision, without direction, the tail wagging the dog, without accountability, without high performance expectations, or undemanding. As if there were anything left, allow me to elaborate.

1. Trust & Inspire leadership is not weak

Historically, there have been traditional ideas about what is strong and what is weak. A predominant idea has persisted that leaders must exhibit strength, and even a form of dominance, through decisive behavior and strong control. Anything other than this is often seen as weakness.

Even the thought of engaging in a dialogue versus giving directives is viewed by many with skepticism, as it could indicate that the leader doesn't have things well in hand. While there has been a gradual shift around what strength truly means, many still view certain practices as inherently "strong" or "weak." In fact, many leaders are often hesitant to implement certain "soft skills" because they don't want to appear soft. For many, admitting fault, apologizing, listening empathically, asking for help, discussing feelings, delegating responsibility, or relinquishing control in any way diminishes what it traditionally means to be a strong leader.

As a child, I loved the musical *Camelot*. I recently rewatched it and found in it a great depiction of leadership. King Arthur had struggled to wrap his head around the idea of "strong" leadership. He explored the prevailing norms of his time as summed up in the phrase "Might

Is Right"—or in other words, using strength and force to push one's agenda. This was exhibited in the behaviors of lords and knights throughout his country who served him without question and also exerted their own unquestionable will over the people under their rule.

Dissatisfied with this method of leadership, King Arthur transformed this idea and phrase into one of inclusion and progress by saying instead, "Might *for* Right." He introduced the round table, where knights could speak freely, represent different points of view, and work together—something previously unheard of and completely revolutionary. His land went from one of dominance to one of collaboration, where ideas and innovation were allowed to prosper. That, in turn, inspired more and greater collaboration and innovation. While this approach didn't endure because of the prevailing norms at the time, it raised the bar regarding what was possible—it became an ideal, even if only for "one brief, shining moment."

Strength in leadership comes not through force and control but through openness, authenticity, and trust. A Trust & Inspire style of leadership is not soft. It is not weak; the reality is that Trust & Inspire demands enormous strength. It is not sitting around discussing feelings all day and hoping for the best. There are practical steps and results-driven actions—stewardships—that go hand in hand with Trust & Inspire leadership. A Trust & Inspire leader exemplifies all of the qualities of a strong leader, such as decisiveness, confidence, and credibility, and those qualities are actually enhanced through intentional listening and deliberate trusting.

In reality, it takes far more strength for a leader to listen to and implement feedback than to feel challenged by those on the team with new ideas. It takes far more strength to acknowledge and benefit from the strengths of others that may exceed your own.

It takes far more strength for leaders to collaborate with their people than to micromanage them. It takes far more strength for leaders to extend trust than just give orders and manage their execution. I'll put it this way: the success of Command & Control leaders is limited by the boundaries of their own strengths. By contrast, the success of Trust &

Inspire leaders is virtually limitless, as their strengths are magnified by the strengths of a team that is ready and inspired to contribute their best. Wielding this level of compounding creativity, passion, and commitment is not for the weak but rather for the remarkably strong.

> *To share your weakness is to make yourself vulnerable; to make yourself vulnerable is to show your strength.*
>
> —CRISS JAMI, PHILOSOPHER AND POET

2. Trust & Inspire leadership is not a lack of control

Anyone who has held a leadership position understands the need for control. Try leading a large workforce without any control mechanisms, or try teaching a classroom full of sixth graders while having no control over the students—it just doesn't work.

Every organization needs some level of control. Obviously, processes, systems, and structures are critical components for a healthy organization. Compliance with certain organizational controls or standards is an absolute necessity, like safety and ethics, for example. These can help protect organizations and people, streamline work, and lead to effective outcomes. Trust & Inspire leadership is not asking leaders to give up control; rather, it enables leaders to *increase* control by extending trust and enlisting the people leaders serve.

The reality is that there is more control in a strong, principled Trust & Inspire culture than is ever possible in a rules-based, Command & Control culture. When people feel trusted, their engagement and level of self-accountability increases. Research shows that a lack of engagement leads to dramatically higher voluntary turnover rates. When people don't want to stay, the leader has lost control. Even worse is when people quit *and* stay—they remain on the payroll but give only the bare minimum, hampering and sometimes even sabotaging the work to be done.

True control comes from strong, engaged teammates and teams that are mutually committed for the long haul. Can you imagine how much more control and stability your organization would have if you were able to cut employee turnover by 50 percent? Or increase engagement by 20 percent? Or if your people became truly inspired? Can you imagine how much more streamlined and efficient things would be if coworkers, partners, students, and teenagers *held themselves* accountable?

A Trust & Inspire style of leadership helps people tap into a deeper drive to perform rather than to simply be compliant. When people feel engaged, personally committed, and inspired to do their work, and to do it well, the need for external forces of control decreases. For many organizations, the standard of professionalism is for employees to "not break the rules" or "do no harm." I argue that not breaking the rules and doing no harm are the bare minimum of what employees should and will want to do if they are given the chance to become personally invested—inspired—in the work. As educator Karl Maeser once said,

> Place me behind prison walls—walls of stone ever so high, ever so thick, reaching ever so far into the ground—there is a possibility that in some way or another I may escape; but stand me on the floor and draw a chalk line around me and have me give my word of honor never to cross it. Can I get out of the circle? No. Never! I'd die first!

In an effort to control for a desirable outcome, so many well-meaning organizations, managers, parents, and even friends attempt to Command & Control their way to that outcome and end up building taller, deeper, and thicker walls. Rules and controls may help to keep people preoccupied, but they often give only the illusion of accountability. You'll get people's hands and backs, but not their hearts and minds. Rules and controls taken too far (which they often are) may ensure a level of compliance (albeit artificial), but they will also stifle creativity and extinguish the inspiration needed to operate effectively today.

It's human nature to feel resentful of excessive rules, and many will seek (and find) ways around those rules that often carry significant risk. Others will simply leave the situation altogether.

However, when people are inspired and trusted, they don't need to be contained. They will govern themselves because they want to, and they can do so far more effectively than anything or anyone else. They don't want to let down a leader, or their peers, with subpar work or by breaking company policy.

More importantly, they don't want to let themselves down. Their word and reputation mean something. They carry value, and that value puts in place intrinsic controls that external incentives, systems, positions of authority, or organizational hierarchy simply don't have access to or reach of. Again, there's far more control in a Trust & Inspire culture than can ever be sustained in a rules-based Command & Control culture.

How much more could those you serve accomplish if instead of monitoring for compliance you were mentoring for creation?

3. Trust & Inspire leadership is not a lack of structure

At the extreme, some might erroneously assume that a Trust & Inspire leader gets rid of all organizational structure and simply moves to a boss-less holocracy where people do their own thing, flying by the seat of their pants! Let me be clear: by advocating for a style of Trust & Inspire, I am *not* advocating for a lack of structure. The reality is that we need structure. Structure can be helpful when it's aligned to the strategy and to the new realities of both the marketplace and the workplace. Structure can be hurtful when it's misaligned. But it's needed—in some form.

Remember the Five Emerging Forces? The first three forces are 1) the nature of the world has changed, 2) the nature of work has changed, and 3) the nature of the workplace has changed. As a result of these forces, structure may also need to change to maintain alignment and relevance. Technology is enabling many organizations to dramatically shift not only their business models in the marketplace but the way in which they produce and deliver that business in the workplace.

Increasingly—especially in the aftermath of COVID-19—many

people find themselves with more opportunities to work from anywhere, to collaborate with others more frequently and via different modes, and to produce in less traditional office settings. All of this may have an impact on structure, but it doesn't eliminate the need for it. It may just look different, given the changing nature of both work and the workplace. There is not a one-size-fits-all structure.

Structure can look different from industry to industry, from organization to organization, from team to team, and even from family to family. Some organizations operate with a lighter, flatter, more free-flowing structure where there are no walls or no doors, and in some cases no traditional bosses. Others may be more formal or may even embrace a more traditional top-down structure. While there is not a one-size-fits-all structure for Trust & Inspire leaders and organizations, in light of the Five Emerging Forces, we *are* seeing shifts from hierarchical to more of a "hivelike" approach, with fluidity and agility.

Management thinker Gary Hamel writes of what he calls *Humanocracy* replacing the traditional bureaucracy. The premise of "humanocracy" is that organizational design has not kept pace with changes in the environment and in the workplace, and that we need to create and structure organizations today "as amazing as the people inside them."

Does the structure in your organization, on your team, or in your family work for you? Is it helpful? Aligned? If so, keep it; if not, redesign it. If you lead within any structure from a style of Trust & Inspire, you can produce a far different and far greater outcome than almost anything you can accomplish operating out of Command & Control.

Structure and systems are programs, while people are programmers—they're the ones who write the programs. Structure and systems flow from style, and style flows from paradigm. So when we operate out of an inaccurate paradigm based on beliefs of scarcity and control, we not only tend to manage that way, but we also tend to create scarcity and controlling systems and structures from that same paradigm.

Be the designer of your world and not merely a consumer of it.

—JAMES CLEAR, AUTHOR OF *ATOMIC HABITS*

If the structure isn't working, you can always change it to achieve better alignment. But if you or your organization find yourself restructuring again and again (usually in the name of change), let me suggest that the problem might not be the structure! Instead, it may be time to take a closer look at the prevailing style of leadership operating within that structure.

4. Trust & Inspire leadership is not a lack of vision or direction

Some might worry that Trust & Inspire leadership means that everyone gets a say in every decision. That progress can't be made until everyone agrees. That the direction and vision for a company is dictated uniformly by the desires of each and every stakeholder. In fact, some might feel a resistance to the ideas of consensus and collaboration because to them that means letting their vision and goals for their organization get molded by others or get changed frequently based on the whims of the moment or of a person.

This is not the case. While a Trust & Inspire leadership approach is conducive to consensus and collaboration, it is also clear that leaders can and should strive to have a clear and compelling vision. You steer the organization; you don't let the organization steer you. Every employee doesn't need to sign off on every idea. That would be a disaster.

> *If I had asked people what they wanted, they would've said "a faster horse."*
>
> —HENRY FORD

A Trust & Inspire leadership style doesn't mean leaders can't or shouldn't have a strong vision for their team and a decisive strategy to execute. A parent's decision is not made by the children. As leaders, we should have a consistent vision if we hope to inspire those we serve and hope to produce long-term results.

A surgeon entering an operating room knows what the plan is for the procedure and communicates that to the operating team—not the other way around. Yet a good surgeon knows that operating team members who believe in the plan, who can contribute to it in meaningful ways, and where there is psychological safety will have more engagement and better focus throughout the procedure and beyond. When modeled authentically, Trust & Inspire leadership will lead to *more* commitment to the plan. In the end, the enthusiastic support brought out through Trust & Inspire leads to far different outcomes than the spiritless subordination of Command & Control.

Once a vision has been created, it is vital for Trust & Inspire leaders to listen to, and even inspire, people to understand, buy into, and champion that vision. This is where true collaboration comes into play. Leaders can listen to feedback that might help enhance the vision without abandoning it. Leaders can also learn from stakeholders how to make that vision accessible and actionable in an everyday work environment.

Even as an organization might shift over time due to growth, technological advances, or significant change of any kind, its vision and the employee buy-in to that vision can remain constant while improvements to practice, structure, and methodology occur.

It's a matter of understanding which decisions are best made top-down and which are best made bottom-up.

I think of the coffee shop chain Starbucks that has expanded to more than thirty thousand stores worldwide since its founding in 1971. When Howard Schultz became CEO, he brought and created a compelling vision around what became their mission statement, "to inspire and nurture the human spirit—one person, one cup, and one neighborhood at a time." This mission for their company is known, taught, and, more importantly, embraced throughout their stores located all throughout the world—and it is a constant amid a changing world.

This constant does not keep Starbucks from improving the way they do business or from introducing a new Frappuccino flavor now and then—in fact, it provides the necessary agility to do just that, along with many other things on a global scale. The company seeks to learn from employees and customers alike based on the needs of different locations precisely *because* of their universal and strong company vision. Employees feel trusted and also trust their leaders. They are connected to, and therefore inspired by, the company's vision. Trust & Inspire leadership allows leaders to have a clear vision without compromising it while also affording them the opportunity to enhance their vision with the valued ideas and input of their people.

5. Trust & Inspire leadership is not a lack of high expectations and accountability

Have you ever asked someone to do something for you and they didn't come through? If you haven't experienced this, then you've led a truly blessed life, my friend. Most of us know the pain and awkwardness of having to follow up with someone about a task they never completed. Just ask your teenage child to clean their room for the second or third . . . or hundredth time. Holding people accountable can be hard, and some might think that operating with a Trust & Inspire style means you don't have high expectations for others or that you don't hold them accountable.

In reality, it is just the opposite. Low expectations inspire no one, and trust doesn't work without accountability. A Trust & Inspire leader knows that every person has great potential that needs to be unleashed. In order to have integrity to that belief, these leaders instinctively expect great things from their people. It's natural to work with them to drive accountability to those standards.

A Trust & Inspire leader is not afraid to talk straight to others in helping them achieve their highest potential. Some of the most demanding people I've ever worked with were Trust & Inspire leaders. While not blindly demanding perfection, such leaders know their people and teams can produce at high levels—so they expect it. However, instead of micromanaging, they communicate and extend trust to their people based on clear expectations and a mutually agreed-upon process of accountability. They inspire their people and offer support, help, coaching, and resources.

Most importantly, they have the same, if not higher expectations for themselves. Imagine telling your nephew to drive more carefully even though you consistently text while you drive. High expectations begin with each of us.

Trust & Inspire leaders are more loyal to principle over person, and they see times to hold people accountable as opportunities to encourage and foster growth rather than to punish. Bottom line, Trust & Inspire leaders see greatness inside everyone, and they work to unleash it.

> *The greatest danger for most of us lies not in setting our aim too high and falling short; but in setting our aim too low and achieving our work.*
>
> —MICHELANGELO

Is there ever a time *not* to be a Trust & Inspire leader?

You might be wondering if there is a time when Command & Control is the right way to go. I've had people explain a situation to me and then say, "And that's when I felt like I had to go all 'Command & Control.'" Maybe you can think of a time where you've felt like you had no choice. What if your child is about to run into a busy street? Should you slow down, focus on the relationship, and try to find a way to inspire him to come back to the sidewalk? Obviously not.

So, this situation and many others beg the question *Is there ever a time when a Command & Control style is a better approach?* The short answer, simply put, is no.

Let me explain. Anyone who has spent more than a few minutes with a toddler knows that toddlers don't exactly have the best impulse control. Okay, more like *no* impulse control. My now-grown son, Christian, was perhaps the best example of this as a toddler. Like most young children, there was very little space between stimulus and response for him. His temper led to a lot of broken things and some dicey situations—including him driving and crashing our pickup truck into the neighbor's fence at the age of five. There were multiple times when my wife or I had to grab him before he ran out into the road because he refused to listen.

Maybe some of you can relate to this—whether as a parent, a sibling, a babysitter, or just an observer at the park or a restaurant. When a toddler is about to run out into the road or touch a hot stove or knock over a stack of cans in the grocery store aisle, nobody would think about trusting the toddler to change his or her mind. Nobody would think about trying to inspire the toddler away from the road or the stove or the cans. We would instead take action immediately, decisively, to protect the child from injury. The reality is, we would appear pretty Command & Control in that moment. So does this mean that Trust & Inspire doesn't apply?

No. I would say that being a Trust & Inspire parent, grandparent, or guardian is more important in that moment than in almost any other. Because being a Trust & Inspire leader means that you are *always* a Trust & Inspire leader. That doesn't mean that you never command someone or act with authority or even dole out discipline. A Trust & Inspire leader can do all of those things, and in the case of a toddler running into a road, such a leader absolutely should. But when a moment like that comes, Trust & Inspire leaders have already built credibility and relationships that allow them to act decisively as needed, yet with integrity.

The difference between a Command & Control leader and a Trust & Inspire leader, even if their actions are exactly the same, is that their behavior is interpreted completely differently, because it comes from a different place. To act decisively, or be firm, or be authoritative, or show "tough love" or discipline from an established Trust & Inspire style is completely different from attempting the same things when you're perceived as Command & Control. Your mindset and intent make all the difference, and your track record tells people loud and clear how to interpret your behavior.

A Trust & Inspire leader can see the greatness and potential in everyone—even a toddler in the midst of his terrible twos. With my own son Christian, there were a few years where it was difficult *not* to be in a state of perpetual Command & Control with him, simply because of how much attention he required. My wife, Jeri, and I had to make a conscious choice to view our son with a Trust & Inspire mindset—even if we did have to be more authoritative with him at times to keep him safe or help him learn. Most parents are sure that they may be doing something for their child's own good, and it means so much more if the child believes it, too. That's equally true for leaders of adults.

But too often our style gets in the way of our intent.

As parents, Jeri and I, although imperfect, always tried to approach Christian and our relationship with him through the lens of Trust & Inspire. If you don't work to make Trust & Inspire *your* style, whatever your current style or approach is will almost certainly get in the way of your intent. Our method helped us focus more explicitly on our intent—what were we trying to achieve in each interaction with him? Were we trying to control and punish him? Or were we trying to teach him and help him reach his potential? What did he believe our intent was?

Sometimes that process of teaching him was best done by setting up rules and consequences that showed our intent to help him rather than to control him—to parent for his growth, not for compliance. It also meant not blindly extending trust in situations where he wasn't ready for it. Because of this, Christian came to know that he could trust his mother and me—and to genuinely believe that we had his best interests at heart, even if we had to be strict at times. He knew that we trusted him as well—that we knew he was more, and would be more, than the moment he was in.

I'm happy to say that Christian outgrew his childhood temper and has become one of the most gentle, kind, and caring people I know. I used to beg him to show a little more fierceness during his high school basketball games—a far cry from the intense games he used to play with his brother during his high-temper days. He is also a diligent and competent person with a tremendous amount of discipline and self-control.

When I look back at our relationship, I think of how differently things could have gone had I approached him with a Command & Control mindset. Christian always had this kindness and self-control inside him—he was just a bit of a late bloomer and needed time to grow into it. Imagine how those good qualities of his might have been stomped out had my wife and I tried to Command & Control him during those formative years. The obedience and compliance we could have forced out of him would have left him entirely unprepared to make his own important choices as an autonomous, contributing adult, much less achieve the enormous potential that was inside him all along.

How much differently do you think a child regards the moment where you grab them from out of the road if you have a relationship built on Command & Control versus one built on Trust & Inspire? A child whose parent has a Command & Control mindset might see that moment as just one in a hundred examples of a time where Dad hurt their arm or yelled at them. This usually is confirmed by how the Command & Control parent responds to the child once the danger has passed. The style manifests so plainly in whether the parent's words convey love and concern for the child or frustration and inconvenience for the parent. A child whose parent has a Trust & Inspire mindset might see the moment as proof of that parent's love—a time when that parent saved the child's life.

The paradigm with which you approach your relationships—whether at work or at home—will define the long- and short-term outcomes of the high-stress and high-pressure moments you encounter before you've even encountered them.

Employees who trust their boss and are inspired by their boss will be more willing to forgive a misunderstood situation or to trust the feedback from a performance review.

So I reiterate, with an emphatic *no*, there is never a time *not* to be a Trust & Inspire leader. There is too much resting on tomorrow to sacrifice for Command & Control today. There will be times when you have to act with authority. You can be authoritative without being authoritarian. There will be times when you can't extend trust, and there will be times when you have to correct someone's behavior. But there is never a time not to see each person you interact with as someone with potential not just to stop behaving in a certain way, but to become great in spite of that behavior.

When we believe in the unseen potential within each person, we're inspired to treat people according to their potential rather than their behavior.

A Way of Being

Being a Trust & Inspire leader is a lens for life and a way of being—not merely a tool that you use when convenient or beneficial. And as I've explained, it doesn't mean you can't be a strong leader with vision, structure, expectations, and accountability. On the contrary. It means that each of those things is informed by your fundamental belief in people and your paradigm of leadership.

For instance, when you see leadership as stewardship, the strength of your vision, structure, expectations, and accountability are enthusiastically enabled and reciprocated by the people you lead. Both you and they feel that they can and should be both trusted and inspired. Both you and they feel that they can create meaningful contributions and find a sense of purpose. And together, both you and they can produce something far greater than you could ever do on your own.

As you think through your own life, where do you see room for improvement?

Time to Change!

Now that we more clearly see why Trust & Inspire is the only truly effective and relevant approach to leadership for our time, the next step is to *become* a Trust & Inspire person in order to adopt a Trust & Inspire style. Change can be daunting, but I'm here to tell you it is possible, it will be worth it, and it happens all the time. The world is changing all around us, whether we like it or not, and we can seize the opportunity to change with it.

By becoming a Trust & Inspire leader, your outcomes and those of the people around you will be better than ever before. As you lead in this new way, you will see far greater results in every area of your life—in your home, in your work, in your community.

You can become a Trust & Inspire leader. You can influence and change the culture of the situations around you as you yourself change. And what a glorious transition and transformation it will be. I'm confident that you can do this!

COMMAND & CONTROL	TRUST & INSPIRE
Might is Right	Might for Right
Hierarchy	Hive
Bureaucracy	Humanocracy
Goals and Plans	Vision and Strategy
Force	Persuade

PART THREE

Overcoming the 5 Common Barriers to Becoming a Trust & Inspire Leader

Every year, I go on a short weekend trip with some of my old friends. This is a tradition we've been doing for years, and it means a lot that we've been able to stay close. Each year, someone different is in charge of organizing the trip. One year, my friend decided that we should rent Harley-Davidson motorcycles and drive around Northern California.

Here's the thing you should know about me: I had just gotten my motorcycle license the day before this trip, and I had no prior experience in riding. In fact, I had to borrow my neighbor's scooter to pass my license road test.

As my friends and I practiced in the parking lot on the big Harley-Davidson motorcycles, I thought to myself, *This isn't so bad*. But minutes later, as we pulled onto the freeway, the wind started to gust while the cars were zipping around me at seventy to eighty miles per hour. I struggled to keep the bike steady. My panic rose. *What am I doing?* I thought to myself. *I have no idea how to do this!*

Maybe when you think of Trust & Inspire, you feel like I did as I got on the freeway—completely out of your element, concerned that forces outside your control might prevent you from enjoying the ride.

It's understandable to be apprehensive about a new approach, especially when you've spent most of your life operating in a different way. Many of us relate to this feeling of uncertainty when it comes to shifting our style of leadership. As I did on the bike, we realize, "I haven't been trained in Trust & Inspire." "I haven't been mentored in this." "I don't know how to do this!" Maybe you've seen someone else try it without success. Or maybe you yourself have already tried it and it didn't work, so you reverted to your old style.

This part of the book will explore the roadblocks that are getting in the way of you succeeding with a Trust & Inspire style. As I mentioned at the outset of this book, the overarching barrier in becoming a Trust & Inspire leader is that we think we already are one! As a result, the problem is always "out there"—in other words, the problem is everyone else. While that mindset is the generic, universal roadblock, there are five very particular and specific barriers that keep us from becoming Trust & Inspire leaders.

These 5 common barriers are the mindsets, thoughts, and attitudes that many of us have experienced at some point on our leadership journey. Collectively, they comprise nearly all of the reasons why people struggle to change and why they remain trapped in their old style. Too often we let these barriers get in the way of the beliefs of a Trust & Inspire leader. When these barriers are at the forefront of our minds, we begin to question the greatness in people or to question our ability to unleash that greatness.

Some of these barriers might really resonate with your own experience, while others may be something you've seen in or experienced with other people. I will give the headline names of these barriers below (I think you'll "get" them instantly), and then we'll dive into each of the barriers and explore solutions for each.

Barrier # 1: "This Won't Work Here"

Barrier # 2: Fear—or "But What If ..."

> "... I Lose Control?"

> "... It Doesn't Work?"

> "... I've Been Burned Before?"

> "... I Don't Get the Credit?"

> "... I'm Not As Confident As You Think I Am?"

Barrier # 3: "I Don't Know How to Let Go"

Barrier # 4: "I'm the Smartest One in the Room"

Barrier # 5: "This Is Who I Am"

All of these barriers work against our desire to change—and all of them are valid. They all acknowledge real, inherent risk. However, we don't need to use them as excuses for not changing. Risk and return go hand in hand, and the research overwhelmingly shows that the return on being a Trust & Inspire leader is infinitely better than on being a Command & Control leader. That return is measured not only in dramatically increased performance but also in remarkably higher energy and joy—greater well-being.

I've seen people, families, and organizations literally transform as leaders have let go of Command & Control and embraced Trust & Inspire. I've also seen them struggle, not knowing why, as they blindly cling to Command & Control. The irony is, they end up with neither command nor control.

We can't solve a problem that we don't understand. Once we identify and understand some of the thoughts or attitudes that get in the way of making this change, we can focus on overcoming them so we can become Trust & Inspire leaders.

Over the next five chapters, we will go into each of these barriers in depth. For each, I will start by providing a paradigm-level solution—

offering you a *mindset* that can help you think about how to approach this barrier. I will then provide practical things you can learn and do— a *skill set*—that will help you develop the competencies needed to address and overcome these barriers. Finally, in many instances, we can use the "stewardship agreement" process we discussed earlier—a *tool set*—to overcome each of these barriers.

Simply stated, the right mindset, skill set, and tool set are needed to overcome the 5 common barriers in order to become a Trust & Inspire leader.

Whatever barriers may apply to your situation, take heart in knowing that you can overcome them and become the Trust & Inspire person and leader you want to be.

CHAPTER 10

Barrier #1: "This Won't Work Here"

Start where you are. Use what you have. Do what you can.
—ARTHUR ASHE, TENNIS CHAMPION

"This all sounds really great, but it could never work *here*. You don't know my boss." "You don't know my company." "You don't know my industry; we're highly regulated and controlled." "The focus on quarterly earnings . . . or patient satisfaction scores . . . or test scores is everything." "I don't have the time." "I wouldn't have buy-in from my colleagues." "You don't know my family." "I'd be doing this all on my own."

These are often very real concerns for many. As we get started, I invite you to list several reasons why a Trust & Inspire style *won't work* in your particular circumstance:

_____

_____

_____

_____

_____

Looking at your list, underline the items that are in your circle of concern—things you can't do anything about, such as the economy or the weather.

Now circle the items that could be in your circle of influence—things you might be able to influence or impact, even if only a little.

There is no question that there are very real circumstances and limiting factors for every scenario. There are some industries and organizations where a Trust & Inspire style of leadership will fit more easily than in others. But there is no industry, no organization, no team, no family, no relationship that will not benefit enormously from a Trust & Inspire approach.

Furthermore, no matter your position in whatever situation you find yourself, you can lead by going first. I recognize that you can't manage your boss. But you can *lead* your boss. You can be the catalyst for change. With the way our world is changing, waiting on others to start a change is simply not an option. Start where you are—whether that be with your team, your colleagues, your organization, your partner, your family, your friends, or even just yourself—working from the inside out to become a Trust & Inspire Leader.

I'm Okay—but *You've* Got Problems!

Several years ago, I was working with a leader who loved the Trust & Inspire material and training I presented to him. He wanted to implement it in his company. He said, in effect, "This is great material and a great approach—we need this at our company. The problem is that my boss will get in the way of this; he won't understand it. Until my boss gets on board, this is not going to happen."

We did the logical thing and went to his boss to present the approach. We were surprised when the boss liked the approach. Then the boss said, "This is great. I can see that we need this here. But we need to get the executive vice president on board. It won't work unless she supports it."

So, we went to the executive vice president. She said the same thing: "Wow, this is great material, and a great process! We need it badly here. But nothing here gets done without the buy-in of the CEO. We need to talk to him."

So, we went to the CEO. Can you guess his response? He told us, "This is great stuff—it could really help our company and our culture. But I'm powerless on this; the board controls everything. Nothing happens without the board! And the board is completely Command & Control, so there's no way this will work."

We didn't have a chance to go to the board, but if we had, I'm pretty sure the board members would have told us, "This is great material . . . but the problem is Wall Street!"

The data irrefutably shows that the common, underlying mindset is "I'm doing great; the problem is everyone else. It's not me—the problem is 'out there'!"

> *If you think the problem is out there, that very thought*
> *is the problem.*
>
> —DR. STEPHEN R. COVEY

When I run a cultural assessment with teams and organizations, people consistently rank themselves high on their own credibility and behavior while they simultaneously mark the rest of their colleagues low on the same traits. This is true almost without exception. Similarly, there is a gap regarding inspiration. People rank it as the most valued characteristic of leaders and also among the most underdelivered by those leaders.

In other words, everyone thinks everyone else is the problem.

This incongruence leads to a lot of misunderstandings and even more unmet expectations. Above all, it leads to people not holding *themselves* accountable first because they're too busy trying to hold *everyone else* accountable. Everyone is looking to pass the buck because in their minds, they're not the problem. They didn't cause the problem, so they don't need to fix it. In their minds, there's nothing they can do about it. They live with a victim mentality. To be clear, you embrace victimhood when you insist on the equivalent of "this won't work here" or accept the status quo of your current situation as unchangeable.

We often feel like nothing can be done when we see the misalignment between strategies, structures, and systems. Indeed, in a rapidly changing world, almost all organizations struggle with alignment; systems and structures often pit employees against each other as different groups have competing priorities. Infighting within cultures is often systemic as people compete for scarce resources. Such misalignment can feel impossible to overcome. And those systems and structures operate independent of people; in fact, they are bigger than the people in an organization and not beholden to whims.

Does that mean you have no ability to create change? No.

As we discussed earlier, systems and structures are programs; people are the programmers. At the end of the day, systems and structures are really the arms and legs of style. And style flows from paradigm— from our fundamental beliefs. If we embrace or even change our beliefs about people and leadership to those of Trust & Inspire, and if we help those around us to do the same, our style, our actions, and eventually our systems and structures can change, too. When the paradigms of the leaders change, the leaders write different programs.

It can be easy to get overwhelmed when looking at the big picture; it's easy to feel, "There's nothing I can do about it." But don't sacrifice who you want to be as a leader on the altar of a Command & Control culture. There is always one part of the picture, no matter how small, where we can start.

All of us have the power to create change in at least some areas of our life and work. We can make a difference and impact our environments for good, whether we are a CEO or an intern. Whether we are a stay-at-home parent or a retiree. Obviously, there might be some things that we really can't change. If our organization has specific compliance or legal rules imposed externally, we might not be able to do anything about those. However, we can change the way we communicate about those rules. We can change our attitude toward them. And we can *influence* systems, even if we aren't in a position to directly change them.

Above all, we can change our mindset to recognize that we can be part of the solution—regardless of whether we created the problems. And when we do so, we will be surprised how positively it affects the people around us.

Solution: A Trust & Inspire leader first models, then mentors.
Mindset: I become the solution and help others become their best selves.

The solution to believing that "this won't work here" is to first model, then mentor, creating a ripple effect.

You can model a Trust & Inspire way of leading regardless of how anyone else acts. Rather than thinking the problem is *out there*, which renders you helpless to change it, *you* become the solution to the problem. You, within your circle of influence, become an island of excellence in a sea of mediocrity. An island of trust in a sea of micromanagement. An island of inspiration in a sea of indifference. You lead the way. You look in the mirror and ask yourself how you can change. You model the behavior for those around you.

You change the culture by changing yourself. And then by changing your team. And then by influencing the other teams with which your team interacts. If you can do this (and you can), then another person can, too. And then another, and another. People will see you. Your performance and track record will speak for themselves. You will have built enduring influence from the inside out.

Then you move from being a model to becoming a mentor. As we discussed in the stewardship on modeling, a model is someone who shows what is expected by leading the way themselves. A mentor is a model with a trusted relationship, one who works for the success and progress of another. When people see a model, they want to emulate that person. When people see a mentor, they get personal help on how to do it. A model focuses on developing self; a mentor focuses on developing others. This is an inside-out process.

> *I think mentors are important and I don't think anybody makes it in the world without some form of mentorship. Nobody makes it alone. Nobody has made it alone. And we are all mentors to people even when we don't know it.*

> —OPRAH WINFREY

One of our great client success stories came when we were working with an upper-midlevel leader named Janita at a very large company. Janita worked in a hard-driving, results-oriented, Command & Control culture. The environment was far from Trust & Inspire. We worked with Janita to develop a better way to lead her team. She was convinced it was a better way to operate than the Enlightened Command & Control style in which her company was currently entrenched.

Janita decided that rather than trying to get approval from her superiors, she would first start implementing a Trust & Inspire approach with herself and her team. As she did, she began to have great success. People saw what she and her team were doing and noticed the success she was having, and they started asking her, "How did you do this? How did you get these results?" She responded by sharing her approach and mentoring others on how to do the same. As she did, her influence began to ripple through the company.

Eventually the ripple effect of Janita's modeling and mentoring made its way to the CEO. He was inspired by her. She had modeled a style of leadership and produced results that he wanted to see on a larger scale. He held up Janita's team as a model for the whole company, and she was put front and center as a mentor. Her influence ultimately helped the CEO transform the entire organization, but it all started with just one person—Janita—working from the inside out.

What makes this story all the more remarkable was that in the middle of working to change the culture, the company hit serious economic turmoil—so Janita's efforts weren't changing direction in calm seas but rather in a perfect storm. Janita also wasn't an executive-level officer or decision maker, yet she was able not only to elevate herself and her team as leaders, but she was ultimately able to elevate the entire company. As a result of this, she was promoted. Her decision to go first—to take responsibility for her team and their culture— eventually led to a company-wide culture shift, and the company produced better results coming out of the storm than they had in the prior decade.

Many will look at this example and say, "Wow, that would be so great if we had a CEO like hers who was willing to implement that style!" But that wasn't how it happened at all. Janita was the one who took the initiative. She didn't know how her CEO would react. But she didn't let competing priorities or misaligned systems hold her back from starting where she could. She didn't ask permission. She simply began within her circle of influence, modeling and mentoring those around her.

A proactive leader will look at this, as Janita did, and say, "What can I do? Where can I start?" She didn't wait for the perfect CEO or situation to start making changes. She simply began. And her work— her ability to model the change she wanted to see—inspired everyone around her and put her in a position to mentor. Others wanted to be like her, and she helped them make that change.

Don't underestimate your ability to influence others—your family, your team, and even an entire organization. I know that every situation is different, and the circumstances will never be perfect. The point is that you can do *something*. This is an action item. Remember, start with yourself and focus on being a model. Then move out to your relationships as you aspire to become a mentor. Rather than thinking, *This can't work here*, instead choose to think, *How can this work here?* Then get to work! Start now.

Start now. Start where you are. Start with fear. Start with pain. Start with doubt. Start with your hands shaking. Just start.

—MEL ROBBINS, AUTHOR OF *THE 5 SECOND RULE*

COMMAND & CONTROL	TRUST & INSPIRE
Start with Others	Start with Self
Work *in* the Systems	Work *on* the Systems
"This Can't Work Here"	"How Can This Work Here?"

CHAPTER 11

Barrier #2: Fear—or "But What If . . ."

Ultimately, we know very deeply that the other side of every fear is a freedom.

—MARILYN FERGUSON, AUTHOR

Anytime we are about to make a difficult decision or try something new, we instinctively consider the risk. We ask ourselves a whole host of questions that begin with "But what if . . ." That phrase is then followed by any number of potential concerns with varying degrees of likelihood based on past experience, fears, and worst-case scenarios. This chapter presents five different scenarios, but all of them revolve around the same concept—fear.

Everyone has fears. Some fears protect us from very real threats, while others irrationally paralyze us. I'll explore what I've identified as the most common fears that get in the way of transitioning from Command & Control to Trust & Inspire. We'll take on each fear in turn and offer a solution that will help you shift both the mindset and the skill set.

- **"But What If I Lose Control?"**
I'll never forget the time I was invited to speak at a management conference for a large bank. I had actually been invited by the company's

executive leadership team as part of their effort to reach their CEO—unbeknownst to him—and help him change his leadership style. He was the ultimate Command & Control leader. True to form, the CEO even took over the event from his planning team. He decided to organize it around *his* four principles of leadership—two of which happened to be "command" and "control"!

You can imagine how awkward I felt when the speaker before me, a retired military general and a good friend of the CEO, expounded the virtues of both commanding and controlling your people in order to get better results. Needless to say, the team's plea to the CEO for a new style of leadership wasn't quite landing. Despite feeling awkward, I moved forward with my presentation because of my confidence in the idea and in the principles of leading people. I shared nearly the exact opposite of everything that had been said before me, but I reframed it in the language of the CEO, who wanted more rules in order to have better control.

My position was this: there is actually *more* control in a Trust & Inspire culture than in a rules-based culture. You can never come up with enough rules for people you don't or can't trust. Rules can never exert more control over a person's action than what a person can do when inspired. If you really want to increase control, then extend trust in a smart way, allow people to exercise good judgment, and let them "manage" themselves.

Like this bank CEO, many of us have been taught that leadership is all about being in control. Many people can't let go, and most don't want to. They want to be hands-on leaders. They want to know what's going on everywhere, at all times, at all levels. They want to see compliance with their decisions and directions. Pushed to the extreme, this quickly becomes the clearly labeled, always decried "micromanagement."

All of us have probably spent time around someone like this. In fact, a survey showed that 79 percent of us have experienced being micromanaged. Moreover, I hardly know any, well meaning or otherwise, who haven't done it themselves to some degree or another. It's exhausting for everyone involved.

The great irony is that we're never truly in control anyway. Principles are in control. Violating principles is like trying to violate gravity. When an airplane takes flight, it isn't defying gravity. It is simply aligned with the principles that govern flight: lift, thrust, drag, and weight. Principles rule our world, and no matter how hard we might try, we can only ever *create the illusion* of control. The more we align ourselves to principles, the more predictable outcomes become.

Adherence to or rejection of principles governs our results. While our behavior is based on our values, the consequences of that behavior are based on principles.

For example, if we don't trust people, they remain uninspired and uncommitted—perhaps complying to avoid punishment or to gain a reward, but never fully investing. All the while, they reciprocate that distrust right back at us. On the other hand, if we trust people, they tend to trust us back, want to perform, and rise to the occasion. When we trust people, they become more committed and engaged. In turn, it becomes easier to trust them. This creates a virtuous upward cycle of trust and confidence that inspires and actually creates greater trust and confidence. Trust is contagious. This is why I emphasize again that there is more control in a Trust & Inspire culture than a Command & Control, rules-based culture.

The retailer Nordstrom has created a high-trust culture that at the same time is characterized by strong control. But it's a different type of control. Over the years, they have created a great reputation with their customers for outstanding customer service. They trust their customers. But that trust extended to their customers is simply an extension of the trust they first give to their own people.

The Nordstrom employee handbook, for example, is short and simple; it might not even be considered a handbook. It's a single card that states, "Welcome to Nordstrom; we're glad to have you with our company . . . We have only one rule: Use good judgment in all situations. There will be no additional rules."

Through this one rule, Nordstrom has extended trust to their employees. This rule speaks volumes, telling their people that they are trusted and respected. It also tells them that they have, and are to use, good judgment. People want to live up to that kind of trust. They're inspired by it. They want to behave so as not to lose the trust. People simultaneously help each other out and hold each other accountable to this trust that's been given. As a large, publicly traded company, Nordstrom still has other policies, along with expected legal and ethical compliance standards. But this one-rule approach of "use good judgment in all situations" powerfully influences their strong culture—including how they recruit, hire, train, coach, mentor, and lead.

Nordstrom's method features control—a built-in self-control. Because people wouldn't think of breaking them, excessive rules become unnecessary and irrelevant. Micromanagement stifles while trust inspires.

Solution: A Trust & Inspire leader extends "smart trust."
Mindset: I start with a high propensity to trust.

The best way to overcome the fear of losing control is to extend smart trust. Notice that I said *smart* trust. Not every situation is the same nor does every situation carry the same risk, so you cannot blindly extend trust in every situation. If you do that, you're going to get burned, and you will galvanize the fear of losing control. You must take the time to assess the situation, the risk, and the credibility of the people involved. There will be times when extending trust is not smart and therefore shouldn't be done, either because the risk is too high or the credibility of the people too low—or a combination of both.

But I've found that when you've hired good people, most people can be trusted. I've also found that in most situations, not extending trust to others actually carries greater risk than extending it. People respond to being trusted, and they respond just as strongly, and often more strongly, to being distrusted.

Extending trust is not a "one-size-fits-all" approach; rather, it's a "use-your-good-judgment" approach. Build it into your culture. Recruit and hire people who want to be trusted. When you mentor people, help them learn how to exercise good judgment. Make it a staple for the way your team operates. By doing so, you can spend your time leading instead of monitoring for compliance to excessive rules. Good judgment supersedes granulated rules, and it allows trust and inspiration to thrive.

A. G. Lafley, the former longtime CEO of Procter & Gamble, described this approach as follows:

> No single set of rules can provide explicit guidance for every situation that might be faced . . . So ultimately P&G relies on every employee to use good judgment in everything he or she does.

If you really want to keep control as a leader, you can't do it with rules. You *can* do it by extending smart trust.

> *The right people will feel far more pressure to perform well when they are trusted.*
>
> —HECTOR RUIZ, CEO OF ADVANCED
> NANOTECHNOLOGY SOLUTIONS

- **"But What If It Doesn't Work?"**

Leaders are responsible for outcomes. The thought of trying a new way of leading when it could jeopardize the perceived certainty of the usual outcome can be frightening. It might fail. It might not work. There is a risk.

However, the game has changed. If you haven't already, you'll soon find there's a far greater risk in assuming you can continue to get the "usual outcomes" with the usual approach. Operating in today's world with yesterday's Command & Control style of leadership is a risk few of us can afford to take.

Solution: A Trust & Inspire leader balances risk and return.
Mindset: I believe the potential return can outweigh the risk.

Amazon founder Jeff Bezos once said, "Failure and invention are inseparable twins." Moreover, in a letter to shareholders, Bezos also noted, "If you're good at course correcting, being wrong may be less expensive than you think, whereas being slow is going to be expensive for sure."

This has become the new paradigm for innovation in the technology sector: *fail fast, learn faster*.

The reality is that risk and return go together. Whenever you try something new, there is a chance that it might fail. But there is also a chance that it might succeed! There are situations where the risk might outweigh the return. Assess the job to be done and then ask questions such as What are the risks involved? How likely and serious are those risks? Are your people ready and equipped to take this on? Do you believe they will respond to your belief in them and rise to the occasion? What might the potential return look like? What will this do for the culture? Is it worth it?

As always, try to balance risk and return. In doing so, I find that most focus on trying to minimize the risk and less on maximizing the return. Rather than thinking about what might go wrong, imagine all that might go right when you have an empowered, engaged, even inspired team.

When I worked with a provincial civil service government agency of a foreign country, they wanted to build a Trust & Inspire culture as a means of serving both their constituents and their own employees better. This client said that most agencies seemed to focus almost exclusively on minimizing risks—to make sure nothing could go wrong so they couldn't get blamed for a mishap.

But this particular agency took the exact opposite approach. They asked the provocative questions "Yes, we want to be aware of risk, but how can we maximize all that could go right? How do we maximize the possibilities?"

They were still mindful of risk, and they managed it appropriately, but that didn't define them. What *did* define them was their focus on maximizing all that could go right.

The emphasis at Netflix from the beginning has been based on trust—trust for their customers and trust for their employees. During their early years as a company, they courageously took a risk and disrupted themselves. They created two separate companies, one for their traditional model of delivering movies through the mail, and the other for their new streaming service.

Creating two separate companies wasn't necessarily a bad decision. But they made a pretty significant blunder when they required customers to subscribe to both services separately. Customers hated it. They felt taken advantage of, and they lost trust in the company.

Netflix paid a price for their mistake. But they quickly course-corrected. They came back and said, in effect, "We hear you. You're right, and we trust you." They went back to the model of one company that offered both services. Look at their success today.

Netflix calls their trust with their people "freedom and responsibility." It's an illustration of both smart trust and of the principles of risk and return. Their leadership team communicates this idea to their employees in a statement on company culture that says,

> Our goal is to inspire people more than manage them. We trust our teams to do what they think is best for Netflix—giving them lots of freedom, power and information in support of their decisions. In turn this generates a sense of responsibility and self-discipline that drives us to great work that benefits the company . . . You might think such freedom would lead to chaos. But we also don't have a clothing policy, yet no one has come to work naked. The lesson is, you don't need policies for everything. Most people understand the benefits of wearing clothes to work.

In other words, the return is far greater than the risk that's taken. The output is exceptional. They continue, "On rare occasions that freedom is abused . . . But those are the exceptions, and we avoid over-correcting. Just because a few people abuse freedom doesn't mean that our employees are not worthy of great trust."

Their style is Trust & Inspire. Yes, there's a risk, but the return is extraordinary—far greater than what a traditional organization might elicit. It leads to the kind of performance that people just don't give in response to Command & Control.

Those principles don't apply just at Netflix. Remember the study showing that high-trust organizations are eleven times more innovative than low-trust organizations. There's no question that some of these leaders along the way asked the same question: "What if this doesn't work?" If you truly believe there is greatness in people, leaving that potential on the table represents an unacceptable risk.

The ultimate freedom for creative groups is the freedom to experiment with new ideas. Some skeptics insist that innovation is expensive. In the long run, innovation is cheap. Mediocrity is expensive—and autonomy can be the antidote.
—TOM KELLEY, PARTNER OF IDEO DESIGN FIRM AND AUTHOR OF *CREATIVE CONFIDENCE*

A small business client of ours who runs a chain of retail jewelry stores knows how to balance risk and return. He started with a high propensity to trust, telling his employees, "I know you'll make some mistakes along the way in exercising your judgment, but I want you to know something: I forgive you in advance." He also extended large amounts of trust to his customers by offering lifetime warranties. No matter what the problem, whether something broke or even if it simply got lost, a customer could get a full refund. Because he trusted them.

Even though he's taking risks by operating this way, the rewards have been worth it. He has a 97 percent customer satisfaction rating and an employee turnover rate that is one-tenth the industry average. He also has an inventory shrinkage rate that is one-hundredth the industry average. He has inspired his people and customers through the way he treats them.

- **"But What If I've Been Burned Before?"**

Of all the barriers we discuss, this might be the most poignant. It is heartbreaking to see the pain in people's eyes as they approach me and ask how they can ever trust again after experiencing great betrayal. The reality is that all of us at some time have probably felt the sting of broken promises and broken trust, even sometimes in the form of great betrayal. It is natural to feel wary about extending trust again once we've been burned.

The truth is that some people can't be trusted. Those who engage in a pattern of repeat offenses dig the grave of their own credibility. It is right—and in fact sometimes necessary—to withhold trust, or at least a degree of trust, from certain people. Especially from those who cause harm or who show no remorse or desire to change. Those who have been burned before often double down on a Command & Control style as an instinctive defense mechanism without ever really considering the cost. Again, let's stipulate: it is always smart to exercise judgment when it comes to trusting and to not extend trust to the untrustworthy. However, as the expression goes, a few bad apples don't spoil the whole bunch. In my experience, most—though not all—people can and want to be trusted.

One of my colleagues shared an experience he'd had in leading a two-day Speed of Trust program for a group of nurse managers, administrators, and teams that work with military veterans:

> The first morning, I asked everyone what they hoped to take away at the end of the program. "Clint," who works with the homeless vets, said, "I'd like to learn how to trust again." When I asked him to say more, he replied, "After what happened in Afghanistan, it's hard for me to trust anybody." He then told us his story.
>
> After a twenty-two-year military career, two deployments to Iraq, and two to Afghanistan, he was sent on a final tour in Afghanistan, where he led a unit that was training the Afghan army to take over security when the U.S. troops left. Clint and

his team worked side by side with the Afghans for weeks, train-ing, eating, sleeping, and fighting together. Then one day, the Afghan soldiers turned their weapons on their American train-ers. Clint was severely wounded in the firefight. "That's why I can't trust anybody," he concluded. "It can get you killed." I could tell from his sharing that his trust issues were deeply af-fecting his relationships at home, especially with his son.

Sobered, I told Clint that I couldn't begin to understand what he'd gone through, but I asked him to stay open with the hope that over the next two days he might find tools and language that might help. He agreed, but I wondered how far this class could move someone with his experience of betrayal.

At the close of day two, Clint had committed to take the lead in building trust with his son. He was willing to try again.

Several months later, I ran into Clint again, and the change in the man was phenomenal. He'd just returned from a camp-ing trip with his son where the two of them had enjoyed a great time together. Clint looked like a different person altogether. He'd changed from gruff, ominous, and intimidating to warm, open, and approachable, and it was clear he'd built a great re-lationship of trust with his son—and likely with others as well.

Clint's experience was incredibly personal, and I've had others share similar experiences of being betrayed by a spouse, a family member, a close friend, or a business partner. It's excruciatingly hard to overcome such painful and often debilitating experiences. They can script us for a lifetime—but they don't have to. Sometimes the relationship can be salvaged and sometimes it can't. But the fact that we can't trust some doesn't mean that we can't trust others.

> **Solution:** A Trust & Inspire leader doesn't let the one tell them about the many.
> **Mindset:** I believe most people can and want to be trusted.

After one of my speeches, a person approached me and told me about his experience with being burned. While he was the head of internal audit for a major company, one of the company's senior executives committed a very serious fraudulent offense. The audit leader had the job of digging into all the details, identifying every way the senior executive had twisted and cheated his way to personal gain.

While the audit leader was in the process of this audit, the company's CEO approached him to discuss the case. As the audit leader vented his serious disappointment about this executive's behavior to the CEO, he was surprised when the CEO interrupted him. "After all that you've seen, do you think it will be possible for you to be able to trust again?"

The audit leader thought for a few moments before replying, "Honestly, I don't know. I don't know if I can trust people like I did before."

The CEO said, "Well, that is a problem, because if you can't trust, you can't lead."

This resonated with the audit leader. He wrestled with it for months but concluded that the CEO was right. Without trust, there could be no real collaboration, no real partnership, no real leadership. "That's why I had to approach you!" the audit leader said to me. "Because I can vouch for what you said about trusting. Even though I witnessed wrongdoing, I couldn't let it tell me what others would do. That would be no way to lead. I learned that being able to trust is vital to being able to lead."

Don't let the one tell you about the many. Don't let the 5 percent you can't trust tell you about the 95 percent you can. Just because one person betrays your confidence doesn't mean others will.

That doesn't mean you should trust everyone blindly—we've already discussed the importance of smart trust and good judgment. But extend trust to those who have given you reason to trust them. The audit leader I spoke to at the conference used the inappropriate behaviors of the senior executive to reinforce to his people the need for trustworthiness rather than to punish them for something they didn't do.

How many of us remember being in a classroom where the teacher punished the entire class for the actions of one? It's as frustrating and illogical now as it was then. One person's actions might mean you can't trust that person. One person's actions don't mean you can't trust others.

This doesn't mean that it's easy to extend trust after being burned. It's not. But it is possible. And with the right safeguards in place, using good judgment as you extend trust to those who deserve it will yield great benefits.

• "But What If I Don't Get the Credit?"

People naturally want to be recognized for the work they do. Everyone wants others to know they put in time and effort to make something successful. This isn't just about ego or wanting to look great in front of others. There's a level of security and confidence that comes from knowing that your efforts and contributions were not only valuable but needed. If your efforts and contributions don't seem to be making a difference or adding value, then your efforts could feel irrelevant.

The problem with our desire for receiving deserved credit is that it can lead to a scarcity mindset. Since a scarcity mindset sees the world as a finite pie, whenever someone else gets a piece of that pie, there's less for us. When someone else succeeds, it diminishes our own success, and therefore our relevance.

When it comes to getting credit, we could start to feel threatened by the competence of others. What if someone on my team is more competent than I am? We start to question people's motives. We start to worry that maybe people don't really want to collaborate but rather just co-opt and steal our good ideas instead. As a leader, we start to think that if we have to take all of the responsibility if the team fails, then we should also get all of the credit when the team succeeds—or at least more credit than others.

This scarcity mindset is not only misguided, it also leads to bitterness and rigidity. It's hard to work with others when you don't trust them or don't want to see them succeed as much or more than you. It's definitely not inspiring—for you or for them.

It's amazing what you can accomplish . . . where you have people who don't care who gets the credit.

—HARRY S. TRUMAN

Solution: A Trust & Inspire leader has an abundance mentality. Mindset: I know that others' success does not diminish my own because there is enough for everyone.

You can shift from a scarcity mindset to an abundance mentality. An abundance mentality doesn't see the world as a finite pie or as a "zero sum game." Instead, it's an all-you-can-eat buffet. Just because someone else grabbed the chicken wings doesn't mean you won't get any. In fact, we can all have some chicken wings! The buffet is constantly being refilled.

There *is* enough for everyone, especially of what matters most: love, kindness, trust, inspiration, generosity, energy, credit, recognition, success, significance.

Someone else succeeding doesn't take away from your success. Someone else getting credit doesn't mean you've failed. The best leaders want their people to perform *better* than they did. Imagine how counterintuitive it would be if parents didn't want their child to have a better life than they did. If a teacher felt threatened by his students scoring higher on the SATs than he did. If a coach didn't want her players to win more championships than she won. True excellence comes in helping others achieve their highest potential, regardless of whether their achievements are "better" than yours. Getting credit loses its importance when you change your mindset to one of contribution rather than accumulation.

I would love to redefine success to say it's not just what you achieve, it's also what you help other people to achieve.

—ADAM GRANT, PROFESSOR AND
AUTHOR OF *THINK AGAIN*

Abundance flows out of our credibility, because integrity and authenticity breed inner security. When we are credible and secure, we are not dependent on comparisons or the opinions of other people. This enables us to be genuinely happy for others' successes. But when we're not credible or secure, we tend to operate out of a comparison-based identity where we're threatened by the success of others.

The most important thing to know is this: abundance is a choice, not a condition! A great example of this was Jon Huntsman Sr. A self-made billionaire, he became a game-changing philanthropist and sought to instill the same mentality in his children. Some people might say that it's easy to be generous when you have so much. But Jon Huntsman Sr. started giving money away when he didn't have any money to give! His generosity of spirit was a mindset, not a condition. Some people who have nothing give so much, and some people who have so much give nothing. But Huntsman didn't stop giving once he became wealthy.

If you operate with an abundance mentality, your people will feel valued, and they will thrive. And the reality is that you will, too. It's a sign of a great leader if your people are doing well; it's a sign of a mediocre manager if you're doing well but your people aren't.

If you are seeking to raise your people up, regardless of whether you get credit, people will respect and trust you more. They will be inspired to continue to give their best. When you're able to say to those you serve, "Yes, I care about my win, but I care about your win as much as I do my own"—and mean it—you'll truly have adopted an abundance mindset. You'll also find that you now have a team of people who truly care about your win as well.

• "But What If I'm Not As Confident As You Think I Am?"

Have you ever felt underqualified? If so, you're not alone! It's estimated that approximately 70 percent of the population experience "imposter syndrome" at some time in their life. *Imposter syndrome* is a phenomenon characterized by feeling underqualified, not experienced or talented enough to be doing what we're doing. At the same time, we believe that other people *are* qualified, experienced, and talented enough. Anyone ever in charge of raising a child knows these feelings especially well.

When we operate with this mindset, we heap feelings of inferiority onto ourselves. This makes it harder to work with others, and it certainly makes it harder to lead. It's difficult to trust others if you don't trust yourself. It also can be threatening to extend trust to people, because what if it proves that they are indeed smarter and more qualified than you?

People always say "fake it till you make it," but what do you do when you've been faking it the whole time and you genuinely get the feeling that you might not make it?

These types of thoughts can be exhausting, and they lower our ability to operate at our highest levels and to help others to do the same. Many people compensate for this with increased volume, or bravado, or micromanagement, or a lack of communication, or a lack of transparency. As a result, they cut themselves off from the growth that would help them become the leader they're pretending to be.

> **Solution: A Trust & Inspire leader intentionally builds credibility through modeling the behavioral virtues.**
> **Mindset: I can increase my credibility and self-trust and help others do the same.**

How do you overcome self-doubt? Go back to what we discussed in the 1st stewardship, modeling, and focus on modeling the behavioral virtue pairs: humility and courage, authenticity and vulnerability, empathy and performance. Leaders increase their credibility through modeling the behavior. Leaders work from the inside out. Leaders go first.

As you focus on who you are, your confidence will grow. The basis for self-trust or self-confidence is your credibility—your character and competence—along with your moral authority. You don't have to be perfect, but you do need to recognize what you are capable of and work toward it. The more you build trust in yourself, the more you can extend trust to others. The more you believe in yourself, the more you can help others believe in themselves.

In my discussions with brand-new "C-Suite" senior leaders, many of them explain how nervous they were or how out of place they felt as they began leading at that high a level for the first time. Looking around at veteran C-suiters, they began to experience imposter syndrome and wondered if they truly belonged. However, once they stopped comparing themselves to others and instead began to focus on building their personal credibility with their colleagues and team members, they began to feel more confident and see more success.

We are never perfectly qualified for what life throws at us. But that doesn't mean we can't become qualified.

Fear—or But What If . . .

All of the fears we have addressed in this chapter are valid and present a reality that we may need to confront. However, *trust is the antidote to fear*. Great leaders not only extend trust to others, they also help others gain trust and confidence in themselves. The resulting self-trust can be greater than their fears.

> *It's about giving people confidence.*
>
> —INGA BEALE, FORMER CEO
> OF LLOYD'S OF LONDON

Fear is a reaction; trust is a choice. As we use good judgment, weigh risk and return, operate with an abundance mentality, and focus on building our credibility, we will be able to overcome our fears and their accompanying baggage.

You could spend your whole career or your whole life playing the "what-if" game and coming up with scenario after scenario of the myriad ways things could go wrong. This is one of the ways we tend to go Command & Control on ourselves.

I've always loved the phrase, "Worry is the interest paid, in advance, on a debt you may never owe." Rather than pay wasted interest, I'd like you to make an investment.

Instead of asking yourself, "What if I lose control?" or "What if it doesn't work?" ask yourself the question, "What if it does work?"

COMMAND & CONTROL	TRUST & INSPIRE
Minimize the Risk	Maximize the Possibilities
Formula	Judgment
Finite	Infinite

CHAPTER 12

Barrier #3: "I Don't Know How to Let Go"

When I let go of what I am, I become what I might be.
When I let go of what I have, I receive what I need.

—LAO TZU

Watching a teenager struggle to complete a simple task that you want done a certain way is frustrating. Watching a teen attempt to load the dishwasher or lackadaisically fold clothes can be irritating when we know we can do it better and faster. How many of us have redone a task simply because we needed to know it was done right? How many of us never even let someone else *attempt* the task? As the common expression goes, "If you want something done right, you have to do it yourself."

As prevalent as this might be with our friends or family, it can also be a reality in our jobs and careers at work, or even in community and volunteer work. For many of us, ceding control—letting go—can feel impossible. The desire for constant control feels like a necessity rather than a luxury. Being in control of the little things can help us feel like we are in control of the big things. For some people, this feels like a fundamental part of who they are.

My children experienced this when they were asked to help plan and decorate for a youth event for a local congregation. After their planning and hard work, the adult leaders swooped in and "fixed" everything. My son rolled his eyes and asked, "Why did they even ask for our help if they really just wanted to do it themselves?" The event did indeed look better and run more smoothly, but the youth left feeling disenfranchised and bitter.

The inability to let go can be damaging to morale and stifling to creativity. Regardless of our reasons for not letting go, the outcomes are the same.

> **Solution: A Trust & Inspire leader has a high tolerance for failure with a focus on learning and course correction.**
> **Mindset: Failure is the pathway to growth and innovation.**

Letting go doesn't mean you have no control. We've already established that Trust & Inspire leaders use clear expectations, guidelines, accountability, and structure—including stewardship agreements—to accomplish their work. However, Trust & Inspire leaders also know that appropriately trusting others is crucial to engaging them, inspiring them, and earning their buy-in. It's also vital to others' own growth and development.

We should always remember that people have greatness inside them, and that the life and power is in the seed—knowing that people have untapped potential. We should create an environment where people can experiment and try to gain their own experience, even if that means failing. We can't do this without letting go. The gardener can't pull the seed up through the soil; the seed has to sprout and break through on its own.

A high school teacher told me of an experience she had where letting go not only sparked her students' creativity but also bolstered their autonomy. Instead of a standardized, one-size-fits-all assignment, she decided that for the final project of the semester, students could turn in anything they'd like. Of course, she still had guidelines, as the projects had to be relevant and demonstrate mastery of the competencies the students were learning. But she let go of controlling the normal conventions.

At the end of the semester, she received an array of creative, thoughtful works presented in different mediums, from films to robots to art pieces to poems. One student even choreographed and performed a dance. Students who were less likely to participate in traditional classroom instruction turned in meaningful pieces. A few months later, a group of students formed a band, using a poem one student had created for her project as their inspiration and first song. The song is even on Spotify! The assignment meant so much to the students that they took it into their personal lives.

By letting go, this teacher enabled her students to do much more than before. They created inspiring works that she never could have gotten out of them through Command & Control.

Many, if not most, policies are either relics of the industrial age in disguise, or they represent organizational scar tissue from being burned when trust went awry. Even though we are well past the industrial age, when it comes to policies, there is still a strong tendency for organizations to operate with the "can't let go" mindset. A better way to think about a policy is this: if we didn't already have this policy in place, would we create it today? If the answer is no, then let it go.

I was conducting a public seminar on trust one time when a senior leader from a large, regional grocery chain stood up in the middle of my session and excitedly told me and the entire audience of a jarring learning experience her grocery store chain experienced—and how the company turned their failure into growth and improvement.

She told us that one day, a frequent customer returned to their store with a carton of eggs, several of which were cracked, and asked for a refund. The customer had left the receipt at home. The cashier explained that they couldn't refund the money for the eggs due to store policy—no receipt, no refund. The cashier maintained that without a receipt, they wouldn't know where the eggs came from.

The customer began to get irritated—the grocer's logo was prominently stamped right on the egg carton. Still, the cashier refused to budge from the policy.

"But you know me! I come in here every week!" the customer exclaimed in exasperation.

Still the cashier stuck to store policy and wouldn't issue a refund. So the customer appealed to the store manager, who—shockingly!—also clung to store policy and wouldn't issue a refund. The customer angrily declared that he would never shop at that chain again.

As you can imagine, it wasn't really about the eggs for the customer—it was about not being trusted. The cashier and the manager couldn't let go of control, which was most likely because the policy was made precisely so they wouldn't.

This story made its way up the ranks to the senior leaders. When they heard it, the leadership team was aghast and embarrassed. They didn't blame their cashier and manager for following the policy; instead, they blamed themselves for having such a policy in the first place and for having a culture where following the rules was a higher value than serving the customer. They realized they immediately needed to make a change. They needed to let go of an antiquated policy that was based on distrust, and empower their people to use their good judgment instead of strictly adhering to rules.

So the company let go of that policy—and several others—in order to better trust and empower their employees and customers. Today, they are one of the most trusted food brands and have enjoyed nine straight years of same-store sales growth. Their willingness to learn from their failure, and to grow from it, helped them achieve better outcomes for everyone.

COMMAND & CONTROL	TRUST & INSPIRE
Failure is Bad	Failure is Growth

CHAPTER 13

Barrier #4: "I'm the Smartest One in the Room"

None of us is as smart as all of us.
—KEN BLANCHARD, AUTHOR OF
THE ONE-MINUTE MANAGER

Many years ago, I consulted with a client organization where the president of one of the company's business units had a mantra he would repeat at the outset of almost every meeting he led. "Remember," he would say to everyone, "the best idea wins!" It was a great expression because it meant the president was looking for the best idea, no matter who or where it came from—an idea meritocracy.

Or at least that's how it appeared.

But the reality of how the meetings played out was a far cry from his rallying call. He continually acted like he wanted to hear all ideas, acting as if they were all valid. The group went through a long, drawn-out process and exhausted ideas—and people—until finally the president decided that his idea was the one the company would go with, a conclusion he had arrived at long before the meeting began. At the end of the day, what *he* wanted always won out.

While he said the best idea would win, the fact was that nobody won. People quickly learned that what he projected didn't match his intent, so they stopped trying. Instead, they just worked through the charade as quickly as possible so they could stop wasting time and just get to work on his idea. On the flip side, he missed many great ideas simply because they weren't his own. As the saying goes, he was "often wrong but never in doubt."

Do you think this president knew he was coming across this way? He had no idea. It's important to note here that while you may not see yourself or label yourself as the "smartest in the room," your Command & Control approach—even your *Enlightened* Command & Control approach—might be doing that for you. Now would be a really good time to ask yourself the question "Could my style be communicating to people that I think I'm smarter, or better, or more qualified?" Many leaders I work with are often surprised by the answer to this question.

Letting our style get in the way of our intent may well be the most common thread running through the "smartest in the room" problem. Many leaders push for "collaboration" but instead practice control. This is demoralizing, dehumanizing, and exhausting. It is cynicism inducing. And in the end, only one person feels good about it. The leader says, "Thanks for the input, everyone; I feel good about where we ended up!" Everyone else is thinking, *No one else feels good about where we ended up.*

It's almost better to work with someone who essentially says, "If I want your opinion, I'll give it to you!" than to work with someone who asks for your opinion but then doesn't acknowledge it—or completely ignores it altogether.

On several occasions, I've spoken with groups of health-care workers who often expressed this very frustration. They said administrators ask for feedback and input but implement none of it—and sometimes don't even acknowledge they received it. It's okay as a leader to make decisions and ask people to support those decisions, but don't act like you want input when you're not really open to it. This makes people doubt their instincts and experiences, and it insulates you as a leader from the real value your people can bring to the table.

I knew a Trust & Inspire leader who before discussing any issue, identified whether she was asking for the team's input or simply for their support. The team was very clear before the discussion if the decision was already made. Because her style was Trust & Inspire, she had the credibility to say either, "I really want to discuss different options, and I need your input," or, "I've already made the call on this particular item—can we discuss the best way to move forward?" Both options can be perfectly appropriate; what's needed is clarity. As a Trust & Inspire leader, you can be authoritative without being authoritarian. There is power in being authentic.

Being smart is more than just intelligence or credentials. It includes your ability to reach people, to inspire them, to open their minds rather than to shut them down so that everyone (including you) can benefit by what they bring to the table. By that definition, if you think you're the smartest in the room, then you're automatically not. If you think you're always right, you'll find that when it comes to people, you're more often getting it wrong.

I imagine that some of you might have been gearing up for this chapter ever since you saw it in the Table of Contents. You might be ready to explain to me, "No, Stephen, really. I *am* the smartest one in the room. I may not be the smartest in *every* room, but I'm certainly the smartest in the room I'm in."

Nothing is more frustrating than feeling like you're the only one pulling your weight or that your colleagues and team members, or even your boss, don't have the same skill set or perspective that you do. And sometimes you aren't wrong.

I saw a very basic version of this when my then-thirteen-year-old daughter complained to me that her boss at the summer "snow-cone shack" was incompetent—and she wasn't totally wrong. Her boss also happened to be her fifteen-year-old brother! He wasn't trying very hard. She could see it, and it really bothered her.

Maybe you're on the flip side of the situation and you're the boss, like my son was, and feel like the people you're working with just don't get it. Most of us have been taught somewhere along the line that the leader is *supposed* to be the smartest in the room. A leader isn't supposed to show weakness, right? So you treat everyone accordingly, either unwilling or afraid to ask for help. In essence, you begin to Command & Control them because you know best, or at least want to appear that you do.

The reality is that both sides of this have some validity. Sometimes you might be on a team that seems disengaged and unskilled. Sometimes you might be treated that way by a boss or a colleague, and therefore you become more disengaged and unwilling to contribute your skills or ideas. In most cases, if you are treating others as if you are the smartest in the room, even if you're really nice about it, they will stop trying and you *will* become the smartest in the room—because you're the only one left in the room. Or, at the very least, you'll be the only one left in the room who cares.

If you want to be a leader to those around you—whether they are your colleagues, your family, or even your actual boss—there's little value to being the smartest one in the room.

Solution: A Trust & Inspire leader is a multiplier.
Mindset: I need the strengths of those around me.

When Indra Nooyi was a finalist being considered for the position of CEO of PepsiCo, the other finalist the board was considering was Mike White, a comparably qualified and talented leader. Both had been at the company for years, and both were excellent choices. The board ultimately chose Indra. Rather than seeking to consolidate power, Indra's first move was to try to persuade Mike to stay and work with her. She told Mike how much she both wanted and needed him to stay. She knew that someone as talented as he was could immediately step into a CEO position anywhere (and many runners-up typically leave and do exactly that). She also knew that both she and the company would be far better off with him there.

Indra didn't think of herself as the smartest in the room. She wasn't threatened by Mike; instead, she had an abundance mentality and recognized her need for his strengths and capabilities. They had built a relationship of trust and, while he was disappointed in not getting the top job, Mike felt valued by Indra and was inspired to stay for several years before becoming CEO of DirecTV. Together, they were able to chart a new path for PepsiCo that took the company to new heights.

The solution and mindset to overcome the smartest-one-in-the-room syndrome start with believing that there is enough for everyone. And with understanding the importance of elevating caring above competing.

A favorite African proverb of mine is "If you want to go fast, go alone. If you want to go far, go together." I've seen the truth of this saying many times over in my life and in the lives of others. However, it's not enough anymore to just go far, or even just to go fast—we have to do both. To align this statement with what we need today, I would say: "If you want to go far fast, go together with trust." We're better together than we are by ourselves, but just going together isn't enough. If we try to go together with a Command & Control style, we won't be able to generate the agility, innovation, or inspiration needed to keep pace as the world around us continues to change.

> *You can do what I cannot do. I can do what you cannot do. Together we can do great things.*
>
> —MOTHER TERESA

Those who understand the need for speed and want to go fast often consider themselves the smartest in the room. They don't have time for others, and they believe they have the skill set they need to accomplish the job by themselves. If they need other people, what they need is for those people to dependably do what they're told. In a few cases, this might give them an edge, but there's a price to it, and it's not sustainable. And more often than not, it yields mediocre results.

Those who go far are those who go together. These people recognize that not one of us is smarter than all of us together. The collective ethos and knowledge of teams is what brings about true innovation and creativity. It's what allows for better ideas, deeper understanding, and happier teams. Those who go far fast never think they are the smartest in the room; they depend on others being more capable than they are and bringing diverse thought and opinion to the team. They seek to work together to innovate—but they do it on the basis of trust, allowing them to go faster as they eliminate misunderstandings and hidden agendas while allowing people to focus on and contribute their greatest strengths. They produce better results in a faster and more effective way. They inspire each other to do their best work.

> *Alone we can do so little; together we can do so much.*
>
> —HELEN KELLER

As a leader, you should strive for engaged, trusting teams working together—but remember that your intent is just as important as what you project. It's one thing to say it; it's another thing to believe it. Someone might say the words *we're better together*, but their paradigm might still be *I'm the smartest in the room*. People can see right through it.

For those of you who are "the smartest one in the room," have you ever thought about what it feels like to be with you? For those around you, it is mentally and physically exhausting. It's both insulting and marginalizing at the same time. Others' desire to engage and contribute sinks immediately once they realize they won't be listened to or taken seriously. This becomes a damaging cycle where you as the leader start to see those around you as unmotivated and uninspired, not realizing you are the one demotivating and sapping inspiration!

This also plays out frequently in families where parents "know best" and raise children to be obedient and compliant rather than discover who they are and what they're capable of. You want to know the biggest limitation you put on yourself if you have this belief? It's this: you cannot, with integrity, treat others as equals when you see them as inferior.

If people truly are the smartest in the room, it will not occur to them to see themselves as the smartest person in the room. If they truly are the most intelligent, they will recognize that everyone else can still bring a different life experience filled with perspective and creativity that they don't have. They can be a multiplier instead of a diminisher.

What does that mean? In her masterful book *Multipliers*, leadership authority Liz Wiseman describes how leaders who are multipliers can enhance conversation, help spark ideas, share credit, and uplift others. They lead to greater outcomes and more unity. They multiply the strengths of everyone around them—and make everyone smarter.

> *The person sitting at the apex of the intelligence hierarchy is the genius maker, not the genius.*
>
> —LIZ WISEMAN, AUTHOR OF *MULTIPLIERS*

Diminishers, whether intentional or accidental, do the exact opposite. They stifle conversation, snuff out ideas, praise themselves, and criticize others. They effectively make any team collectively dumber. They lead to mediocre outcomes and disunity—frustrated disunity. Is it any wonder the data show that people don't leave organizations but leave bad bosses?

I saw this firsthand as I watched a good friend toil for years at his company with a boss who thought he himself was the smartest in the room. My friend was extremely bright, hardworking, and proactive— a model contributor in every way. And yet he told me how he always felt that he wasn't smart enough, that his ideas weren't good enough, that he was always deficient in some way. He hated being around his boss, not because his boss was a bad person, but because of how his boss made him feel.

My friend eventually decided to leave the company. A few months after he started a new job at a different organization, I came across him at a social gathering. He called out "Stephen!" from across the room as he ran toward me. As this was not normally how we greeted each other, I approached him somewhat confused, not knowing what to expect.

When he got to me, he gave me a hug and excitedly declared, "I'm not dumb, Stephen! I'm not dumb!"

He went on to explain that his ideas and insights were greatly appreciated at his new company. That he felt respected and like a contributing member of the team. "I had been working with my old boss for so long, and he had shut me down so continuously for so many years, that I honestly started to believe I was dumb. I forgot that I have a lot to offer! That I have capabilities and drive and desire to make a difference. I'm telling you, it's like a breath of fresh air."

Even I could see as we talked that a weight had been lifted from his shoulders. He was full of energy and excitement for the first time in a long time. Even though my friend's boss had never demeaned him personally, the boss's constant need to be the smartest in the room—to one-up everyone—made my friend feel like he had nothing to offer.

I think we've all known someone like my friend's boss at some point in our lives. Maybe we've even been that person at some point as well. If you still are saying, "But I *am* the smartest in the room," please recognize the way this belief shows up and the price you may be paying because of it.

If you're willing to be challenged by this, following is a three-step process that will help.

1. Start with Humility

Too often, our pride is what gets in the way. True leaders are humble. True leaders are more concerned with *what* is right than *who* is right.

Regardless of whether they have more skills or experience than the members of their team, they are confident enough in who they are that they don't feel a need to flaunt themselves. They've built enough trust with those on their team that they don't feel the need to frequently remind people of their capabilities and accomplishments. Trust & Inspire leaders check their ego at the door.

2. Listen First and Demonstrate Respect for What You Hear

While my kids were growing up, they could always tell when I wasn't listening. Most of the time I was really good at listening. But sometimes I nodded my head and even made a comment at the appropriate moment as they chattered on about their dream from the night before—but inside, I was going through my work schedule or thinking about tomorrow's presentation. They always pulled me away from my thoughts by yelling, "Dad! You're not *really* listening!" And they were right.

Listening seems pretty basic and obvious. But as we've measured trust for more than fifteen years now, listening shows up consistently as one of the lowest-rated behaviors for nearly every leader, team, and organization.

We *all* struggle with listening, but the "smartest one in the room" especially struggles. Often, those who see themselves as the smartest in the room don't listen with the intent to understand—because they think they already do understand. They are thinking about their next line of argument in their head to prove why their idea or perspective is best. They are, in effect, just waiting their turn. This habit causes them to miss out on great ideas.

When we listen with the intent to understand, it's amazing how much we can learn. People have ideas that make our organization smarter and better. When parents say they learn from their kids, it isn't just a trite saying. Children can often be more insightful and resourceful than adults. But we will never learn from them or others if we don't first take the time to listen.

Good leadership requires you to surround yourself with people of diverse perspectives who can disagree with you without fear of retaliation.

—DORIS KEARNS GOODWIN, HISTORIAN
AND AUTHOR OF *TEAM OF RIVALS*

While it's true we miss good ideas when we don't listen, what we really miss is something much bigger than an idea. We miss a huge opportunity to demonstrate empathy and understanding, connection with people we care about. We miss a chance to show someone we believe they are of worth. We miss a chance to show they are important and valuable to us. More than missing out on one idea, we miss all the ideas that person has to offer. We don't just miss the bucket of water, we miss the well.

If we don't listen to and respect what we hear from others, it sends a signal to them that they don't matter. Team members stop trying to contribute if they don't feel they are respected. On the other hand, it's amazing how engaged people are when they feel respected and listened to.

Once we've listened to people, we must demonstrate respect both for their ideas and for the person who offered them. This doesn't mean all ideas are winners. Just as children are capable of coming up with profound suggestions, they are also capable of coming up with utterly absurd ones. However, demonstrating respect for ideas—even for ones we disagree with or that may not work—is fundamental in building a relationship of trust.

If you want to encourage those around you to take chances, to try new things, to share their ideas, you need to communicate respect for them and their ideas, the good and the bad equally. Again, that doesn't mean you have to act on all the ideas. But listening respectfully shows them that they matter to you. It's important to note that there's a difference between genuinely having respect for someone versus merely being respectful—and people can tell the difference.

When someone's respectful behavior flows out of an honest respect for the person, it has the ability to inspire in big ways. Few things are more Command & Control than behaving disingenuously toward someone to placate them or manage their reaction.

3. Embrace a Growth Mindset—Not Just for Yourself

You're likely familiar with Dr. Carol Dweck's seminal book *Mindset*, in which she discusses the difference between a fixed mindset and a growth mindset. In the initial juxtaposition I shared at the start of this book, I put a "fixed mindset" on the Command & Control side and a "growth mindset" on the Trust & Inspire side. A *fixed mindset* generally reflects an acceptance of things as they are and doesn't tend to do too well with change. A *growth mindset*, on the other hand, not only does well with change, it actively seeks out change. It's difficult to become a good leader without embracing a growth mindset, and many are very aware of a constant need to continue to develop themselves.

Most Enlightened Command & Control leaders have a strong growth mindset. That's especially true of those who tend to see themselves as the smartest one in the room, consciously or otherwise. They are constantly working on improving their capabilities. They're often extremely well read, and they are usually disciplined in how they approach their work and their life. This helps them to be extremely effective and further sets them apart from others with whom they work.

Now, I know this doesn't sound right. I just acknowledged that having a growth mindset falls on the Trust & Inspire side, so how does that coincide with having a Command & Control style?

Let me clarify. Here's the challenge as I see it: most Enlightened Command & Control leaders have a strong growth mindset *for themselves*—and at the same time often project a fixed mindset *on others*.

They tend to size up or assess people very quickly, and they often hold to that initial assessment throughout the relationship. When you work with someone who sees himself or herself as superior, it's very difficult for you to grow out of that initial perception. It becomes a label that is hard to shake. The very act of attempting to do so can be seen as an effort to prove that person wrong.

By contrast, Trust & Inspire leaders know that there is power in the seed, that whatever people are capable of when they meet is only a starting point for what they can become. Command & Control leaders believe that the power is in the gardener, and they work hard to become a better, smarter gardener, but they often fail to nourish the seed. When the seed doesn't grow, they often assume it was the seed, and they just try a new seed.

Trust & Inspire leaders have a strong growth mindset for themselves *and* for the people they lead. They see greatness in other people, and they know that others have the potential to grow, change, and get better. They also encourage those people to have a growth mindset for themselves, and they see that eventual growth in others as a potential source for their own growth as well. In short, they not only grow themselves, they grow people.

> *With the right mindset and the right teaching, people are capable of a lot more than we think.*
>
> —CAROL DWECK, PROFESSOR
> AND AUTHOR OF *MINDSET*

The Three-Step Process in Combination

Listening first and demonstrating respect both flow from humility. I've known many Command & Control leaders who do well in these first two steps, but because of how they see or label others, they still fail to inspire or unleash the talent of those with whom they work. It is the combination of all three steps—humility, listening first and demonstrating respect, *and* embracing a growth mindset for others (not just yourself)— that allows you to create an environment of collaboration and innovation. It is what gains you the respect of those around you and allows you to have influence with them and support their growth along with your own. It is what makes you trustworthy, trusting, and inspiring.

It's great to be smart, but remember that none of us is as smart as all of us. As leaders, we *need* the greatest strengths of those around us. We need a truly complementary team that values differences. Valuing the differences is where the greatest potential and growth lies.

COMMAND & CONTROL	TRUST & INSPIRE
Authoritarian	Authoritative
"If I Want Your Opinion, I'll Give It to You!"	"What's Your Opinion?"
Diminisher	Multiplier
Who is Right	What is Right
Listen to Respond	Listen to Understand
Growth Mindset for Self	Growth Mindset for All
Individual Contributors	Complementary Team

CHAPTER 14

Barrier #5: "This Is Who I Am"

Through learning, we re-create ourselves. Through learning, we become able to do something we were never able to do. Through learning, we reperceive the world and our relationship to it.

—PETER SENGE, AUTHOR OF *THE FIFTH DISCIPLINE*

"I Can't Change"

We all face situations in life that are difficult. When presented with a tough situation, many of us have probably said or heard one of the following:

"This is just who I am."

"I can't change."

"What can you do?"

"It is what it is."

While these are relatable and understandable phrases, they are also very uninspiring. They operate out of a fixed mindset. Carol Dweck's important work helps us see that it doesn't need to be this way—that growth is possible and even necessary. Yet it's understandable, and far easier, to throw up our hands and say, "I am what I am!"

The reality is that most people have been heavily scripted in Command & Control from their upbringing and from early mentors, whether in their family, school, work, sports, or the military. Habit is strong. If you're one of the few who didn't grow up in a Command &

Control home, you've almost certainly experienced it at school or at work. That's what has been consistently modeled, and for all our progress, it remains the prevailing norm today.

Additionally, you may feel that a Command & Control style has served you well. You might think, *I don't know if I can change who I am, and I don't know if I want to change who I am.* You may feel that your style was what got you to where you are today.

But as executive coach Marshall Goldsmith said, "What got you here won't get you there." While your style may have worked in the past, in the disruptive, multigenerational, and ever-changing world of today it will only grow in irrelevance and ineffectiveness.

You must unlearn what you have learned.

—MASTER YODA

Solution: A Trust & Inspire leader rescripts.
Mindset: I'm the programmer, not the program.

Many people have committed to a career path only to have that path be altered under their feet by our rapidly changing world. I have a friend who built a successful career selling advertising in the Yellow Pages phone book. If you're scratching your head right now wondering what I'm talking about, there used to be a large book, printed on paper, that listed all the phone numbers of homes and businesses in the area in which you lived. As in many evolving industries, technology eliminated the need for this business, so there came a time when he had to decide if he "was what he was" or if he had the ability to change. A similar thing has happened to many as a consequence of the global COVID-19 pandemic, as entire professions and industries have been significantly altered—some even upended, and people were laid off.

The good news is that however you've operated in the past doesn't control who you can become. You have the ability to say, "This is not who I am." Instead, you can say, "This is the style I've used." We are not programs on a set course, laid out by someone else, unable to choose our own path—we're the programmers. As the world changes around us, we can reprogram our path. We can create our own future.

Consider the age-old question: Are leaders made, or are they born? Leaders are less either made or born as much as they are *reborn*, again and again, through the choices they make. Leaders are now tasked with making choices that consider the different world we're navigating. The opportunity today, noted London Stock Exchange Group CEO David Schwimmer, is that "people are looking . . . for a different kind of leadership."

We're not robots who have been programmed to operate in a certain way until our programmers give us a new update. We are the ones writing the program, so we can update ourselves anytime we'd like! As Microsoft CEO Satya Nadella stated, "Anyone can change their mindset." We may have been deeply scripted in Command & Control, and it may have even worked—but we can rescript. And the possibilities of rescripting are exhilarating.

The first step to rescripting is to find new models of Trust & Inspire that can replace the old models of Command & Control. If all we've known from our work, education, family, and community lives are models of Command & Control, then we should seek out Trust & Inspire models as replacements. In addition to models, we should also seek out mentors—people we can learn from and, if possible, work with to become the leaders we want to become.

The problem is never how to get new, innovative thoughts into your mind but how to get the old ones out.

—DEE HOCK, FOUNDER AND CEO EMERITUS OF VISA

The Power of Rescripting in Leadership

April Wensel is a perfect example of rescripting, even more so because she is an actual programmer, and has reprogrammed herself. April runs a company called Compassionate Coding, where she teaches programmers and others in the tech industry the benefits of taking a more people-centered approach to their very technical work. She notes in an article entitled "Confessions of a Recovering Jerk Programmer" that her work today often leads people to believe that she is a naturally "nice" person. April identifies herself as having entered the tech field as "the stereotypical jerk programmer," falling in line with what she called the "old tech values" in the industry. Those values, not dissimilar to a Command & Control style, are things like ego, elitism, competition, being "smart," and being a "rockstar."

In the beginning, April thrived in this setting. She was making great money and doing interesting work. She was engaged in her work, but soon found that her life lacked meaning and connection, and without that, the other things weren't enough. After wading through a period of burnout and disillusionment with the tech industry, she rescripted herself. Discovering her own values, she learned that what was missing from her life and work was compassion. She opened up and began caring more for others and realized the value they had to offer. She rediscovered a love for programming and has found meaningful success in helping and inspiring others. April's company works to empower individuals and companies to create *collaboratively* all over the world. She continues to work to rescript not only herself, but her industry as well.

Ralph Stayer is another example of rescripting. He is the owner, chairman, and former CEO of Johnsonville Sausage. After leading the company successfully—at least financially—for many years, he came to realize that he was leaving far too much value on the table. Morale was low, product quality had begun to decline, "people didn't seem to care," and "the gap between potential and performance" was widening.

After considerable self-reflection, it dawned on Ralph that *he* was the problem, or at least his *style* was. His style was Command & Control, and he made almost every decision in the company, which diminished the capacities of his people as they became dependent on him and "less capable than when they were first hired." While he had always cared deeply, his style was definitely getting in the way of his intent! So, he consciously and intentionally moved to a Trust & Inspire leadership style.

After a short transition period of learning, both for him and his team members, he and they have had enormous sustained success, not just financially but also culturally—and have gone on to new heights. They created "The Johnsonville Way" as a way of codifying these principles of leading and developing people.

> *Other companies use their people to build a business, but at Johnsonville we use our business to build our people.*
>
> —RALPH STAYER, OWNER AND CHAIRMAN
> OF JOHNSONVILLE SAUSAGE

Andy Pearson is yet another example. As I mentioned earlier, he might have been considered the epitome of a demanding Command & Control CEO when he ran PepsiCo for some fifteen years, being named by *Fortune* magazine as one of the ten toughest bosses in business. After retiring and teaching at the Harvard Business School for nearly a decade, he then was lured out of retirement by David Novak to become chairman of YUM! Brands.

Considering how David had been leading YUM! and how Andy had led PepsiCo, this appeared to be a complete mismatch of style. But Andy Pearson chose to dramatically and completely rescript himself and fundamentally change the way he operated as a leader at YUM! He became enthusiastically influenced by, and aligned with, David Novak's Trust & Inspire leadership style. Andy went on to help David create a great culture of recognition and collaboration within YUM!—one that also performed remarkably well. After all these years, Andy found a better way to lead.

> *You say to yourself, if I could only unleash the power of everybody in the organization, instead of just a few people, what could we accomplish? We'd be a much better company.*
>
> —ANDY PEARSON, FORMER CHAIRMAN
> OF YUM! BRANDS

All of us have the ability to rescript ourselves and become a transition figure through our leadership—not only for our teams and organizations, but also for our families and communities. Just because we've operated one way does not mean we need to continue that way. Just because our parents raised us one way does not mean we need to raise our own family that way. Just because we were taught one way does not mean we have to behave that way. We don't need to let past experiences define us. We can create new habits.

We are not our style—therefore we can choose to rescript our style. We can choose a growth mindset and inspire others to do the same. Doing so creates infinite possibilities for us and everyone around us.

Perhaps Albert Einstein described the possibilities of rescripting best when he stated that "imagination is more important than knowledge."

The Power of Rescripting in Life

In 2002, Elizabeth Smart was kidnapped from her family home at the age of fourteen. After nine horrific months of enduring unimaginable ordeals, pain, and suffering, she was finally rescued. Elizabeth had every right to let this experience shape, and possibly even define, the rest of her life. She had been a victim of incredibly cruel and demented acts, and the scripting she had been force-fed for those nine terrible months easily could have become her script for life. But while the experience terribly impacted her, it didn't shape her life—*she* did. She chose to rescript.

With the help of her family, community, and professionals, Elizabeth chose to transcend the programming she'd been given, and she became a programmer. She used her experience to help others. She created a foundation dedicated to helping kidnapping victims and also trying to prevent future kidnappings. She not only became a model of how to overcome hardship but a mentor to people everywhere. She went from survivor to thriver. She is a true transition figure and continues to use her platform to contribute to and benefit people around the world.

> *Life is a journey for us all. We all face trials. We all have ups and downs. All of us are human. But we are also the masters of our fate. We are the ones who decide how we are going to react to life.*
>
> —ELIZABETH SMART

Write Your Own Story

If you've felt stuck, take heart! You don't have to remain that way. You can change your style. You can let go. You can rescript your leadership. You can rescript your life. You can program new behavior. You're not a character in someone else's story. You write your own.

> *You are capable of reinventing yourself, as a company or as a leader, while preserving the core of what you are.*
>
> —BRAD SMITH, FORMER CEO OF INTUIT

COMMAND & CONTROL	TRUST & INSPIRE
Stagnation	Growth
Program	Programmer
Top-Down, Bottlenecked Decision Making	Distributed Decision Making
Scripted	Rescripting

A Quick Assessment of the 5 Common Barriers

Now that you have a deeper understanding of the 5 Common Barriers, it may be helpful to take a quick inventory of which of these barriers you most relate with.

Identify which barriers get in your way of fully transitioning to becoming a Trust & Inspire leader. Circle the number for each barrier:

DEFINITELY NO ←→ SOMEWHAT ←→ DEFINITELY YES

This won't work here.	1	2	3	4	5
Fear: But what if I lose control?	1	2	3	4	5
Fear: But what if it doesn't work?	1	2	3	4	5
Fear: But what if I've been burned before?	1	2	3	4	5
Fear: But what if I don't get the credit?	1	2	3	4	5
Fear: But what if I'm not as confident as you think I am?	1	2	3	4	5
I don't know how to let go.	1	2	3	4	5
I'm the smartest one in the room.	1	2	3	4	5
This is who I am.	1	2	3	4	5

PART FOUR

The New Way to Lead in a New World

As the walls that separate our public, private, and inner lives are becoming increasingly thin, the premium on *how* we lead cannot be overstated. While leadership is a choice, the reality is that all of us are being called on to lead, regardless of whether we seek leadership. We lead at work, we lead at home, we lead in our communities, and we lead ourselves.

Becoming a Trust & Inspire leader is first about becoming a Trust & Inspire *person*. That's applying the inside-out process to ourselves. We begin by recognizing there is greatness in people—including in ourselves—and that people surround us in every dimension and aspect of our lives.

This final section will explore the application and extraordinary impact a Trust & Inspire person can have on others in some of the everyday aspects of life. It will conclude with a most uncommon, in-depth illustration of what can be accomplished by a group of Trust & Inspire individuals working together as a complementary team with a remarkably inspiring purpose.

CHAPTER 15

Trust & Inspire in Any Context: Parenting, Teaching, Coaching . . . and More

The potential for greatness lives within each of us.
—WILMA RUDOLPH, OLYMPIC CHAMPION

When Jonathan Horton was three years old, he was at Target with his parents. His parents turned their backs for just a few seconds, and when they turned around, Jonathan was gone. While his parents were frantically searching for him, Jonathan saw a giant pole in the middle of the store that ran thirty or forty feet all the way to the ceiling. By the time his parents found him, he had climbed all the way to the top, and his head was touching the ceiling.

Most parents naturally would be really worried and upset—and they might scold the child and warn him for his own safety to never do anything like that again. Jonathan's parents felt the same way, saying to themselves, "We've got to do something with him. Number one, he's going to kill himself." Then they added, "And number two, he's got some talent."

So they put Jonathan in gymnastics.

You can bet there was no shortage of discipline, commitment, structure, or firmness on Jonathan's road to becoming a two-time

Olympian and a two-time U.S. National All-Around Champion. His parents saw his potential for greatness—and they helped him develop and unleash it.

> *The most important decision we will make: how to remove barriers to people's unique capabilities.*
>
> —DR. FRANCES FREI, PROFESSOR
> AND AUTHOR OF *UNLEASHED*

Your Various Roles in Life

Think of a role in your life that really matters to you. Maybe it's a family role, such as a parent, grandparent, spouse, sibling, aunt, uncle, or child. Maybe it's a work-related role, such as an executive assistant, HR manager, team leader, or department head. Maybe it's a community-related role, such as an activist, neighborhood chair, or a summer camp director. Or maybe it's any of a variety of church or volunteer organization roles.

You can be a leader in any role. You don't have to be given the title to be a leader. You can make a difference to the people you interact with in that role. Regardless of what role came to your mind, please plug it into the following question:

Am I a Command & Control _____, or am I a Trust & Inspire _____?

Whatever your context is, please recognize the difference that occurs when you approach it with a style of Trust & Inspire.

Now ask yourself this question:

How does it affect the people around me (my coworkers, colleagues, customers, friends, kids) when I am a Command & Control _____ versus a Trust & Inspire _____?

When we have a Command & Control style, the reality is that the people around us are paying for it. On the other hand, people around us benefit enormously when we adopt a style of Trust & Inspire. People trust us more and feel inspired when they are around us—even if our interaction with them is just a brief encounter.

The example you model can inspire others to change their lives. The way you parent might inspire your neighbor. The way you care for your customers might inspire your colleague. The way you speak about others might inspire your friends. There's no telling how your life will be blessed as you seek to bless the lives of others.

I hope you see that Trust & Inspire truly does apply to any context, even yours. It can even help you simply in the way you view and treat yourself. *Don't forget that you have greatness within you.* Above all, if you seek to become Trust & Inspire in one area of your life, it can naturally seep into the other areas as well. Trust & Inspire people are authentic, and it wouldn't be very authentic if you turned on your Trust & Inspire style at work and then turned it off when you got home or in the way you speak to yourself.

Trust & Inspire is not just about what you do, but who you are. This style demands that you strive to be congruent in all parts of your life. This might take time, but it is possible.

With that being said, I want to highlight a few specific roles in our society that most people have some experience with and a connection to. I'd like to focus on three of these—parenting, teaching, and athletic coaching—but I will also briefly address a few more. If I don't specifically address your job or role, please know that this is still meant for you! Pull lessons from these and make them your own. These principles are timeless and transcend the various roles in everyone's life.

Trust & Inspire Parenting

I used to have no kids, and lots of theories on parenting. Now I have lots of kids, and no theories on parenting!

While not all of us are parents, all of us have been kids.

Let me just say this: being a parent is a difficult, rewarding, often thankless, and often inspiring job! To all of the people who parent in some capacity—as a parent, a guardian, a foster parent, a grandparent, a godparent, a brother or sister, an aunt or uncle, a close family friend—let me say thank you. It truly takes both a parent and a village, and your efforts are important and valuable.

All of us can remember how our parents or caretakers raised us (or in some cases didn't) and the profound impact their choices had on our lives. Far into adulthood, some of our most painful or most joyful memories still come from childhood. When you think back to the home in which you grew up, place it in the context of this book. Was it an Authoritarian Command & Control home? Maybe an Enlightened Command & Control home? Or was it a Trust & Inspire home? And what kind of home are you creating for the children you parent?

Former Florida governor Jeb Bush shared how his mother, Barbara Bush, described her parenting style. While speaking at her funeral, Jeb humorously remarked, "[Mom] called her style a benevolent dictatorship. But honestly, it wasn't always benevolent."

A Command & Control parent often relies on the old-school attitudes of "I'm the parent, so I have ultimate authority" and "Because I said so!" The challenge with this fundamental paradigm is that it's easy to evaluate children based on their most recent behavior but to miss their inherent goodness and potential. Like a seed, every child is filled with power, but it's stored inside. It's easy to forget that children are whole people capable of great things. Regardless of whether parents are aware of it, they often suffer from the I'm-the-smartest-in-the-room mentality—because, generally, they *are* the smartest in the room! However, as we described earlier, this mindset dictates that children need to be controlled and contained rather than inspired and unleashed.

Command & Control parents often parent their children for compliance—and will use various methods of carrot-and-stick to get it. Generally well meaning, they sometimes overlook the fact that children won't remain with them forever. We all hope to raise children not simply to be obedient to a parent, but to be prepared to leave the nest and fly, even soar, on their own. Children might comply with your moral code while living in your home to avoid punishment, but what will they choose to do when they set out on their own?

Command & Control parents are still modeling, but the lesson children often take from that scenario is not what the parent truly wants. "My way or the highway" eventually leaves a lot of people on the highway, unprepared to find *their* way. Children don't feel trusted or inspired if they are not given the opportunity to grow or if they're not involved in meaningful and age-appropriate decisions to contribute to their family life. In some ways, disengaged children are not too dissimilar to disengaged employees—just punching their time card, running out the clock, waiting for the day they turn eighteen and can seek new employment elsewhere.

A Command & Control parent often parents a child for the most obedient version of themselves or the most risk-averse version or the most parentlike version—"the best version I can make out of them"— as opposed to the best version the child can become. A Trust & Inspire parent knows that children are capable of growing into the best version of themselves. They see that the greatness truly is in the seed, and they're able to see beyond the relentless demands of daily schedules and routines.

Like leadership, parenting is more like being a gardener than being a mechanic. As you teach, nurture, and lead your children, you bring out the life from within them rather than "inject" life into them. You work *with* children rather than *on* them. You create the conditions of a healthy garden where children can flourish. You are the gardener.

> To plant a seed, watch it grow, to tend to it and then harvest it, offers a simple but enduring satisfaction. The sense of being the custodian of this small patch of earth offered a small taste of freedom. In some ways, I saw the garden as a metaphor for certain aspects of my life. A leader must also tend his garden; he, too, plants seeds, and then watches, cultivates, and harvests the result.
>
> —NELSON MANDELA

Ensuring your child practices the piano is important, but what's more important is that she learns discipline and explores musicality. Discipline is vital for children to learn, and good parents teach it—but the point is for children to learn discipline so that they learn to discipline themselves (Trust & Inspire), not so they operate as a function of someone else's discipline (Command & Control).

Trust & Inspire parents encourage good behavior by first modeling it. They are the ultimate example to their children of good behavior and ethical living. Such parents mentor their children, helping them learn how to make decisions rather than forcing decisions on the child. They spend time trying to help the child discover his or her passions and gifts, not just ascribing certain passions and gifts to the child.

Ask yourself this: Does your child feel contained or empowered? This is not an endorsement of hands-off, laissez-faire, free-range parenting. Structure, discipline, and sometimes firmness are vital. Remember, we manage *things* (bedtime, meals, practices, technology, and responsibilities), and we lead *people*. Children who feel managed respond the same way you do: they become disengaged, uninspired, distrusted, and apathetic. Do your children feel like they are being managed or led?

Seeing a child's potential isn't always easy, especially when you are dealing with behavioral issues and tough circumstances. But it is crucial to a child's success and well-being.

My parents learned this the hard way while I was growing up as they struggled to help one of my brothers. At the time, he was doing poorly in school and was quite immature for his age, not to mention being gangly, skinny, and uncoordinated. My parents worked hard to help him improve his performance in school, in sports, and in social settings. They were constantly reminding him and pushing him to be better. In response, he cried and tried to escape situations; he wanted to quit baseball and to stop going to school.

Only through deep reflection did my parents realize they were not seeing his potential. They wondered if perhaps they might have been caring more about what others thought of their son and of them as parents than they did about seeing and accepting their son for who he was. They realized they needed to return to the fundamental belief of seeing greatness in the seed.

> *A great thought begins by seeing something differently, with a shift to the mind's eye.*
>
> —ALBERT EINSTEIN

Once they did this, they changed their approach to parenting him. They loosened up and stopped judging him so much; instead, they tried to enjoy him. They didn't set him up against social expectations or even their own expectations; instead, they tried to appreciate him for his individuality. The tactics they had used before fell by the wayside, as those tactics now felt manipulative and inauthentic. Instead of communicating his failures to him with the unspoken message of "You need to fix yourself," they tried to communicate his worth and potential to him, expressing, "You are valid just the way you are."

It took time, but eventually this new line of parenting took effect. My brother started to gain more confidence. He also started to grow and change at his own pace, eventually becoming an all-state athlete, student body officer, and straight-A student. The parenting tactics weren't what changed my brother. He had that greatness inside him all along. His greatness just needed the right conditions to blossom. My parents changing the way they *saw* him made all the difference.

As parents, we need to see our children's potential for greatness, communicate it, develop it, and unleash it. Even if they make choices we wouldn't. Even if they don't end up the miniature clones we'd hoped they'd be. Even if their life doesn't end up the way we thought it would. We must appreciate them for who they are and who they can be. We cannot control how our children come to us, but we can control how we love them, nurture them, and perceive them. Real love is putting our bias aside and seeing children for who they truly are and for who they truly can and want to be.

I believe we should consistently examine how we see and perceive each of our family members individually. To help with this, I invite you to complete this brief exercise:

Who in my family would benefit the most from being more trusted and inspired by me?

_____

How am I "seeing" this person that may be limiting me?

_____

This is how I will now choose to see this person (include one unique gift):

_____

How will I communicate the greatness I see within this person?

_____

How can I develop and cultivate this person's greatness?

_____

How can I unleash this person and free him or her to become even greater?

_____

What might be the impact?

_____

How do you become a Trust & Inspire parent? Through the same model we've been using. First you focus on modeling. No one in the world has a better radar for "do as I say, not as I do" than children, and they'll never buy what you're telling them if you're not doing it yourself. Many parents slip naturally into the realm of Enlightened Command & Control—great intentions, fueled by genuine love and concern—but their style gets in the way of their intent. You don't just *tell* your kids what it means to be disciplined, charitable, hardworking, and forgiving—you *show* them.

When your children think of honesty, do they think of you?

When they think of patience, do they think of you?

When they think of kindness, do they think of you?

When they think of selflessness, do they think of you?

When they think of humility, do they think of you?

When they think of authenticity, do they think of you?

When they think of a leader, do they think of you?

A child who sees his parent getting up early to exercise learns far more about the importance of a healthy lifestyle than any words or statistics could ever convey. A child who sees her parent apologize for bad behavior learns to apologize for her own.

> *Everyone thinks of changing the world, but no one thinks of changing himself.*
>
> —LEO TOLSTOY

Second, you actively look for and seek out opportunities to trust your children and to communicate that you trust them. For example, you might consider having family meetings and ask for their age-appropriate input or advice. Let them help you come up with family systems and rules, and trust them to follow through with those systems and rules.

One of the things my wife, Jeri, and I tried to do with our kids while they were growing up (and even since) was to have family meetings where we'd ask one of the kids to take charge of planning a family service or work activity—or, even better, our next family vacation! Of course, some of our early attempts at such meetings bordered on disaster, but as we persisted, we found that our kids really responded to being trusted. Trusting your children inspires them and brings out the best in them. Not trusting them may cause them to feel or wonder if you don't view them as trustworthy.

I remember one time overhearing a father berating his child, saying, "What's wrong with you? You're so untrustworthy. Why do you behave this way?"

The child replied, "Because that's the way untrustworthy kids behave, Dad."

They were trapped in a vicious downward cycle; the child was living down to the label his dad had given him. How do you respond to that?

Finally, inspire your children by connecting with them personally, showing your love and care for them as well as connecting to what matters to them.

I'll never forget seeing my dad taking my younger sister Catherine to all the *Star Wars* movies during the years she was growing up. My dad wasn't a science-fiction fan, and he didn't really care for those particular movies. But he knew my sister loved them, so he went with her to the movies. He went not because the movies meant anything to him, but simply because they meant everything to her—and *she* meant everything to him.

Don't miss this connecting step. What do children feel inspired by, and how do they want to make a difference—and do they believe they can? How can they contribute to your family culture in meaningful ways? Build stewardship agreements *with* them to give the children opportunities to grow and thrive, like my father did with me in "green and clean."

Whenever my children were close to getting their driver's license, my wife and I sat down and made a stewardship agreement with them. We wrote it up, printed it out, and even had them sign it (and so did we). We normally didn't make stewardship agreements in our home that formal, but with something as important as driving, we decided to do it that way. We trusted our children to drive safely because they had agreed to it and knew the natural consequences of not doing so.

Does this ensure the agreement isn't violated? Absolutely not. If you want an example of this, my oldest son, then sixteen, violated this agreement. He was pulled over for going eighty-three miles per hour in a twenty-five-mile-per-hour zone! The stewardship agreement, which we'd all agreed to and built together in advance, governed. It was hard, he was embarrassed, and he had to pay a large fine, but he learned to discipline himself as a result. And because everything was specified in advance, he didn't resent us when he lost the privilege to drive for the agreed-on period.

As a parent, you can do this with anything! Does your child need to be better at cleaning their room? Think of "green and clean," and create a stewardship agreement together. But remember the most important adage from that story for a parent: *Raise kids, not grass.* It's not about the final product but about the growth of your child. Manage things, lead people. Yes, you want a clean room from your child, but the more important thing is that you're developing someone with good habits who values cleanliness, not simply someone with the ability to pick things up and put them away. It's not about the room; it's about the growth of your child. You're seeing and developing potential, not containing it. The greatness is in the seed, not the gardener.

Trust & Inspire Teaching

Nearly all of us can remember a teacher who made a difference in our lives. For me, it was my high school history and psychology teacher, Mr. McKay. Not only did he make both history and psychology interesting, relevant, and accessible, but he inspired me. I looked up to him and wanted to be like him. He taught me how to be a good student, but more importantly, he taught me how to be a good person.

Every day, there are students like me who are changed, uplifted, and inspired by the incredible teachers in their lives. Perhaps you were one of those students and can remember the teacher(s) who improved your life.

I'm a little biased because, as many people know, my father was a university professor the entire time I was growing up. And as I mentioned earlier, my daughter McKinlee is a teacher. I believe that teaching is one of the most noble and important professions in the world. The future of our society is in large part shaped by those who teach children. Teachers are the ultimate models and mentors to our children. They don't just teach a specific subject; they teach how to be kind, how to work hard, how to develop a love for learning. They teach students to believe in themselves. They help students plan for a bright and exciting future in which they can contribute to society.

Teachers also work in an industry that is highly regulated for many valid reasons. Maintaining student safety, tracking student outcomes, and seeking ways to improve are all important and necessary measures on which districts and schools focus. However, many would describe the education industry in general as deeply Command & Control. Too often, the rules and regulations—even the necessary ones—become the sole focus of education systems. Focus on test scores and measured learning outcomes dominate the national stage, while specific rules and regulations abound in every school district. Strict policies combined with overloaded classrooms and underfunded schools can lead both teachers and administrators to adopt, and in some cases embrace, a Command & Control style.

Because there are so many moving pieces and because teachers are entrusted with student lives, leaders in education can feel that they *have* to oversee every detail. That they *have* to micromanage, because children are too important not to double-check everything or to err on the side of caution.

The end result, however, is that teachers and administrators often feel stifled and overwhelmed. Regardless of whether that was the intent, this Command & Control style often leads to compliance being valued over creativity, scores being valued over growth, and rules being valued over people. And while there is great merit to being very cautious with our children and their protection, in the end a Command & Control style hurts teachers, administrators, and students. Remember, a Trust & Inspire style can work in even the most highly regulated industries. This doesn't mean throwing rules out the window. Instead, it means increasing the abilities of people to comply with those rules and thrive while doing so.

Trust & Inspire can and does work extraordinarily well in education. I know that because in many schools and districts throughout the nation and world, it already is.

As mentioned earlier, recent surveys found that half of teachers in the United States were actively seeking a different job, with only slightly more than 30 percent being fully engaged. These statistics aren't because people have lost interest in helping children—all the people in these studies worked to become teachers, so the passion for the profession was there at one point. But teachers, like people in any other profession, need to be both trusted and inspired. And too often they feel the exact opposite way. Just consider the passion and potential that could be unleashed in a school system by an administrator "going first" in becoming a Trust & Inspire leader and building a Trust & Inspire culture!

Instead teachers too often feel overwhelmed and burned out. Instead of being unleashed to develop creative lessons and activities, they are burdened with paperwork and meetings. We know that teachers aren't in it for the money (because we all know they should be paid more)—they're in it because they love students and they love education. They become teachers because they care. But as the data shows, if they don't feel valued—if they aren't supported, both financially and emotionally—their love for students can go only so far. And it *should* go only so far. Teachers, like everyone else, are whole people—body, mind, heart, and spirit. They shouldn't be asked to sacrifice their emotional and physical well-being simply because they love helping children. Their desire to help children should instead be nourished and supported.

Teachers long to achieve the same feelings of safety, belonging, pride, and achievement as all other people do in their jobs. Administrators have the power to help this happen. They can create policies that advocate for teachers. They can create Trust & Inspire environments in their offices, their districts, their schools. They can be leaders in changing the narrative in education.

What's good for teachers is also good for students. Trust & Inspire administrators trust their teachers to know and serve their students best. A Trust & Inspire administrator not only seeks the best for teachers in terms of resources but looks to inspire them, simply because the teachers deserve it.

Administrators also face huge challenges in education; they are often overworked and underfunded as well. But they can be the turning point for an entire school, for an entire district. Imagine what would happen if you as a principal decided to transform your school to become a Trust & Inspire school. If you as a superintendent worked to create a Trust & Inspire culture in your district. What possibilities and outcomes might come into view? What creativity, passion, and drive might you be able to ignite? What sense of purpose could you spark in your team if they felt trusted and inspired instead of feeling unappreciated and undervalued?

Often, the Command & Control style found in the upper echelons of education carries over into the classroom. This style may even feel necessary for some teachers in order to keep structure and order in the classroom. While this is understandable, it is also the least inspiring method of teaching and connecting with students.

In my daughter McKinlee's first year of teaching, a veteran teacher told her, "You need to establish your credibility with the kids by talking about your credentials and showing them how tough you are. Explain why you're an expert in your subject and show them that they need to respect you." McKinlee tried that out only to find that this approach flopped in a major way. Kids didn't care about her degree or how long she'd been teaching. And they definitely did not respond to her demands for respect.

What they *did* care about was how she treated them and whether she wanted to invest in them. The same adage also applies here: they didn't care how much she knew until they knew how much she cared. She couldn't Command & Control her way to student respect or buy-in. And she definitely couldn't help them achieve anything academically.

McKinlee course-corrected and instead built her credibility by showing students who she was. She spent time with each individual student, trying to learn about his or her life and establish meaningful relationships. She worked to help her students feel safe in her classroom and to have a sense of belonging. She gained credibility through her character, her competence, and her consistency. Above all, she modeled the behavior she wanted to see.

This didn't mean that she threw out the rules of her classroom. She still had high expectations for her students and held her students accountable. But the students learned *why* she did those things. She didn't set and enforce expectations to punish them but to push them—to *grow* them. And she didn't do it because she was mean but because she cared. When they understood who she was—what her intent was, what her goals were, why she did what she did—they got onboard with her ideas, rules, and structures.

Of course, there were still problems. She definitely had some bad days and difficult situations that first year. But the connections she had made with individual students helped carry her through. The positive classroom environment where students felt they belonged was as big a blessing to her as it was to her students. And in turn, the students worked harder and achieved more than they would've had she just commanded and controlled her way through the year.

McKinlee didn't wait on an administrator or any other forces outside her control. She became a Trust & Inspire teacher, and the impact of that was seen and felt at a broad level. In fact, her classes had the highest academic growth rates of any in the entire school—by far—and she was recognized at the district level as one of the top two teachers in the school.

Many teachers have probably had similar experiences. Teachers who share and live their *why*, build caring relationships with individual students, and foster a teamlike feeling in the classroom where everybody belongs are able to help their students care more and achieve more than those who simply teach their subject and demand students listen and comply.

> *I am not a teacher, but an awakener.*
>
> —ROBERT FROST

This doesn't always mean that you will achieve the highest academic scores or have the best results. There are things that educators simply can't control, including a student's situation at home, that impact test results and other quantitative measures. But there is one thing that you can always control: the way you see and treat your students. The way you express belief in them. The way you are there for them. And if you do these things consistently, it will yield great results—even if it's not always a result that other people can see. You will see it in the way your students respond to you, trust you, and work for you—and for themselves.

There are students whose life paths can be changed forever all because of the belief of one teacher. The way a teacher treats the most difficult student sends a message to the rest of the class about how that teacher views each of *them*. It's easy to get along with the students who comply. It takes a lot more to work to get along with those who don't. But how you treat that student speaks volumes to every other student.

A Trust & Inspire teacher sees the inherent value of each student, especially those who struggle. A Trust & Inspire teacher doesn't just focus on rules or outcomes but on student development. A Trust & Inspire teacher's classroom becomes a refuge: where students know they are valued and feel a sense of belonging. A Trust & Inspire teacher is driven by the fundamental belief that there is greatness in people and that the life and power is in the seed. That each child has potential, even if it might take a while for that potential to reveal itself. But as my father said, "Leadership is communicating to people their worth and potential so clearly that they come to see it in themselves." Perhaps no one can do this—see potential and communicate it—better than teachers can.

> *You can never teach a person anything; you can only help him find it within himself.*

> —GALILEO

Author and thought leader Les Brown experienced this firsthand during his school days. He struggled in school and was even once diagnosed as mentally disabled. Much to his chagrin, his twin brother did well in school, leading Les to be called the "DT" or the "dumb twin." This went on for years. As a result, he had incredibly low self-esteem, developed depression, and felt lethargic about his abilities. One day, while working with a teacher in high school, Les exclaimed that it was pointless—that he couldn't learn because of his diagnosis of having an intellectual disability.

The teacher looked Les directly in the eyes and said, "Don't you ever say that again. Someone's opinion of you does not have to become your reality."

That was a turning point for Les. It opened his mind and gave him a new view of himself. He saw his potential for the first time. And he started working to achieve it. He overcame difficulties and has become an author of many books and an Emmy Award–winning speaker. All because a teacher saw more in him than he saw in himself.

What students are sitting in your classroom right now who, like Les, need their worth and potential to be communicated to them? Which students need you to help them achieve that potential?

Another great example of looking for the potential in both students and teachers comes from the development of "The Leader in Me" program. In 1999, principal Muriel Summers of A. B. Combs Elementary School in Raleigh, North Carolina, read my father's book *The 7 Habits of Highly Effective People*. She felt deeply inspired by the content. Her school was failing at the time, and she was looking for ways to change that. She had a subsequent personal interaction with my father, where she asked with great sincerity whether "the habits could be taught to children as young as kindergartners to get them life ready."

He answered, "I don't know why they couldn't. Why don't you test it and find out?"

Muriel decided to begin teaching the 7 Habits in her school fueled by the belief that every student is a leader and can learn and implement the leadership principles. She got her staff and teachers onboard, asking for their help and trusting them to help her. The students responded to this belief in them, and soon her school's test scores began to rise—significantly.

She continued this process and even went deeper, believing in the leader inside every student and helping students see this leader in themselves. Both the students and school began to thrive as never before. Since implementing this process, A. B. Combs Leadership Magnet Elementary School has been named the number one magnet school in America—on two separate occasions!

Muriel's work ultimately became "The Leader in Me," a schoolwide program that has now been adopted in thousands of schools in more than fifty countries. It all began with her belief in students. She saw value in each of them, even though statistically and by traditional measures, they showed up as both low potential and lower performers. She felt that each child needed only to believe that "there is a leader in me," and her desire was to unleash that belief and bring it out in each student. She extended that same trust to her teachers as they also learned and taught the 7 Habits. She and her staff modeled the behavior and trusted that students were capable to do the same.

I've visited Muriel's school a couple of times, and I cannot tell you how inspiring it is to see students empowered with the knowledge that they have greatness within. In fact, some of my grandchildren attend that school today, and I couldn't be prouder.

You don't need to create a new program like Muriel did to be an effective teacher or administrator. She started with herself, and she worked from the inside out within her role. You can do the same.

Nothing else in education—not new technology, new curriculum, or a new building—can make up for a lack of trust and inspiration. We need leaders who believe in those around them and who lead with that belief. It begins with the way you view those you teach. It begins with your fundamental beliefs about students and teachers. Do you see their potential? Do you see greatness in them? They are waiting to be unleashed. You can be the one to unleash their potential. Like the teacher who inspired Les, like Mr. McKay who inspired me, like the administrator who trusted my daughter in her first year of teaching, like Muriel Summers who unleashed the potential of an entire body of students, you can be the catalyst in changing the way a student, a school, a district, a community operates.

I want to be the pebble in the pond that creates the ripple for change.

—TIM COOK, CEO OF APPLE

Trust & Inspire Athletic Coaching

Have you ever been to a Little League game and seen *that* person? You know the one I'm talking about—the one yelling at the players and the coaches and the officials. The one who can't help but tell #10 (usually his own child or grandchild) to "Keep your elbow up! No! Not like that!" for the tenth time. This person might also be the one who gets in a shouting match with a parent from the opposing team or with the officials.

Sadly, this person might be the coach.

Unfortunately, coaching is probably the last bastion of seemingly acceptable "Neanderthal" Command & Control in our society. This may be born out of the desire to get the best out of players by pushing them to their physical and mental limits. However, it is often manifested through extreme yelling and demeaning behavior. And for far too long, we as a society have accepted it and sometimes even embraced it.

But does it have to be this way? Do we have to tolerate the guy yelling at an eight-year-old's baseball game? Can an effective Trust & Inspire coach truly exist?

Absolutely. Trust & Inspire doesn't mean you can't have high expectations or demand the best from people. It also doesn't mean there aren't moments when you have to discipline people or push them. But you do so from a mindset of Trust & Inspire, having built a relationship of trust first. When you do push and challenge them and the relationship of trust is already there, they will see themselves as being as capable as you see them, and they will be inspired by it!

Again, the full pattern for this virtuous cycle is the fourfold process we described earlier: to *see*, *communicate*, *develop*, and *unleash* the potential inside people. Trust & Inspire coaches lead and coach this way. Pete Carroll and Dabo Swinney are this way in football. Cori Close is this way in basketball, as was her mentor, John Wooden. So is Becky Hammon today. Diljeet Taylor coaches her track team this way. The great San Francisco 49ers football player Joe Montana had this to say about his legendary coach, Bill Walsh: "His goal in life was to convince us that we could be great. And he did, and we were. That's why he was such a great leader."

The four most powerful words are: I believe in you.

—BILL WALSH, FORMER 49ERS
HALL OF FAME COACH

A current NFL player highlighted the importance of Trust & Inspire coaching when he recounted his athletics journey. He was athletically gifted, to say the least, and he had a hulking frame. While in high school, he received offers to play both Division 1 football and basketball. He ended up choosing football. Undeterred, the basketball coach at the university he chose approached him to see if he would consider playing for their team as well. He decided that he would play for both teams. When he stepped onto the court, it seemed clear to most people watching that he had a body built for basketball. He made great progress his freshman year and did better in basketball than he did in football.

Many people thought he'd end up quitting football to focus solely on basketball. Much to their surprise, he ended up doing the exact opposite. The basketball staff was known for their Command & Control style and had used negative tactics with players in the past. This athlete decided that he'd rather work with the football coaches, who he found to be much more trusting, inspiring, and caring.

Fast-forward a few years, and he is now playing in the NFL. As he discussed his decision to quit basketball, he said, "You know what? I would've loved to have stuck with basketball. The reason I left is because one of the key assistant coaches left. And I couldn't work in that environment without him. If he had stayed, maybe I'd be playing in the NBA right now instead of the NFL."

This assistant coach was such a Trust & Inspire leader that this young man would have changed his entire career trajectory had that coach remained. Instead, he chose to leave because of the remaining coaching staff's controlling style—and the negative impact it had on him (remember—people don't leave organizations, they leave bad bosses). The assistant coach who left became a head coach at another university and saw great success there, elevating the program to new heights. He had high expectations and pushed his players, but they loved him for it because of the way he treated them. Because of the way he saw them. Because of the way he believed in them. Because of the way he trusted and inspired them.

Which coach would you rather play for?

We all parent, we all teach, and we all coach in one form or another. You can operate with a Trust & Inspire style to unleash greatness in anyone, and in any setting.

Other Types of Jobs or Roles

There are many other roles that warrant mentioning due to their significance in our society. Any role can be seen through the lens of Command & Control or Trust & Inspire. For example, consider lawyers. While they are the butt of many jokes and some negative stereotypes, lawyers play an essential role in our society and can help bring both justice and mercy to many people. Trust & Inspire lawyers are out there, and they're extraordinary. How does a Trust & Inspire lawyer operate compared to a Command & Control one?

Religious, civic, and community leaders also impact our neighborhoods and communities, yet they might not often think of the way they interact with their stakeholders, be they parishioners or constituents or citizens. For those of you serving in one of these roles as a leader, does your style get in the way of your intent?

While outsiders may think the military is all about Command & Control, those involved will also tell you that to be effective, military units must operate with trust. I had the privilege of spending time with the former chairman of the Joint Chiefs of Staff, General Martin Dempsey (Ret.). He strongly believed that trust was "the secret sauce of the military." I earlier mentioned how General Dorothy Hogg of the air force extended trust to her team as a means of becoming innovators. Similarly, General Stanley McChrystal, former four-star commander, shared a mantra his leadership team used in the field that demonstrated extending trust to their soldiers: "If, when you get on the ground, the order that we gave you is wrong, execute the order we should have given you." As a military leader, are you focused both on executing missions *and* building relationships of trust?

Trust & Inspire is a way of being, regardless of your different roles in life. Its value is central to the human condition. Of all the roles described in the various stories and situations in this book, perhaps the most significant is the role of being a transition figure. In both large and small ways, a transition figure is a person who changes the trajectory of someone else's life.

Two extraordinary Trust & Inspire transition figures are illustrated beautifully in Victor Hugo's *Les Misérables*. After serving nineteen years of hard labor in prison for stealing a loaf of bread to feed his sister's starving child, Jean Valjean is finally released on parole. When a woman sees him trying to find shelter, she tells him to go to the church, where he encounters Bishop Myriel of Digne.

The bishop treats Valjean with kindness and dignity, feeding him and giving him a place to spend the night. Desperate and believing he has no other options, Valjean steals the bishop's silverware and flees under the cloak of night. He is quickly apprehended by the police, who return him to the bishop to face his punishment.

In an astonishing display of mercy, the bishop welcomes Valjean and assures the police that he *gave* the silverware to Valjean as a gift, and goes on to say that he forgot to take the candlesticks as well—thus sparing Valjean an arrest and the inevitable return to prison. Once the two are alone, the bishop communicates to Valjean a belief in his own potential. Even after Valjean's term in prison, the bishop sees greatness in the ragged man—he sees the power that is in the seed; sees what hopefully someone else has seen in each of us.

In that moment, the bishop becomes a powerful transition figure in the life of Valjean. His belief in Valjean changes the trajectory of his life.

Inspired by the bishop, the second Trust & Inspire leader is Valjean himself. What happens next illustrates the ripple effect created by a Trust & Inspire leader, a phenomenon in which goodness spreads throughout the tapestry of connected lives.

Valjean becomes a benefactor to countless souls in need—including becoming a kind, devoted father to the orphaned Cosette. He becomes the mayor of the town, and uses the wealth he amasses to finance orphanages, hospitals, and schools. Valjean becomes a transition figure in the lives of many, including Fantine, Cosette, Marius, and even his archenemy Javert.

As humans, we all have a desire to become a transition figure in the lives of those we love. As leaders, we all have an opportunity, and perhaps even a stewardship, to become a transition figure in the lives of those we lead.

The key to becoming a transition figure is to first become a Trust & Inspire person.

Conclusion

It's not about me. It's about what you do for other people.

—INGA BEALE, FORMER CEO
OF LLOYD'S OF LONDON

On May 25, 2001, Erik Weihenmayer became part of the largest team ever to make it to the top of Mount Everest. Erik also became the first person to climb Mount Everest—blind. His story is incredible and is a tribute to the triumph of the human spirit. It is also a Trust & Inspire story.

It's estimated that only approximately 29 percent of people who've tried have made it to the top of Mount Everest. Erik had been mountain climbing since he was a teenager but had never considered climbing Everest—the odds were stacked against anyone, let alone him as an unsighted person.

He met expedition leader Pasquale Scaturro (or PV, as he's called) at a trade show. When PV asked Erik if he had ever considered scaling Everest, Erik felt something stir inside him. Together they began to devise a plan for Erik to take on the mountain. PV knew that the only way this would work would be for Erik to be surrounded by climbers that he knew and trusted.

Although their skills were critical and foundational to their success, it was the attitude and the relationship among team members that took their performance to the level necessary to accomplish this unprecedented feat. As they put their team together and throughout the long training process, Erik's excitement grew.

But that excitement was crushed after Erik's first day of climbing left him exhausted, bloodied, and bruised. The team knew they needed to do more to help him, and Erik knew he needed to dig deeper to find the belief that he could do what he set out to do.

As he worked with his team, Erik's climbing skills began to improve, and things started to go more smoothly. Every night, PV called a tent meeting so the group could discuss any issues or problems they saw. This method of frequent, open communication enabled expectations to be clear and helped the team to grow closer through understanding.

Erik inspired the team with his skill and dedication, making it from Base Camp to Camp 2 in less than five hours, beating the times of most sighted climbers. In return, the team worked to become better at guiding Erik.

The trust between everyone became a catalyst for incredible performance and galvanized everyone around an amazing goal. Erik later told me personally, "Being roped together when crossing an ice field riddled with crevasses is the ultimate trust scenario. In the mountains, my life is often in my teammates' hands and theirs in mine."

However, Erik was still worried he might not make it to the summit, which would ruin the ascent for the teammates, who would need to help him if he needed to turn back. Everyone rejected this notion, reminding him that they had only one goal and purpose: to get *him* to the top of Everest.

Never would their commitment to their purpose be tested more than when PV became ill with malaria. He made the decision to go back down the mountain so he wouldn't slow down the team.

A few days later, a storm hit, and the leaderless group had to decide whether to continue onward or to turn back. Michael Brown, the film-maker who documented the event, said, "Most of the time on Everest, it's every man or woman for himself, saying, 'I want to be on the top...' Our team had a loftier goal, to get behind Erik and make sure he was able to safely get to the top and back down ... everybody on the team put aside their own self-serving need to get to the top to get behind Erik's summit." The team decided to continue onward.

More challenges arose, but the team continued to meet and beat them. When Erik made it to the top, he shed tears of joy. But Erik wasn't the only one to make it. With the exception of PV, all nineteen members of the expedition team did, too—making it the largest team to ever make it to the top and one of the most successful expeditions to summit Everest. Ever. When PV learned they had made it, he was overcome with joy knowing the two years they had spent preparing for this expedition had been worth it.

Erik achieved something remarkable, and it was made possible by a Trust & Inspire team. They relied on one another and built trust before and throughout the journey. The group became connected and unified in purpose—focused on helping Erik achieve something that nobody had ever done before. The dedication they all had to Erik, and to one another, was absolutely inspiring and gave them the extra push they needed to make it to the top.

PV saw the greatness inside Erik and his potential to make it. Together they completed one of the most incredible feats in human history by trusting the process—and each other.

There was no fear. They trusted each other to succeed because they knew there was greatness in their team. They each saw the greatness not only in the team but also in each other, including in Erik. Where others may have looked at Erik and doubted, they had total belief. Where others might have seen limitations, they saw potential and greatness. And he had complete belief in them.

There was no complaining. They worked to inspire each other because they knew that this climb wasn't just physical, but mental, emotional, and spiritual as well. It simultaneously taxed and brought joy to the whole person, to every part of their beings. Motivation wasn't enough—they needed inspiration. They looked beyond the physical and made this a journey for their whole selves.

There was no internal competition. They elevated caring over competing because they knew that one person's success could be *ev-*

erybody's success. Jealousy wasn't part of the picture; caring and love is what drove them all. Erik's success became all of their success. There was enough for everyone on the mountain.

There was no small-minded selfishness. The entire team felt a stewardship—to Erik and to each other—to get Erik to the summit. That sense of stewardship and service enabled there to be so much shared leadership among the team that when PV needed to go back, the team could still go forward.

There was no short-term mindset. The enduring influence of Erik and his team was built on the foundation of their work on themselves first—and it continues to this day and beyond. And it all started because Erik, PV, and others each chose to go first and model both the beliefs and the behavior.

These, indeed, are the five fundamental beliefs that make up the paradigm of a Trust & Inspire leader, which Erik and his team beautifully represented:

- People have greatness inside them . . . so my job as a leader is to unleash their potential, not control them.

- People are whole people . . . so my job as a leader is to inspire, not merely motivate.

- There is enough for everyone . . . so my job as a leader is to elevate caring above competing.

- Leadership is stewardship . . . so my job as a leader is to put service above self-interest.

- Enduring influence is created from the inside out . . . so my job as a leader is to go first.

Individually and collectively, Erik and his team on this summit demonstrated a wonderful mastery of all 3 stewardships of a Trust & Inspire leader—modeling, trusting, and inspiring.

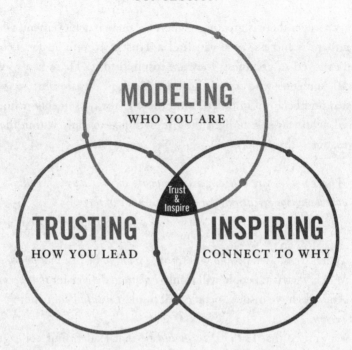

They modeled the behavior, demonstrating who they were as leaders of credibility and moral authority, each one choosing to go first in their modeling.

They trusted each other, as well as the entire team—and even the process—and by doing so, they unleashed the team to achieve one of the greatest feats in the world. They demonstrated how they led through trusting.

And they inspired each other by connecting with people and by connecting to purpose in answering why it matters. Despite the difficulty of the journey, they tapped into purpose, meaning, and contribution—inspiring everyone to incredible heights.

We might not ever attempt to summit Mount Everest, but we can all do great things. The world is a better and more noble place when filled with Trust & Inspire people and leaders. Amazing feats, and equally amazing leadership, are made possible through modeling, trusting, and inspiring.

Wherever there is greatness, wherever there is achievement, wherever there is success—you can find a Trust & Inspire leader. People aren't moved to greatness; they are inspired to it. There is always a model, someone who paved the way. There is always someone who trusted and believed in others. And there is always someone who inspired, who was able to light the fire within—not only within themselves, but within others.

What's within you is stronger than what's in your way . . . I think everybody has a yearning for greatness inside of them.

—ERIK WEIHENMAYER

When we model, people will think, *I want to* be like *that person.*

When we trust, people will think, *I want to* deliver for *that person.*

And when we inspire, people will think, *I want to* contribute with *that person.*

We can be that leader. We *should* be that leader. Our colleagues need it. Our organizations need it. Our family and friends need it. Our communities need it. Our society and world need it.

And as we become the leader we strive to be, we will find that life is made all the better for it.

This, indeed, is the new way to lead, and a better way to live: Trust & Inspire.

Acknowledgments

It takes a village to write a book! At least for me it does.

There are countless people in my village who have helped make this book possible. I feel deeply thankful for others' contributions to this book and to my life. Albert Einstein's expression rings true and humbles me: "Every day I remind myself that my inner and outer life are based on the labors of other people, living and dead, and that I must exert myself in order to give in the same measure as I have received and am still receiving."

So it is with this book. It could not have been written without the help of many people for whom I am grateful.

In particular, I want to express profound gratitude to my three collaborators on this book: David Kasperson, McKinlee Covey, and Gary T. Judd. Individually and collectively, they have created such tremendous value that I feel compelled to recognize their synergistic contributions by giving them attribution on the book cover itself.

David Kasperson is my original collaborator around the idea of this book. Brilliant as always, when David would help me in my speaking engagements, we found ourselves talking about how the world had changed but how our style of leadership had not. We began to identify and articulate the new kind of leadership that is needed today—Trust & Inspire. His remarkable insight, creativity, and understanding of people and leadership is matched only by his ability to help me on the speaking side of the business—not only in filling my calendar with engagements but also in helping me prepare and customize my presentations to meet client needs exactly. Exceptionally capable and passionate, David was the original spark that ignited the fire within me to write this book.

McKinlee Covey, my immensely talented daughter, is the collaborator who initially helped me put this book down in writing. For me, the first draft is far and away the most difficult to produce. With her magnificent assistance and productivity, she helped turbocharge our writing efforts while also adding additional insight, wisdom, examples, and stories. She helped make the book readable and relatable. Without her creative help, we'd still be talking about this book rather than reading it.

Gary T. Judd, my longtime business partner and superb leader of our Trust Practice, added an unparalleled understanding, wisdom, and application into what makes up a Trust & Inspire leader and how to build Trust & Inspire cultures. Time and again, he provided profound insights and practical implementation into this work, without which it would have been significantly diminished. Not only does Gary understand people and leadership, he also understands principles and how to apply them. And, best of all, he models what he believes.

Special thanks also to:

• Julie Judd Gillman, my extraordinary Executive Assistant, for her talent, expertise, creativity, and "make it happen" abilities. She has been indispensable in the creation of this book, including doing all of the graphics. She not only makes my life more productive, she also makes it better!

• Doug Faber, our outstanding FranklinCovey Global Trust Practice Leader, for not only passionately believing in this book, but especially for helping us turn this content into learning modules, programs, curriculum, and tools so that we can help our clients succeed in developing Trust & Inspire leaders and cultures.

• Kathryn Jenkins for her exceptional writing and editing help as we focused on making this book more accessible and readable. Her significant contributions have been invaluable to me, and they gave me far greater clarity and confidence in the expression of my voice. I'm enormously grateful to her.

• Barry Rellaford, for his ongoing collaboration, coaching, and expertise. Among other things, Barry worked with Doug and our team in helping to modularize and operationalize the *Trust & Inspire* content with clients.

• Greg Link—my longtime visionary friend and business partner—for his continued influence for good on me, on this book, and in my life.

• My terrific research assistants, Maureen Fitzsimmons and Cynthia Hall, for their hard work, diligence, and resourcefulness in helping to identify and bring data, examples, and illustrations to this book.

• My wonderful editor at Simon & Schuster, Stephanie Frerich, for her belief in the project from the outset and for her affirming and constructive guidance along the way in helping me to do what this book is about—trust my reader. Stephanie not only made this book significantly better, she was an invaluable and creative collaborator.

• Jonathan Karp, my publisher, for believing in this book from the first time he heard the idea, and for being such a model of a Trust & Inspire leader that the Simon & Schuster team could immediately see and understand what I was talking about.

• The entire extended team at Simon & Schuster, including Emily Simonson, Jackie Seow, Martin Karlow, Phil Metcalf, and others for their valuable contributions.

• Rebecca Merrill, my longtime collaborator from past projects, and Roger Merrill, my longtime business partner. Together, they provided enormous insight, wisdom, and advice. Their involvement on this project had a transformative impact on both the book and on me.

• Other members of the extended FranklinCovey team for their ongoing support, help, and encouragement, including Bob Whitman, Paul

Walker, Jennifer Colosimo, Sean Covey, Adam Merrill, Scott Miller, Suzette Blakemore, Matt Murdock, Annie Oswald, Zack Kristensen, Nolan Marx, Muriel Summers, Debra Lund, Ryan Muir, Jimmy McDermott, Lori North, VS Pandian, among so many others.

• The entire FranklinCovey innovation and development team led by Rob Cahill, for their development of learning and training curriculum, modules, assessments, and tools around this Trust & Inspire content so as to help our clients on their journey of creating Trust & Inspire leaders and cultures.

• Our many clients, who provide an ongoing laboratory to apply and validate the Trust & Inspire approach, and for the input and helpful feedback so many have given.

• Many other individuals who generously took the time to read and review various stages of the manuscript, and who gave us invaluable feedback that was instructive yet always affirming: Suzette Blakemore, Donna Burnette, Maria Cole, Jennifer Colosimo, David Covey, Sean Covey, Boyd Craig, Sue Dathe-Douglas, Kameron Haller, John Harding, Julene Judd, Audrey Kasperson, Annie Link, Greg Link, Debra Lund, Annie Oswald, Nolan Marx, Greg McKeown, Rebecca Merrill, Roger Merrill, Cameron Moon, Shawn Moon, and Barry Rellaford.

With deep gratitude, I acknowledge my parents, Sandra and Stephen R. Covey, for their profound influence on my life and on my thinking. I dedicated this book to them for this reason. As I've worked on this book over these past several years, I've begun to feel, in many ways, that I am continuing, and in some ways completing, my father's work from his book *The 8th Habit*.

I gratefully acknowledge my amazing wife, Jeri, for her constant love, support, encouragement, and help along the journey. She makes my life adventurous and fun! She is my true companion. This book wouldn't be possible without her.

I similarly acknowledge my children, Stephen, McKinlee, Christian, Britain, and Arden, along with my daughters-in-law Emily, Emarie, and Leah for their encouragement and support. They've endured me working long hours on this project instead of playing. Now it's time to play!

Most importantly, I acknowledge and thank God for the blessings, insights, and support I have felt throughout this entire book project. For me, God is the source of all principles that bring joy and success in relationships, in leadership, and in all of life.

Appendix

Contrasts

COMMAND & CONTROL	TRUST & INSPIRE
CHAPTER 1	
Compliance	Commitment
Transactional	Transformational
Efficiency	Effectiveness
Status Quo and Incrementalism	Change and Innovation
Fixed Mindset	Growth Mindset
Coordination among Functional Silos	Collaboration among Flexible, Interconnected Teams
Control, Contain	Release, Unleash
Motivation	Inspiration
Manage People and Things	Manage Things, Lead People
Extrinsic	Intrinsic
Require	Inspire
Suffocate	"Breathe Life Into"
Conditioning	Developing

COMMAND & CONTROL	TRUST & INSPIRE
Behaviorism	Autonomy
Leadership Is a Position	Leadership Is a Choice
CHAPTER 2	
Industrial Age	Knowledge-Worker Age
Stability	Change & Disruption
To Know and Not to Do	To Know AND to Do
Informed Acquiescence	Self-Governance
Coercive	Persuasive
Native Tongue	Acquired Tongue
CHAPTER 3	
Micro-management	Macro-leadership
Leadership is a Position	Leadership is a Choice

COMMAND & CONTROL	TRUST & INSPIRE
CHAPTER 4	
Machinist	Gardener
Fragmented Person	Whole Person (Body, Heart, Mind, Spirit)
Scarcity Mentality	Abundance Mentality
Self-Interest	Caring
Compete	Complete
CHAPTER 5	
Formal Authority	Moral Authority
Position	Influence
What You Do	Who You Are
Tell	Show
Directive	Instructive
Courage	Humility and Courage

COMMAND & CONTROL	TRUST & INSPIRE
Seeming	Being
Hidden Agenda	Open Agenda
Give the What	Give the Why Behind the What
Shareholders	All Stakeholders

CHAPTER 6

COMMAND & CONTROL	TRUST & INSPIRE
Trustworthy	Trustworthy and Trusting
The Power Is in the Gardener	The Life—and Power—Is in the Seed
Verify	Trust
Dictate Expectations	Mutually Clarify Expectations
Dictate Accountability	Mutually Agree to a Process of Accountability
Fix People	Grow People

CHAPTER 7

COMMAND & CONTROL	TRUST & INSPIRE
Self-Interest	Caring for Others
Span of Control	Span of Care
"What's In It For Me?"	"How Can I Best Serve?"

COMMAND & CONTROL	TRUST & INSPIRE
Association	Belonging
Exclusion	Inclusion
Success	Significance
Start with What	Start with Why
Connect to What	Connect to Why
Mission, Vision, and Values	Mission, Vision, and Values *and* Purpose, Meaning, and Contribution
Corporate Social Responsibility (CSR)	CSR *and* Creating Shared Value
Accumulation	Contribution

CHAPTER 8

Get the Job Done	Get the Job Done *and* Build the Relationship
Vertical Positioning	Horizontal Partnering
Micromanagement	Self-Governance
Dictate Methods	Establish Helpful Boundaries
"You're on Your Own"	"I Want to Set You Up to Succeed"

COMMAND & CONTROL	TRUST & INSPIRE
"I Hold You Accountable"	"You Hold Yourself Accountable to the Mutually-Established Agreement"
"I Judge You"	"You Judge Yourself"
Artificial and Arbitrary Consequences	Natural and Logical Consequences
Manage/Manager	Coach

CHAPTER 9

Might is Right	Might for Right
Hierarchy	Hive
Bureaucracy	Humanocracy
Goals and Plans	Vision and Strategy
Force	Persuade

CHAPTER 10

Start with Others	Start with Self
Work *in* the Systems	Work *on* the Systems
"This Can't Work Here"	"How Can This Work Here?"

COMMAND & CONTROL	TRUST & INSPIRE
CHAPTER 11	
Minimize the Risk	Maximize the Possibilities
Formula	Judgment
Finite	Infinite
CHAPTER 12	
Failure is Bad	Failure is Growth
CHAPTER 13	
Authoritarian	Authoritative
"If I Want Your Opinion, I'll Give It to You!"	"What's Your Opinion?"
Diminisher	Multiplier
Who is Right	What is Right
Listen to Respond	Listen to Understand
Growth Mindset for Self	Growth Mindset for All
Individual Contributors	Complementary Team

COMMAND & CONTROL	TRUST & INSPIRE
CHAPTER 14	
Stagnation	Growth
Program	Programmer
Top-Down, Bottlenecked Decision Making	Distributed Decision Making
Scripted	Rescripting

Notes and References

Introduction

1 **highest temperature ever recorded:** "Death Valley Weather," nps.org.

1 **Average rainfall:** "Weather and Climate Death Valley National Park," nps.gov.

1 **Sir Kenneth Robinson:** Kenneth Robinson, "How to Escape Education's Death Valley," TED Talks Education, April 2013.

2 **Socrates quote:** Plato and Benjamin Jowett, trans., *The Republic* (Massachusetts: Digireads.com, 2016); Dave Policano, "The Beginning of Good Data Is the Definition of Terms," *Stanford Social Innovation Review*, August 2018. Accessed July 20, 2021.

9 **Eleanor Roosevelt quote:** Zora Simic, "How Eleanor Roosevelt reshaped the role of First Lady and became a feminist icon," TheConversation.com, June 25, 2021. Accessed July 20, 2021.

9 **the Latin root *inspirare*:** "Breathing Life Into 'Inspire'," Merriam-Webster.com. Accessed July 20, 2021.

10 **Albert Schweitzer quote:** Albert Schweitzer, Facebook, @USASLFL, Albert Schweitzer Leadership for Life Nonprofit Organization, July 25, 2020.

Chapter 1: The World Has Changed, Our Style of Leadership Has Not

15 **Peter Drucker quote:** "Managing Knowledge Means Managing Oneself," *Leader to Leader* 16, Spring 2000, p. 8.

16 **Mahatma Gandhi quote:** Suman Guha, "UN affirms relevance of Mahatma Gandhi's message," *Indian Abroad*, October 10, 2008.

18 **Angela Merkel quote:** *Financial Times* interview with Angela Merkel, July 20, 2005.

19 **"the Fourth Industrial Revolution":** Klaus Schwab, "The Fourth Industrial Revolution: what it means, how to respond," weforum.org, January 14,

2016; Alejandro Lavopa and Michele Delera, "What is the Fourth Industrial Revolution?" unido.org, January 2021.

19 **knowledge doubles every twelve hours:** Scott Sorokin, "Thriving in a World of 'Knowledge Half Life,'" CIO.com, April 5, 2019. Accessed September 7, 2021.

21 **multiple generations working:** Richard Fry, "Millennials are the largest generation in the U.S. Labor Force," Pew Research Center, April 11, 2018; U.S. Bureau of Labor Statistics data.

22 **traditional jobholders by 2023:** "The State of Independence in America," MBO Partners State of Independence report, 2018; "Freelancing in America: 2019," Upwork and Freelancers Union study, October 2019.

23 **Satya Nadella quote:** "Satya Nadella Letter to Employees," Microsoft.com, February 4, 2014. Accessed July 20, 2021.

23 **Gary Hamel quote:** Gary Hamel, *The Future of Management* (Boston: Harvard Business School Press, 2007), p. 4.

23 **Marc Benioff quote:** Julia La Roche interview with Marc Benioff, Yahoo Finance, June 26, 2020.

24 **Global Pulse study:** "Stakeholder Trust: A New Frontier in Business Leadership," 2020 YPO Global Pulse study, January 2020.

25 **Bethany McLean quote:** Bethany McLean, "The Empire Reboots," VanityFair .com, October 8, 2014. Accessed July 20, 2021.

25 **Harry McCracken article:** Harry McCracken, "Satya Nadella Rewrites Microsoft's Code," FastCompany.com, September 18, 2017. Accessed July 20, 2021.

25 **In 2014, Apple and Google:** International Data Corporation data, 2014.

25 **cartoonist at the time:** Manu Cornet, Microsoft Organizational Chart cartoon, BonkersWorld.net, June 27, 2011.

25 **Satya Nadella quote:** Satya Nadella, *Hit Refresh* (New York: HarperCollins, 2017), p. 1.

26 **An employee survey:** "Top CEOs 2021: Employees' Choice," Glassdoor.com, 2021. Accessed July 20, 2021.

26 **Microsoft's market value:** Leo Sun, "Microsoft Is Now Worth $2 Trillion— Here's How It Gets to $3 Trillion," Nasdaq.com, June 26, 2021; "MSFT Historical Data," Nasdaq.com. Accessed July 20, 2021.

27 **"Being a leader":** Jessi Hempel interview with Satya Nadella, LinkedIn.com, December 9, 2019. Accessed July 20, 2021.

30 **Abraham Zaleznik quote:** Abraham Zaleznik, "Managers Are Leaders: Are They Different?" *Harvard Business Review*, January 2004.

30 **The definition of *manage*:** *manage*, Merriam-Webster.com. Accessed July 20, 2021.

32 **parable of the flea:** Brandon Alexander, "The Flea Experiment," LinkedIn
.com, October 8, 2018. Accessed July 20, 2021.

32 **Blaine Lee quote:** Author anecdote.

33 **As Pink put it:** Daniel Pink, *Drive* (New York: Riverhead Books, 2009), p. 73.

34 **The Yoga Sutras quote:** Maharishi Patañjali and Thomas Egenes, trans., *Yoga
Sutra* (Iowa: First World Publishing, March 17, 2010).

35 **"the great jackass theory":** Patrick Leddin, "How a Jackass Manager Treats
People," LinkedIn.com, April 6, 2018; Harry Levinson, "Asinine Attitudes Toward
Motivation," *Harvard Business Review*, January 1973. Accessed July 20, 2021.

35 **A recent study:** "Survey Shows Cheating and Academic Dishonesty Prevalent
in Colleges and Universities," Kessler International survey, prnewswire.com,
February 6, 2017. Accessed July 20, 2021.

36 **A humorous example:** "The Incentive," *The Office*, created by Charles
McDougall and Paul Lieberstein, Season 8, Episode 2, 2011.

36 **Simon Sinek quote:** Simon Sinek, *Start with Why: How Great Leaders Inspire
Everyone to Take Action* (New York: Penguin Group, 2009), p. 17.

36 **Indra Nooyi story:** Author interview with Indra Nooyi, July 28, 2010. Also,
Marguerite Ward, "Why PepsiCo CEO Indra Nooyi writes letters to her
employees' parents," *CNBC Online*, February 1, 2017. Accessed May 14, 2021.

38 **Malala Yousafzai:** "Malala Yousafzai Facts," NobelPrize.org, 2014.

39 *Yo Creo en Colombia:* "Yo Creo en Colombia," YoCreoEnColombia.com, 2014.
Accessed July 20, 2021.

39 **157 cities and 26 countries:** "Yo Creo en Colombia," *Pasion por el Logro* [Passion
for Accomplishment] report, YoCreoEnColombia.com, November 21, 2011, p.
14. Accessed July 20, 2021.

40 **Keith Ferrazzi quote:** Keith Ferrazzi, *Leading Without Authority: How the New
Power of Co-Elevation Can Break Down Silos, Transform Teams, and Reinvent
Collaboration* (New York: Random House, 2020), p. 9.

Chapter 2: The Increasing Irrelevance of Command & Control

42 **Margaret Wheatley quote:** Margaret Wheatley, "How Is Your Leadership
Changing?" MargaretWheatley.com, 2005. Accessed July 20, 2021.

42 **historian Arnold Toynbee:** Arnold J. Toynbee, *A Study of History* (Oxford:
Oxford University Press, January 1, 1957), pp. 327, 548.

42 **Warren Buffett quote:** Warren Buffett, Berkshire Hathaway Annual
Shareholders' Meeting panel, May 5, 2018.

43 **Blockbuster Video:** Christopher Harress, "The Sad End of Blockbuster

Video," *International Business Times*, December 5, 2013. Accessed May 14, 2021.

46 **Great Place to Work:** "The Best Workplaces for Millennials," Great Place to Work study, 2018.

46 **ADP Research:** Mary Hayes, et al., "Global Workplace Study 2020," ADP Research Institute study, 2020.

46 **Bain & Company:** Michael Mankins and Eric Garton, "Engaging Your Employees Is Good But Don't Stop There," *Harvard Business Review*, December 9, 2015. Also, Michael Mankins and Eric Garton, *Time, Talent, Energy: Overcome Organizational Drag and Unleash Your Team's Productive Power* (Boston: Bain & Company, and Harvard Business Review Press, 2017), p. 19.

48 **Robert Porter Lynch:** Robert Porter Lynch and Paul R. Lawrence, "Leadership and the Structure of Trust," *European Business Review*, May 20, 2011.

48 **LRN consulting:** "For Business, Trust Is the Catalyst for Success—From Governance + Compliance," LRN research study, 2017.

49 **Tim Cook quote:** Tim Cook commencement speech to Auburn University, May 14, 2010.

49 **Eric Yuan:** Author anecdote.

50 **Glassdoor ranked by:** "Glassdoor's Top CEOs for 2018 Announced; Zoom CEO Eric S. Yuan Earns #1 Spot," Glassdoor.com, 2021. Accessed July 20, 2021.

50 **2020 *Time* magazine**: Andrew R. Chow, "Businessperson of the Year: Eric Yuan," *Time*, 2020; "*Time* 100 Most Influential People 2020," *Time*, 2020.

50 **Eric Yuan quote:** Eric Yuan, "Zooming in on Zoom's Success: A Conversation with CEO Eric Yuan," YPO European Impact Summit speech, November 24, 2020.

50 **Zoom provided K–12 schools:** Alex Konrad, "Zoom CEO Eric Yuan Is Giving K–12 Schools His Videoconferencing Tools for Free," Forbes.com, March 13, 2020; "#ZoomTogether: Celebrate the Holidays with Unlimited Meetings from Zoom," Zoom.us, December 16, 2020. Accessed July 20, 2021.

52 **groundbreaking study:** "The How Report," LRN study, 2016.

57 **to paraphrase Oscar Wilde:** Oscar Wilde, *Lady Windermere's Fan*, Dover Thrift Editions (New York: Dover Publications, 1998), p. 38.

58 **As Goethe said:** Johann Wolfgang von Goethe and Thomas Bailey Saunders, trans., *The Maxims and Reflections of Goethe* (London: MacMillan and Co., 1908), p. 134.

60 **Bloodletting:** Tobias Lear, "II, 14 December 1799," Founders Online, National Archives, Accessed July 19, 2021.

61 **researchers Kerridge and Lowe:** Ian Kerridge and Michael Lowe, "Bloodletting: The story of a therapeutic technique," *Medical Journal of Australia*, volume 163, issues 11–12, December 1995, pp. 631–633.

63 **lieutenant general Dorothy Hogg:** Author interview with Lieutenant General Dorothy Hogg, December 6, 2018.

Chapter 3: Style Is Getting in the Way of Intent

65 **Thomas Edison quote:** Thomas Edison and Alex Ayres, *Quotable Edison: An A to Z Glossary of Quotes from Thomas Edison, Inventor and Wealth Creator* (Quotable Wisdom Books, 2016).

66 **Pierre Omidyar quote:** Pierre Omidyar eBay Seller Summit speech, September 10, 2015.

66 **Indra Nooyi quote:** *Fortune* magazine interview with Indra Nooyi, 2008.

67 **An internet search of *leadership*:** "Leadership styles," Google search. Accessed July 19, 2021.

68 **"servant leadership":** Author interview with Art Barter.

70 **Jesse Lyn Stoner quote:** Jesse Lyn Stoner, "Be a leader worth following," SeapointCenter.com, November 25, 2015. Accessed July 20, 2021.

Chapter 4: The 5 Fundamental Beliefs of a Trust & Inspire Leader

79 **Stephanie and Jonathan story:** author anecdote.

83 **Wildflowers in Death Valley story:** Sir Ken Robinson, TED Talk, "How to Escape Education's Death Valley," May 10, 2013.

83 **Buckminster Fuller quote:** R. Buckminster Fuller, *Critical Path* (New York: St. Martin's Press, 1981), p. 26.

86 **Goethe quote:** quoted in *Psychology of Human Development: A Science of Growth*, by Justin Pikunas, (New York: McGraw-Hill, 1961), p. 311.

86 **Margaret Mead quote:** Margaret Mead, *Sex and Temperament in Three Primitive Societies* (New York: W. Morrow & Company, 1935), p. 322.

88 **Judy Marks quote:** C. J. Prince, "Judy Marks on Why She Elevated D&I to Top Priority at Otis Worldwide," chiefexecutive.net, August 21, 2020.

88 **2002 Winter Olympics motto:** 2002 Winter Olympics, en.wikipedia.org.

90 **Iyanla Vanzant quote:** Iyanla Vanzant Twitter post, January 24, 2013.

91 **James Autry quote:** James A. Autry, *Love and Profit: the Art of Caring Leadership* (Avon, January 1, 1991), p. 17.

92 **Peter Senge quote:** Peter M. Senge, *The Fifth Discipline: The Art and Practice of the Learning Organization* (New York: Random House, 1990), p. 321.

93 **John Taft quote:** Mike Kearney, Resilient podcast, episode 26, February 2018.

93 **Dr. Frances Frei & Anne Morriss quote:** Dr. Frances Frei and Anne Morriss, *Unleashed: The Unapologetic Leader's Guide to Empowering Everyone Around You* (Boston: Harvard Business Review Press, June 2020), p. 4.

94 **Fred Rogers story:** *Mister Rogers' Neighborhood*, episode 1065, May 9, 1969.

96 **Nelson Mandela story:** *Long Walk to Freedom* (New York: Little, Brown and Company, December 1994); see also Jean Guiloineau, *Nelson Mandela: The Early Life of Rolihlahla Mandiba* (Berkley, CA: North Atlantic Books, 2002).

Chapter 5: The 1st Stewardship: Modeling, or *Who You Are*

98 **James Baldwin quote:** James A. Baldwin, *Nobody Knows My Name* (New York: Dial Press, "Fifth Avenue, Uptown: A Letter from Harlem," 1961), pp. 61–62.

100 **Albert Schweitzer quote:** Albert Schweitzer, William Larimer Mellon, "Brothers in Spirit: The Correspondence of Albert Schweitzer and William Larimer Mellon, Jr." (Syracuse, N.Y.: Syracuse University Press, 1996), p. 18.

101 **Barry Rellaford story:** Author interview.

101 **A study from LRN:** LRN.com, "The State of Moral Leadership in Business 2019." Accessed July 18, 2021.

101 **Dov Seidman quote:** Dov Seidman, "Why moral leadership matters now more than ever," weforum.org, February 19, 2021.

101 **Thasunda Brown Duckett quote:** Ari Bendersky, "Learn to Let Go of Perfectionism with TIAA CEO Thasunda Brown Duckett," *Salesforce*, the 360 blog, June 25, 2021.

102 **95 percent of leaders:** LRN.com, "The State of Moral Leadership in Business 2019." Accessed July 18, 2021.

102 **Eric Schmidt quote:** quoted in "'Anyone can make a difference' on Small Business Saturday," cbsnews.com, November 24, 2014. Accessed July 18, 2021.

102 **Louise Parent quote:** Marjorie Whigham-Desir, "Leadership Has Its Rewards: Ken Chenault's Low-Key Yet Competitive Style Has Pushed Him Up the Executive Ladder and to the CEO's Chair," *Black Enterprise*, September 30, 1999, p. 73.

102 **Ken Chenault quote:** "5 Practical Leadership Insights from Ken Chenault, former CEO of American Express," robertchen.com, 2015. Accessed July 18, 2021.

103 **Frances Hesselbein quote:** Peter F. Drucker, Joan Snyder Kuhl, and Frances Hesselbein, *Peter Drucker's Five Most Important Questions: Enduring Wisdom for Today's Leaders* (New York: John Wiley & Sons, March 23, 2015), p. 85.

106 **Maya Angelou quote:** Rowena Holloway, "Pray It Forward: Daily Meditations" (iUniverse, August 1, 2007), p. 34.

106 **leaders who demonstrated humility:** LRN State of Moral Leadership study, 2018.

107 **Jim Collins quote:** Jim Collins, *Good to Great: Why Some Companies Make the Leap . . . and Others Don't* (New York: HarperCollins, October 16, 2001).

107 **William Wallace quote:** Randall Wallace, screenwriter, *Braveheart* (1995).

108 **motto of North Carolina:** *North Carolina Manual*, 2012–13.

109 **Diane Sawyer quote:** guest lecturing in General Stanley McChrystal's class at Yale.

109 **In 1931, Mahatma Gandhi:** Eknath Easwaran, *Gandhi the Man* (Petaluma, CA: Nilgiri Press, 1978), p. 112.

111 **Brené Brown quote:** Brené Brown, *Rising Strong: The Reckoning. The Rumble. The Revolution* (New York: Spiegel & Grau, August 25, 2015), p. 4.

111 **Brad Smith story:** Jeffrey Cohn and U. Srinivasa Rangan, "Why CEOs Should Model Vulnerability" *Harvard Business Review*, May 11, 2020.

112 **My brother David:** Author anecdote.

113 **Doug Conant story:** Author anecdote. See also, Douglas R. Conant, *The Blueprint: 6 Practical Steps to Lift Your Leadership to New Heights* (Hoboken: Wiley, February 26, 2020), pp. 240–48.

114 *The Speed of Trust:* Stephen M. R. Covey, *The Speed of Trust: The One Thing That Changes Everything* (New York: Simon & Schuster, July 2018 Updated Edition), pp. 129–240.

115 **Princess Diana story:** "Princess Diana shakes hand of AIDS victim," UPI.com, April 9, 1987. Accessed July 18, 2021.

117 **Doris Kearns Goodwin quote:** masterclass.com, "Doris Kearns Goodwin Teaches U.S. Presidential History and Leadership." Accessed July 18, 2021.

119 **Cheryl Bachelder story:** Author interview, December 16, 2016. Also, Henry Kaestner, "Faith Driven Entrepreneur," episode 142—"The Secret Recipe of Servant Leadership with Cheryl Bachelder."

120 **Dare to Serve:** Author interview, December 16, 2016. Also, Cheryl Bachelder, *Dare to Serve: How to Drive Superior Results by Serving Others* (Oakland: Berrett-Koehler, February 25, 2015).

124 **"One of the things":** *The Sunday Times*. April 16, 2000. Also, Oxford Essential Quotations, Oxford Reference. Edited by Susan Ratcliffe, 2017 Current Online Version.

124 **"First who, then what":** Jim Collins, *Good to Great: Why Some Companies Make the Leap . . . and Others Don't* (New York: HarperCollins, October 16, 2001), p. 13.

125 **Amanda Gorman quote:** Amanda Gorman, USA's First National Youth Poet
Laureate, Poem: "The Hill We Climb," recited during the inauguration of
American president Joe Biden, January 20, 2021.

Chapter 6: The 2nd Stewardship: Trusting, or *How You Lead*

126 **Toni Morrison quote:** "The Truest Eye: On the Greater Good," oprah.com.
Accessed July 22, 2021.

130 **Carl Freudenberg quote:** Author interview, September 5, 2015. Also,
Freudenberg Company history book.

132 **the most stressful part of the workday:** quoted in hoganassessments.com, "Stress
Is Killing You." Accessed July 22, 2021.

132 ***Solo* movie quote:** *Solo: A Star Wars Story*, Lucasfilm, 2018.

133 **Jim Gash/Michael story:** author anecdote.

136 **Siemens story:** "Siemens to establish mobile working as core component of the
'new normal,'" press.siemens.com, July 16, 2020. Accessed July 22, 2021.

137 **Mary Barra story:** Jack Kelly, "General Motors, The Iconic American
Automaker, Offers a 'Work Appropriately' Plan for the Post-Pandemic
Future," forbes.com, April 21, 2021. Accessed July 22, 2021.

141 **Zenger Folkman study:** "Understanding Trust: The Salt of Leadership,"
zengerfolkman.com, August 8, 2020. Accessed July 22, 2021.

142 **Zappos story:** Tony Hsieh, *Delivering Happiness* (New York: Grand Central
Publishing, June 7, 2010), p. 147.

142 **Paul Williams story about Jim Henson:** Paul Williams, "The Elegance of
Kindness," gratitudeandtrust.com, September 2, 2013. Accessed July 22,
2021.

143 **Julia Hartz story:** "Julia Hartz Founded Eventbrite with Her Fiancé, Then She
Took His Job," *New York Times*, January 1, 2019.

145 **David Novak story:** David Novak, "4 Ways Great Leaders Overcome Conflict
by Building Trust," davidnovakleadership.com. Accessed September 7, 2021.

146 **Marshall Goldsmith:** author interview.

147 **Bill McDermott quote:** Bill McDermott, *Winners Dream: A Journey from Corner
Store to Corner Office* (New York: Simon & Schuster, 2014), pp. 271–282.

148 **Anne Frank quote:** Anne Frank, *Anne Frank's Tales from the Secret Annex:
A Collection of Her Short Stories, Fables, and Lesser-Known Writings,* Revised
Edition (New York: Bantam, March 4, 2003).

148 **McKinlee Covey/Leo story:** author interview.

149 **Henry David Thoreau quote:** Henry David Thoreau, *Citizen Thoreau: Walden,*

Civil Disobedience, Life Without Principle, Slavery in Massachusetts, A Plea for Captain John Brown (Berkeley: Graphic Arts Books, 2014), p. 17.

Chapter 7: The 3rd Stewardship: Inspiring, or *Connecting to Why*

151 **Simon Sinek quote:** Simon Sinek, *Start with Why: How Great Leaders Inspire Everyone to Take Action* (Portfolio, 2009), p. 6.

151 **Wayne Gretzky quote:** Wayne Gretzky, *99: My Life in Pictures* (Mint Publishers, 2000). See also, Jason Kirby, "CEOs: Stop debasing Wayne Gretzky's 'I skate to where the puck is going' quote," *Macleans.ca*. October 3, 2014.

152 **Gallup study:** Tom Nolan, "The No. 1 Employee Benefit That No One's Talking About," gallup.com. Accessed July 21, 2021.

152 **75 percent of employees said that the most stressful aspect of their job is their immediate boss:** quoted in hoganassessments.com, "Stress Is Killing You." Accessed July 21, 2021.

152 **Research on student outcome and achievement:** Jennifer Cleary, *"The Number One Factor in Student Success? Relationships with Teachers,"* learningsciences. com, October 24, 2018. Accessed July 21, 2021.

153 **Zenger Folkman study:** John H. Zenger, Joseph R. Folkman, and Scott K. Edinger, *The Inspiring Leader: Unlocking the Secrets of How Extraordinary Leaders Motivate* (New York: McGraw Hill, 2009), pp. 4–6.

154 **Jack Zenger & Joe Folkman quote:** Ibid., p. 6.

154 **Usain Bolt:** Kara Rogers, "How Fast Is the World's Fastest Human?" Britannica.com. Accessed July 21, 2021.

154 **Max Weber quote:** Max Weber, *Economy and Society* (University of California Press, 1922), p. 3.

158 **Oprah Winfrey quote:** Oprah Winfrey, "What Oprah Knows for Sure About Finding Your Calling," oprah.com. Accessed July 21, 2021.

159 **empathy and compassion:** Maria Moudatsou, et al., "The Role of Empathy in Health and Social Care Professionals," January 30, 2020, ncbi.nlm.nih.gov.

160 **John Mackey quote:** John Mackey, "Creating the High Trust Organization," wholefoodsmarket.com, March 9, 2010. Accessed July 21, 2021.

160 **Great Clips story:** David Kasperson interview with Nick Layman and Linda, January 25, 2018.

161 **Maya Angelou quote:** Facebook post by Maya Angelou, March 15, 2014.

162 **Ed Catmull quote:** Mel Cowan, "Pixar Co-Founder Mulls Meaning of Success," news.usc.edu, December 10, 2009.

162 **St. Crispin's Day speech, Henry V:** William Shakespeare, *Henry V.*

162 **Peter Senge quote:** Peter M. Senge, *The Fifth Discipline: The Art and Practice of the Learning Organization* (New York: Random House, 1990), p. 13.

163 **Bain study:** Michael Mankins and Eric Garton, "Engaging Your Employees Is Good But Don't Stop There," *Harvard Business Review*. December 9, 2015. See also, Michael Mankins and Eric Garton, *Time, Talent, Energy: Overcome Organizational Drag & Unleash Your Team's Productive Power* (Boston: Bain & Company and Harvard Business Review Press, 2017), p. 19.

164 **amended his hierarchy of needs:** A. H. Maslow, *The Farther Reaches of Human Nature* (New York: Viking Press, October 1, 1971), p. 26.

165 **Nilofer Merchant quote:** Jukka Niemela, "Nilofer Merchant: Success Formula for Leading in the Social Era," *Nordic Business Report*, December 11, 2015. Accessed September 7, 2021.

165 **A study from Achieve Consulting:** "Inspiring the Next Generation Workforce: The 2014 Millennial Impact Report," casefoundation.org, November 2014.

165 **a study from Imperative and LinkedIn:** "Purpose at Work: The Largest Global Study on the Role of Purpose in the Workforce," 2016 Global Report, business. linkedin.com. Accessed July 21, 2021.

165 **Kathleen Hogan:** Author Interview, July 16, 2021.

165 **Simon Sinek:** Simon Sinek, *Start with Why: How Great Leaders Inspire Everyone to Take Action* (New York: Penguin Group, 2009).

166 **Gary Hamel quote:** Gary Hamel, *The Future of Management* (Boston: Harvard Busines Review Press, September 10, 2007, p. 64).

167 **44 percent of teachers leave:** Richard M. Ingersoll, et al., "Seven Trends: The Transformation of the Teaching Force— Updated October 2018," repository. upenn.edu.

167 **50 percent are considering:** Abigail Johnson Hess, "50% of Teachers Surveyed Say They Considered Quitting, Blaming Pay, Stress, and Lack of Respect," *CNBC online*, August 9, 2019. Accessed September 7, 2021.

167 **Gallup's research on teacher engagement:** Matt Hastings and Sangeeta Agrawal, "Lack of Teacher Engagement Linked to 2.3 Million Missed Workdays," news.gallup.com, January 9, 2015. Accessed July 21, 2021.

167 **Michael Porter story:** John P. Kotter, Michael Porter, Elizabeth Olmsted Teisberg, *Leadership, Strategy, and Innovation: Health Care Collection (8 Items)*, (Boston: Harvard Business Review Press, 2015), p. 1721.

168 **Veterans United Home Loans story:** "Our Values," veteransunited.com. Accessed July 21, 2021.

168 ***Fortune* magazine's "100 Best Companies to Work For":** "Veterans United

Home Loans Ranks for the Sixth Consecutive Year on *Fortune*'s List of 100 Best Companies to Work For." *BusinessWire*. April 12, 2021. Accessed Sept. 7, 2021.

169 **McKinsey & Co. quote:** Naina Dhingra, et al., "Igniting individual purpose in times of crisis," mckinsey.com, August 18, 2020. Accessed July 21, 2021.

170 **Doug Conant story:** Shana Lebowitz, "The former CEO of Campbell Soup sent 30,000 handwritten thank-you notes to employees—here's why it's a great leadership strategy," *Business Insider Australia*, September 2, 2016.

171 **Pepperdine Graziadio Business School story:** "Developing Best *for* the World Leaders," bschool.pepperdine.edu.

171 **John F. Kennedy NASA story:** Jitske M. C. Both-Nwabuwe, et al., "Sweeping the Floor or Putting a Man on the Moon: How to Define and Measure Meaningful Work," ncbi.nlm.nih.gov, September 29, 2017.

172 **Angela Duckworth quote:** Angela Duckworth, *Grit: The Power of Passion and Perseverance* (New York: Simon & Schuster, May 1, 2016), p. 152.

172 **St. Jude Children's Research Hospital story:** "About Us," stjude.org.

173 **Nike purpose statement:** Breaking Barriers, purpose.nike.com. Accessed July 21, 2021.

173 **Starbucks purpose statement:** Starbucks Mission, stories.starbucks.com. Accessed July 21, 2021.

173 **Disney purpose statement:** "About the Walt Disney Company," thewaltdisneycompany.com. Accessed July 22, 2021.

173 **Patagonia purpose statement:** Patagonia's Mission Statement, Patagonia.com .au. Accessed July 22, 2021.

173 **Harley-Davidson purpose statement:** Our Mission, harley-davidson.com. Accessed July 22, 2021.

174 **Andrall (Andy) Pearson story:** Obituary of Andrall E. Pearson, *Journal News*, March 16, 2006.

174 *Fortune* **named Andy Pearson one of the ten toughest bosses in the United States:** Peter Nulty, "America's Toughest Bosses: Stop complaining about your own company's Mr. Big—these guys could scare cream into butter and make money on the deal." *Fortune*, February 27, 1989.

175 **Juliette Gordon Low quote:** gsdsw.org.

176 **Amy Wrzesniewski quote:** Adriana McLane, "Are You a Bricklayer?" linkedin .com, January 27, 2020. Accessed July 22, 2021.

177 **"our ambitions are bold . . .":** Jay Yarrow, "Microsoft's CEO Sent Out a Giant Manifesto to Employees About the Future of the Company," businessinsider .com, July 10, 2014. Accessed July 22, 2021.

178 **"Without that tenacity, resilience, . . .":** Satya Nadella, Ignite 2021 Keynote, March 2, 2021.

178 **"Listening was the most important . . .":** Satya Nadella, *Hit Refresh* (New York: HarperCollins, 2017).

178 **"My approach is to lead with a sense of purpose . . .":** Satya Nadella, *Hit Refresh* (New York: HarperCollins, 2017).

179 **when Nadella took over:** Jordan Novet, "How Microsoft bounced back," cnbc .com, December 3, 2018; Accessed July 22, 2021. Microsoft Corporation (MSFT), finance.yahoo.com. Accessed July 22, 2021.

179 **Valued at more than $2 trillion:** Emily Bary, "Microsoft closes with valuation above $2 trillion, becoming second U.S. company to do so," marketwatch.com, June 25, 2021. Accessed July 22, 2021.

179 **"The number one thing":** Satya Nadella, *Hit Refresh* (New York: HarperCollins, 2017).

180 **Dr. Martin Luther King Jr. quote:** Joan Podrazik, "Oprah's Favorite MLK Quote: 'Greatness Is Determined by Service'" huffpost.com, January 21, 2013. Accessed July 22, 2021.

Chapter 8: Stewardship Agreements

181 **Virginia "Ginni" Rometty quote:** Deepshikha Chakravarti, "12 Inspiring Quotes from IBM's Ginni Rometty," *shethepeople The Women's Channel*, March 26, 2017. Accessed September 7, 2021.

181 **Doug Conant & Mette Norgaard:** ConantLeadership, "In Leadership, Look for the 'and,'" conantleadership.com, April 22, 2016. Accessed July 19, 2021.

183 **Rick Warren quote:** Pastor Rick Warren, Facebook post, May 13, 2013.

184 **up to 8 percent of days worked:** Aki Ito, "America's best work-from-home expert is bracing for turmoil," BusinessInsider.com, April 13, 2021. Accessed September 7, 2021.

184 **More than 60 percent of days worked:** Aki Ito, "America's best work-from-home expert is bracing for turmoil," BusinessInsider.com, April 13, 2021. Accessed September 7, 2021.

185 **Peter Drucker quote:** Peter Drucker, *Managing in the Next Society* (New York: Griffin, September 1, 2003), p. 4.

186 **As my father said:** Stephen R. Covey, *The 8th Habit: From Effectiveness to Greatness* (New York: Simon & Schuster, 2004), pp. 257–58.

187 **Richard Teerlink quote:** Michael A. Verespej, "Invest in People," *IndustryWeek*, December 21, 2004.

193: **"walk the yard":** author interview. July 9, 2020.

195 **Zig Ziglar quote:** Facebook post by Zig Ziglar, July 8, 2013.

195 **Herminia Ibarra quote:** Herminia Ibarra and Anne Scoular, "The Leader as Coach," *Harvard Business Review*, November–December 2019.

Chapter 9: What Trust & Inspire Is *Not*

197 **The Dalai Lama quote:** The Dalai Lama, Howard C. Cutler, *The Art of Happiness at Work* (Hachette UK), p. 25.

198 **Camelot story/quote:** *Camelot*: the Musical.

200 **Criss Jami quote:** Criss Jami, *Killosophy* (Scotts Valley: CreateSpace Independent Publishing, January 8, 2015), p. 82.

201 **Karl Maeser quote:** David Brooksby, "The Circle of Honor," ldsbc.edu, June 5, 2012.

203 **Gary Hamel story:** Gary Hamel, Michele Zanini, *Humanocracy: Creating Organizations as Amazing as the People Inside Them* (Boston: Harvard Business Review Press, August 18, 2020).

204 **James Clear quote:** James Clear, *Atomic Habits* (United Kingdom: Penguin Publishing Group, October 16, 2018), p. 87.

204 **Henry Ford quote:** quoted by Tom Kelley with Jonathan Littman in *The Ten Faces of Innovation* (New York: Doubleday, 2005), p. 37.

205 **Starbucks/Howard Schultz story:** Starbucks mission statement, starbucks.com. Accessed July 19, 2021.

Chapter 10: Barrier #1: "This Won't Work Here"

217 **Arthur Ashe quote:** Colleen Curry, "7 Most Touching Moments from Michael Sam's ESPY Arthur Ashe Award speech," abcnews.go.com, July 17, 2014. Accessed July 19, 2021.

219 **Dr. Stephen R. Covey quote:** Stephen R. Covey, *The 8th Habit: From Effectiveness to Greatness* (New York: Simon & Schuster, 2004), p. 128.

222 **Oprah Winfrey quote:** "An interview with Oprah Winfrey," WCVG-TV 5 News CityLine (Boston, January 13, 2002).

224 **Mel Robbins quote:** @melrobbins, Twitter post, February 10, 2020.

Chapter 11: Barrier #2: Fear—Or "But What If . . ."

227 **Nordstrom story:** The Nordstrom Handbook, Greg Link interview with Nordstrom Human Resources, May 2006.

229 **A. G. Lafley quote:** P&G Business Conduct Manual, pg.com, p. 3. Accessed July 19, 2021.

229 **Hector Ruiz quote:** interview in *Forbes* magazine, 2005.

230 **Jeff Bezos quote:** letter to shareholders, Amazon, 2015.

230 **Bezos also noted:** letter to shareholders, Amazon, 2016.

231 **Netflix story:** Netflix Culture, jobs.netflix.com. Accessed July 19, 2021.

232 **Tom Kelley quote:** cited in *Drive* by Daniel Pink, p. 88.

237 **Adam Grant quote:** Alena Hall, "How Giving Back Can Lead to Greater Personal Success, huffpost.com, June 17, 2014. Accessed July 19, 2021.

238 **Jon Huntsman Sr. story:** Jon M. Huntsman, *Winners Never Cheat* (New York: Pearson), March 23, 2005, p. 160.

238 **"imposter syndrome":** Jeanne Croteau, "Imposter Syndrome—Why It's Harder Today Than Ever," *Forbes* magazine, April 4, 2019.

240 **Inga Beale quote:** Jill Treanor in Davos, Interview with Inga Beale: "Let's use the words people are uncomfortable using—lesbian, gay," theguardian.com, January 23, 2016. Accessed July 19, 2021.

Chapter 13: Barrier #4: "I'm the Smartest One in the Room"

246 **Ken Blanchard quote:** Twitter post, December 13, 2012.

249 **Indra Nooyi story:** Author interview with Indra Nooyi. July 28, 2010. See also "Indra Nooyi's Key Challenge Is to Retain PepsiCo Top Guns," *DNA India*, August 15, 2006. Accessed July 19, 2021.

251 **Helen Keller quote:** Joseph P. Lash, *Helen and Teacher: The Story of Helen Keller and Anne Sullivan Macy* (New York: Dell Publishing Company), August 1, 1981.

252 **Liz Wiseman quote:** Liz Wiseman, *Multipliers* (New York: HarperCollins Publishers, May 16, 2017), p. 5.

254 **Doris Kearns Goodwin quote:** *Parade Magazine*, September 14, 2008.

257 **Carol Dweck quote:** Carol Dweck, *Mindset: The New Psychology of Success* (New York: Random House, February 28, 2006), p. 64.

Chapter 14: Barrier #5: "This Is Who I Am"

259 **Peter Senge quote:** Peter M. Senge, *The Fifth Discipline: The Art and Practice of the Learning Organization* (New York: Random House, 1990), p. 19.

260 **Marshall Goldsmith quote:** Marshall Goldsmith, *What Got You Here Won't Get You There* (London: Profile Books, 2010), p. 72.

260 **Master Yoda quote:** *The Empire Strikes Back* (1980).

261 **Satya Nadella quote:** Matt Rosoff, "The buzzy new term at Microsoft is 'growth mindset'—here's what it means," businessinsider.com, June 25, 2015. Accessed July 19, 2021.

261 **Dee Hock quote:** Dee Hock, "The Art of Chaordic Leadership," Leader to Leader Institute, Winter 2000.

262 **Ralph Stayer story:** Ralph Stayer, "How I Learned to Let My Workers Lead," *Harvard Business Review*, November–December 1990.

263 **Ralph Stayer quote:** "The Johnsonville Way: The Path We Follow and How It Began," cdn.phenompeople.com. Accessed July 19, 2021.

263 **Andy Pearson story and quote:** David Dorsey, "Andy Pearson Finds Love," *Fast Company*, August 2001.

264 **Albert Einstein quote:** *Bite-Size Einstein: Quotations on Just About Everything from the Greatest Mind of the Twentieth Century* (New York: St. Martin's Press, 2015), p. 32.

264 **Elizabeth Smart story and quote:** Elizabeth Smart, *My Story* (New York: Macmillan, September 30, 2014), p. 302.

265 **Brad Smith quote:** Geoff Colvin, "Exclusive Interview: Intuit Names New CEO as Brad Smith Steps Down After 11 Years," fortune.com, August 23, 2018. Accessed July 19, 2021.

Chapter 15: Trust & Inspire in Any Context: Parenting, Teaching, Coaching . . . and More

269 **Wilma Rudolph quote:** @Olympic twitter. April 1, 2021. https://twitter.com/olympics/status/1377667108293726210. Accessed July 18, 2021.

269 **Jonathan Horton story:** Dave Reed, "Horton looks to continue outstanding gymnastics career in Beijing," ESPN.com, August 8, 2008. Accessed July 18, 2021.

270 **Dr. Frances Frei quote:** Dr. Frances Frei and Anne Morriss, *Unleashed: The Unapologetic Leader's Guide to Empowering Everyone Around You* (Boston: Harvard Business Review Press, June 2020).

272 **Governor Jeb Bush story:** Manny Fernandez, "Barbara Bush Is Remembered at Her Funeral for Her Wit and Tough Love," nytimes.com, April 21, 2018. Accessed July 18, 2021.

273 **Nelson Mandela quote:** *Long Walk to Freedom* (New York: Little, Brown and Company, December 1994), p. 312.

275 **Albert Einstein quote:** quotefancy.com (featured in "Albert Einstein quotes"). Accessed July 18, 2021.

277 **Leo Tolstoy quote:** "Three Methods of Reform" (translated from the Russian, 1900).

282 **McKinlee Covey "establish credibility" story:** author interview.

284 **Dr. Stephen R. Covey quote:** *The 8th Habit: From Effectiveness to Greatness* (New York: Simon & Schuster, November 2004), p. 98.

285 **Galileo quote:** Jeffrey Bennett, "Galileo Put Us in Our Place," latimes.com, February 8, 2009. Accessed July 18, 2021.

285 **Les Brown story:** "You Gotta Be 'Hungry,'" medium.com, Buffini & Company, May 8, 2018.

285 **Muriel Summers story:** leaderinme.org.

287 **Tim Cook quote:** Brian R. Fitzgerald, "Apple CEO Tim Cook Plans to Donate His Wealth to Charity," *Wall Street Journal*, March 27, 2015.

288 **Joe Montana quote about Bill Walsh:** Tom Alaimo, "16 Quotes from Bill Walsh That Every Leader Should Read," medium.com, October 21, 2018. Accessed July 18, 2021.

288 **Bill Walsh quote:** Bill Walsh, *The Score Takes Care of Itself* (London: Penguin Publishing Group, June 29, 2010), p. 159.

290 **General Martin Dempsey:** author interview with General Martin Dempsey. October 1, 2014.

290 **General Stanley McChrystal:** Ryan Hawk, *Learning Leader* podcast, learningleader.com, March 24, 2019. Accessed July 18, 2021.

Conclusion

293 **Inga Beale quote:** Jill Treanor in Davos, Interview with Inga Beale: "Let's use the words people are uncomfortable using—lesbian, gay," theguardian.com, January 23, 2016. Accessed July 19, 2021.

293 **Erik Weihenmayer story:** Erik Weihenmayer, *Touch the Top of the World* (New York: Dutton Book–Penguin Group, 2001).

293 **only approximately 29 percent of people who've tried have made it to the top of Mount Everest:** Doug Criss, "These Myths About Mount Everest Feed Its Mystique (and Its Traffic Jams), cnn.com, May 28, 2019. Accessed July 19, 2021.

294 **Erik Weihenmayer later told me:** author interview with Erik Weihenmayer, March 2002.

294 **Michael Brown quote:** "Interview with Michael Brown, Farther Than the Eye Can See," May 7, 2009, hulu.com. Accessed July 19, 2021.

298 **Erik Weihenmayer quote:** FranklinCovey training video. erikweihenmayer. com, motto, About section of the website. Accessed July 19, 2021.

Index

INDEX

About Stephen M. R. Covey

Stephen M. R. Covey

Stephen M. R. Covey is cofounder of CoveyLink and the Franklin-Covey Global Trust Practice. A sought-after keynote speaker and adviser on trust, inspiration, leadership, ethics, and collaboration, he speaks to audiences around the world. He is the *New York Times* and #1 *Wall Street Journal* best-selling author of *The Speed of Trust*, a groundbreaking and paradigm-shifting book that challenges our age-old assumption that trust is merely a soft, social virtue and instead demonstrates that trust is a hard-edged, economic driver. *The Speed of Trust* has been translated into twenty-two languages, has sold well over two million copies, and has been applied and implemented in thousands of organizations around the world.

Stephen is also coauthor of *Smart Trust: The Defining Skill That Transforms Managers into Leaders*. Stephen asserts that trust has become the new currency of our world, and that having the ability to develop, extend, and restore trust with all stakeholders is the number one competency of leadership needed today. He passionately delivers this message and is dedicated to enabling individuals and organizations to reap the dividends of high trust throughout the world. Audiences and organizations alike resonate with his tangible, practical approach to trust.

Stephen is the former CEO of Covey Leadership Center, which, under his direction, became the largest leadership development company in the world. He personally led the strategy that propelled his father's book, Dr. Stephen R. Covey's *The 7 Habits of Highly Effective*

People, to become one of the two most influential business books of the twentieth century, according to *CEO Magazine*. A Harvard MBA, Stephen joined Covey Leadership Center as a client developer and later became national sales manager and then president and CEO.

Under Stephen's leadership, the company grew rapidly and profitably, achieving Inc. 500 status. As president & CEO, he nearly doubled revenues while increasing profits by twelve times. During that period, both customer and employee trust reached new highs and the company expanded throughout the world into over forty countries. This greatly increased the value of the brand and company. Within three years of being named CEO, Stephen had increased shareholder value by sixty-seven times in a merger with then FranklinQuest to form Franklin-Covey.

Stephen has become a respected confidant and influencer with executives and leaders of Fortune 500 companies as well as with mid- and small-sized private sector and public sector organizations he's consulted. Clients recognize his unique perspective on real-world organizational issues based on his practical experience as a former CEO.

Stephen serves on numerous boards, including the Government Leadership Advisory Council, and he has been recognized with the lifetime Achievement Award for "Top Thought Leaders in Trust" from the advocacy group Trust Across America/Trust Around the World. Stephen resides with his wife and children in the shadows of the Rocky Mountains.

You can follow Stephen @StephenMRCovey on Twitter, Instagram, Facebook, and LinkedIn.

David Kasperson

David Kasperson has been building high-trust partnerships, and innovative and collaborative solutions for clients of FranklinCovey's Global Trust Practice as the director of business development for more than fifteen years. An expert on trust, he has consulted with and presented to leaders and Fortune 500 organizations and beyond, in more than twenty countries. He also managed FranklinCovey's premier Leading at the Speed of Trust, Sundance Executive Workshop. David graduated Summa Cum Laude with a BA & AA in Communication Theory & Practice from Utah Valley University.

McKinlee Covey

From a young age, McKinlee Covey's greatest desire has always been to help others reach their potential. She became an educator and athletic coach—earning a master's degree in Human Development & Psychology from the Harvard Graduate School of Education. McKinlee has taught both middle school and high school since 2011, impacting thousands of students' lives along the way. Her passion for helping students and athletes thrive has earned her recognition from both her schools as well as her community. Her greatest joy comes from seeing her students succeed.

Gary T. Judd

Gary T. Judd is passionate about working with others to improve team trust and organizational performance. Before becoming FranklinCovey's Global Trust Practice Leader, Gary was a cofounder of CoveyLink, CEO of a financial services firm, the president and COO of an Inc. 500 company, and led Covey Leadership Center's Time Management Division. As executive adviser to numerous leading enterprises, he brings a rare business acumen and proven perspective to his clients. Gary's engaging presentation style makes him a requested presenter and facilitator. Gary resides with his wife in Harare, Zimbabwe.

About CoveyLink and the FranklinCovey Global Trust Practice

The FranklinCovey Global Trust Practice is focused on measurably increasing the performance and influence of people and organizations worldwide, by enabling them to lead in a way that inspires trust— Trust & Inspire.

Our intent is to see, communicate, develop, and unleash Trust & Inspire leaders and cultures. In doing this, we seek, as George Bernard Shaw expressed it, "to be used for a purpose recognized by themselves as a mighty one."

Through a license with CoveyLink, the FranklinCovey Global Trust Practice provides access to additional resources for individuals and organizations worldwide to increase trust and establish Trust & Inspire cultures, including open enrollment workshops, keynote speeches, on-site programs, virtual events, webinars, train-the-trainer certification, individual and organizational assessments and measurement, application tools, advisory services, and custom consulting.

To inquire about keynote speaking, presentations, workshops, training, coaching, or consulting services from Stephen M. R. Covey, or from the FranklinCovey Global Trust Practice, or to access Stephen M. R. Covey personally, email us at david@speedoftrust.com or go to our website at TrustandInspire.com.

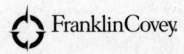

For More Information Regarding Speaking

Stephen's thought leadership, authenticity, and dynamic presenting style have made him a highly sought-after speaker. He has delivered keynotes and workshops on trust and leadership all over the world, from executive teams to audiences of more than 20,000. To inquire about speaking or executive training from Stephen M. R. Covey or another FranklinCovey presenter, email david@speedoftrust.com, or visit our website, trustandinspire.com.